D1453026

The Romance of Adultery

THE MIDDLE AGES SERIES

Ruth Mazo Karras, General Editor
Edward Peters, Founding Editor

A complete list of books in the series
is available from the publisher.

The Romance
of Adultery

Queenship and Sexual Transgression
in Old French Literature

Peggy McCracken

PENN

University of Pennsylvania Press

Philadelphia

Copyright © 1998 University of Pennsylvania Press
All rights reserved
Printed in the United States of America on acid-free paper

10 9 8 7 6 5 4 3 2 1

Published by
University of Pennsylvania Press
Philadelphia, PA 19104-4011

Library of Congress Cataloging-in-Publication Data
McCracken, Peggy.
   The romance of adultery : queenship and sexual transgression in
Old French literature / Peggy McCracken.
      p.   cm. — (The Middle Ages series)
   Includes bibliographical references and index.
   ISBN 0-8122-3432-4 (cloth : alk. paper)
      1. French literature—To 1500—History and criticism.   2. Romances—
History and criticism.   3. Adultery in literature.   4. Queens in literature.
I. Title.   II. Series.
PQ207.M33   1998
840.9'353—dc21   97-49185
                                                                        CIP

For Pauline and Albert McCracken

Contents

Acknowledgments

THIS PROJECT OWES MUCH to the institutional support offered by the Newberry Library and the University of Illinois, Chicago, and to colleagues at both institutions whose encouragement and intellectual example helped to shape it. In particular I am grateful to the University of Illinois, Chicago, whose Institute for the Humanities and Campus Research Board provided generous support for research and valuable time for writing. I also have many individual thanks to offer: this book would be a much different and much poorer product without the many insights, inspirations, and corrections offered by colleagues. R. Howard Bloch encouraged my project in its infancy. Many long conversations with Mary Beth Rose helped me to formulate its conceptual framework. Karma Lochrie and James A. Schultz have discussed these ideas with me for more than six years; this book has been greatly enriched by their insights and by our friendship. I have profited immensely from the generosity of colleagues who read the manuscript: Matilda Tomaryn Bruckner, E. Jane Burns, Jody Enders, John Carmi Parsons, James A. Schultz, and an anonymous reader from the Press offered valuable comments and suggestions for revision. I am also very grateful for the encouragement and suggestions offered by Jerome E. Singerman.

An early version of Chapter 1 was published as "The Body Politic and the Queen's Adulterous Body," in *Feminist Approaches to the Body in Medieval Literature* (Philadelphia: University of Pennsylvania Press, 1993), and an early version of Chapter 3 was published as "The Queen's Secret: Adultery in the Feudal Court," which is reprinted in revised form by permission from the *Romanic Review* 86, 2 (March

1995); copyright Trustees of Columbia University in the City of New York. I thank these publishers for permission to reprint.

I also wish to acknowledge two personal debts: to my parents, whose unfailing support has enriched all my endeavors, and to Doug Anderson, whose contributions to this book I cannot begin to count.

Abbreviations

All translations in the text are mine unless otherwise indicated.

Béroul   Béroul. *The Romance of Tristran*. Ed. and trans. Norris J. Lacy. Garland Library of Medieval Literature, Series A, 36. New York: Garland, 1989.

Caradoc   In *The Continuations of the Old French Perceval of Chrétien de Troyes*. Ms. L, 3.1. Ed. William Roach. Philadelphia: University of Pennsylvania Press and American Philosophical Society, 1952.

Charrete   Chrétien de Troyes. *Le chevalier de la charrete*. Ed. Mario Roques. Paris: Champion, 1958.

Châtelaine   *La châtelaine de Vergi*. Ed. Gaston Reynaud, rev. Lucien Foulet. Paris: Champion, 1921.

Chilton   Marguerite de Navarre. *The Heptameron*. Trans. P. A. Chilton. New York: Penguin, 1984.

Chrétien   Chrétien de Troyes. *The Complete Romances of Chrétien de Troyes*. Trans. David Staines. Bloomington: Indiana University Press, 1990.

Cligés   Chrétien de Troyes. *Cligés ou la fausse mort*. Ed. Alexandre Micha. Paris: Champion, 1957.

Curtis   *Le roman de Tristan en prose*. Ed. Renée L. Curtis. 3 vols. 1963-85; rpt. Cambridge: D. S. Brewer, 1985.

Eracle   Gautier d'Arras. *Eracle*. Ed. Guy Raynaud de Lage. Paris: Champion, 1976.

Erec et Enide	Chrétien de Troyes. *Erec et Enide*. Ed. Mario Roques. Paris: Champion, 1952.
La fille	*La fille du comte de Pontieu, conte en prose, versions du XIIIe et du XVe siècle*. Ed. Clovis Brunel. Paris: Champion, 1923.
Gottfried	Gottfried von Strassburg. *Tristan*. Trans. A. T. Hatto. New York: Penguin, 1960.
Heptaméron	Marguerite de Navarre. *L'heptaméron*. Paris: Garnier-Flammarion, 1982.
Lacy	English translation of: Béroul. *The Romance of Tristran*. Ed. and trans. Norris J. Lacy. Garland Library of Medieval Literature, Series A, 36. New York: Garland, 1989.
Lais	*The Lais of Marie de France*. Trans. Glyn S. Burgess and Keith Busby. New York: Penguin, 1986.
Lancelot	*Lancelot: roman en prose du XIIIe siècle*. Ed. Alexandre Micha. 9 vols. Geneva: Droz, 1978–83.
Lanval	In *Les lais de Marie de France*. Ed. Jean Rychner. Paris: Champion, 1966.
Mantel	"Du mantel mautaillié." In *Recueil général et complet des fabliaux*. Ed. A. de Montaiglon. Paris: Librairie des Bibliophiles, 1872. 3: 1–29.
Ménestrel de Reims	*Récits d'un ménestrel de Reims au treizième siècle*. Ed. Natalis de Wailly. Paris: Renouard, 1876.
La mort	*La mort le roi Artu*. Ed. Jean Frappier. Geneva: Droz, 1964.
Prose Tristan	*Le roman de Tristan en prose*. General ed. Philippe Ménard. 9 vols. Geneva: Droz, 1987–97.
Roman des sept sages	*Le roman des sept sages de Rome: A Critical Edition of the Two Verse Redactions of a Twelfth-Century Romance*. Ed. Mary B. Speer. Lexington, Ky.: French Forum, 1989.

Silence	Heldris de Cornuälle. *Le roman de Silence, a Thirteenth-Century Arthurian Verse-Romance.* Ed. Lewis Thorpe. Cambridge: Heffer, 1972.
Thomas	Thomas. *Les fragments du roman de Tristan, poème du XIIe siècle.* Ed. Bartina H. Wind. Geneva: Droz, 1960.

Introduction: Defining Queenship in Medieval Europe

IN 1148 RUMORS SURFACED that Eleanor of Aquitaine, wife of King Louis VII of France, was involved in an adulterous love affair with her uncle, Raymond of Antioch. Eleanor had accompanied her husband on the second Crusade, and during the couple's stay in the Holy Land stories began to circulate about the queen's close relationship to her uncle. John of Salisbury reported that "the attentions paid by the prince to the queen, and his constant, indeed almost continuous, conversation with her, aroused the king's suspicions."[1] William of Tyre's account of the events focused on the queen's complicity. He wrote that Raymond, frustrated in his effort to enlist Louis's aid in enlarging the principality of Antioch, resolved to deprive Louis of his wife, "either by force or by secret intrigue. The queen readily assented to this design, for she was a foolish woman."[2] Eleanor was never formally charged with adultery, and the rumored liaison did not end the royal marriage. The king and queen were apparently reconciled by the pope when they stopped in Italy after leaving Antioch, and the queen gave birth to a daughter in 1150. Despite the "reconciliation," however, Eleanor and Louis were divorced three years after the events at Antioch on grounds of consanguinity.[3]

Eleanor of Aquitaine's story provides a provocative starting point for a study of the prominent representation of adulterous queens in medieval romances. Eleanor herself has long been associated with medieval love literature as both a patron and a model, and it is possible that Eleanor's experiences may have been well enough

known to have influenced accounts of queenship in medieval romances; the rumors of the queen's adultery predate by about twenty-
five years the composition of the first major French romance about
an adulterous queen, Chrétien de Troyes's *Chevalier de la charrete*, a
work whose patron was Eleanor's daughter, Marie of Champagne.[4]
Whatever direct personal influence Eleanor of Aquitaine may have
had on literary accounts of adulterous queens must remain speculative, however, and the rumors of Eleanor's adulterous liaison with
Raymond of Antioch are more interesting for what they might say
about medieval queenship than for what they might suggest about
this queen's life as a model for fictional representations. The reports
of Eleanor's conduct in Antioch stress the importance of the queen's
chastity, the threat to the king's honor that could be posed by his
wife's sexual transgression, and the importance of undisputed succession in the royal family. All of these issues are featured in romance
representations of queenship and adultery.

The prominence of adultery in many medieval romances has
long preoccupied literary scholars and historians. Critics have idealized adultery as part of the ethic of courtly love, justified it as a
reaction to the practice of arranged marriages, or simply dismissed
it as a literary conceit with no connection to historical situations.[5]
Adultery has yet to be studied as a sexual transgression associated primarily with the queen in medieval romance, and the political implications of that association remain unexamined. Medieval romanciers
do not simply rewrite the stories of Capetian queens like Eleanor of
Aquitaine in veiled form. However, they do represent, sometimes
obliquely, many of the issues debated in the evolution of queenship
during the period in which they were composed: the importance of
chastity and succession in royal marriage; the extent of a royal wife's
influence on her husband; the symbolic importance of the queen in
the display of the king's sovereignty. This study situates romance representations of adulterous queens in the context of medieval monarchy and in relationship to a changing notion of queenship in twelfth-
and thirteenth-century France. It focuses on common issues at stake
in the fiction and the practice of medieval queenship, and it suggests

the contribution of medieval romances to the evolving definition of royal sovereignty as exclusively male.

Defining Queenship

In medieval Europe most queens were queens consort; that is, a woman was crowned only when she married a king or when her husband became king. In early medieval monarchies the queen's position was a precarious and vulnerable one. In Merovingian France, for example, the queen's position in the court was defined entirely by her marriage. There was no special inaugural rite for the queen and her dependence on her husband was complete. Janet Nelson has emphasized the difficulty of identifying "queenship" as an institution during this period: "beyond personalities, episcopacy, aristocracy, [and] kingship can be said to have existed as institutions, but it is much harder to identify anything that could be called 'queenship.' "⁶ Yet the undefined nature of early medieval queenship did not mean that queens had no power in their husbands' courts. Nelson suggests that even the limited parameters of the queen's participation in political and familial structures could offer her some independence and influence in the royal court. Her control over financial resources, the influence that she gained over her husband through affection and sexual intimacy, and her status as mother of a son could all compensate at least partially for the inherent vulnerability of her position.⁷

The queen's circumscribed position in the court, defined largely by her dependence on the king for her status, began to change in the early ninth century as queens became more visibly involved in government. Carolingian queens were still queens consort, but they seem to have gained a new prominence in their husbands' courts. One mark of a change in the queen's status may be seen in her participation in royal documents. As Geneviève Bührer-Thierry notes, the empress Judith, second wife of Louis the Pious, appears five times in royal documents, between 828 and 833. According to Bührer-Thierry, she is the first king's wife to figure relatively frequently in royal docuents; the previous empress, Ermengarde, appears only once.[8] Bührer-Thierry claims that the heightened evidence of the queen's presence is significant because it may suggest that ninth-century queens held a more influential position in their husbands' courts than did their predecessors. She notes the frequent representation of the Carolingian queen as an Esther-figure and suggests that this association may signify the queen's new status for her contemporaries. As *consortium regni*, the title associated with Esther, the queen shares responsibility for the kingdom, and this position prepares the way for her to assume the regency for underage children.[9] Bührer-Thierry further suggests that the increased prominence of the king's wife in the royal court may be signaled by a new political arm used to discredit the queen and her allies: the accusation of adultery. Several Carolingian queens, including the empress Judith, were charged adultery, and Bührer-Thierry argues that in the political context of the early to mid-ninth century, the accusation against the queen demonstrates her new position of power and influence in the Carolingian government.[10]

Medieval queens continued to have a prominent role in their husbands' courts and even to share royal power until the twelfth century. The king was the head of the government, but the queen was associated with his function as ruler. She participated in state decisions, sat in the *curia regis*, and heard lawsuits; she made endowments and signed charters and royal acts jointly with the king. With reference to the French Capetian monarchy, Marion Facinger has suggested that in practice the government of the kingdom was a kind of partnership: the king dominated in the relationship, but the queen had a prominent role.[11]

Facinger identifies the high point in the queen's direct role in government during the reign of Adelaide of Maurienne, wife of Louis VI (1115–37). In royal acts from this period the queen's regnal year appears along with that of the king for the first time, and Adelaide's name appears in forty-five charters. In contrast, her predecessor, Bertrada, wife of Philip I, is not acknowledged as queen in any charters, and her name is recorded only four times.[12] The queen's role in the court also began to diminish during Adelaide's reign, however, and this change became evident during the reign of Adelaide's son, Louis VII, and his first wife, Eleanor of Aquitaine. In the twelfth-century consolidation of royal authority, which included the gradual bureaucratization of the government and the establishment of a permanent group of officials loyal to the king, the ill-defined status of the queen was extremely vulnerable.[13] The queen was slowly excluded from her former right to share royal power and to participate in governing, although she retained potential sources of power in her personal influence over her husband and in her status as mother to the king's heir.

The distancing of the queen from direct involvement in affairs of state accelerated in the reign of Philip II Augustus (1180–1123). Philip's wives, Isabel and Ingeborg, make no appearances in court records in advisory, administrative, or judicial functions. Indeed, Facinger suggests that Philip may have been able to treat his wives as he did precisely because the office of the queen was so unimportant to the goverment of the time. For twenty years, from 1193 to 1213, Ingeborg was queen of France but had no authority or power because Philip refused to recognize her as his wife.[14]

The change in the office of the queen during the twelfth and thirteenth centuries reflects the consolidation and extension of royal authority and the location of royal sovereignty in the person of the king. In France it may also be linked to the establishment of the Capetian family as a royal dynasty. Philip Augustus was the first Capetian king to assume the right of succession to the extent that he did not have his son crowned before his own death. Gabrielle Spiegel has pushed the recognition of this right back a generation. She notes that Philip's father, Louis VII, was the first Capetian king to date some of his charters from the time of his son's birth. This new practice suggests that Philip was considered heir to the throne simply because of his birth and that his succession did not depend on consecration.[15] The Capetians may then have already consolidated their right to rule at the time of Philip's birth, but in earlier generations, before the succession of the son to the father's throne was assumed to be a hereditary right, the queen's lineage was an important part of her son's claim to the throne. This was particularly the case for

queen mothers who could claim Charlemagne as an ancestor, and
their lineage was promoted as a further justification of their sons'
rule.[16] As hereditary succession to the French throne became established, the symbolic importance of the queen's genealogy declined
and her eclipsed status as a mother of exemplary lineage combined
with other forces in the consolidation of royal authority to diminish
her influence in the royal court.

A similar distancing of the queen from sources of influence and
power during the twelfth and thirteenth centuries characterizes the
English monarchy. As John Carmi Parsons has noted, from the time
of Henry II's accession in 1154, the queen's former control over
financial resources was curtailed and she became financially dependent on the king.[17] Parsons suggests that the fact that Eleanor of
Aquitaine did not witness any charters after 1154 signals the queen's
declining role in government, and he also suggests that Eleanor's
imprisonment after encouraging her sons' revolt against the king in
1173 ended queens' regencies, further diminishing the influence and
power available to English queens.[18]

By the thirteenth century, queenship in most European monarchies had become a public office with only symbolic and, of course,
reproductive functions. While the queen's responsibility to produce
a royal heir was always her most important role in medieval monarchies, as the queen was gradually excluded from other functions
in the court her maternity was increasingly emphasized, both in the
public rituals that demonstrated and defined the queen's position in
the royal court and in books of private devotion used by the queen
herself. A male heir guaranteed the peaceful transition of the throne,
and it was the queen's responsibility to provide that heir. The necessity of reproduction was inscribed in rituals, as Claire Richter
Sherman has shown for the *Coronation Book of Charles V of France*,
where the prayers in the queen's *ordo* give the queen's anointing a significance that resembles that of a fertility charm.[19] And if the proper
succession of the kingdom depends on the queen's fertility, it also
depends on God's grace in the form of a son. In a study of the book
of hours made for Charles IV's third wife, Jeanne d'Evreux, Joan
Holladay has suggested that Charles may have considered the piety

of his wife as a way of gaining God's favor to grant him a male heir. Holladay notes, for example, that the maternal imagery in the portrayal of the queen included in an Annunciation scene is reinforced by the presence of babies, rabbits, and other symbols of fertility in the margins of the portrait.[20] Jeanne was thus constantly reminded of the desirability of motherhood and of the importance of children in the royal household: as Madeline Caviness has noted, the embedding of didactic images in a devotional text meant almost constant exposure to the lessons portrayed in the illuminations.[21]

The inscription of the queen's role as mother in these fourteenth-century texts of ritual and devotion corresponds to an emphasis on maternity in the evolving definitions of the privileges and responsibilities of the king's wife. While twelfth- and thirteenth-century queens no longer had a place in the informal ruling partnership enjoyed by earlier queens, they retained access to influence and power through the roles of spouse and mother. As the king's wife, the queen was in a position to intercede with the king on behalf of her own interests or on behalf of his subjects, and it has been suggested that the growing prominence of the queen's role as intercessor during the twelfth century may be linked to the rise of administrative kingship and the queen's concurrent loss of a direct role in government.[22] Yet even though it may have replaced a more direct participation in government, the intercessory model still provided royal women with an alternate access to power that they could manipulate to their advantage. As Lois Huneycutt has shown, Henry I's wife, Matilda, used her position as a successful intercessor to gain power and influence, and as Pauline Stafford notes, whatever the extent of the twelfth-century bureaucratization of government and the concurrent distancing of the queen from centers of power, "influence over the king remained the center of medieval politics, because government was essentially personal rule."[23] Indeed, the queen's role as intercessor was an important part of the functioning of the court. It found a precedent in the Biblical story of Esther, and Esther imagery was used in rituals and in didactic literature to encourage the queen in her duty as intercessor.[24]

The Virgin Mary was another model of intercessor used in descriptions of the queen's mediation between her husband and his subjects, and Parsons has suggested that the shift from Esther imagery to Marian imagery in descriptions of the queen's role as intercessor may be linked to the queen's necessary fertility: Esther is not a mother in the Biblical account of her story.[25] Parsons situates this representational shift within the context of the increasing marginalization of the queen from power during the twelfth and thirteenth centuries, and he suggests that, as the queen became more and more isolated from government, she became more attractive as an intercessor to those distrustful of royal law. He sees the growing importance of Marian veneration, which corresponded to the increasing influence of the church in all aspects of life, including government, as a parallel to the increasing importance of the queen's role as intercessor. The very marginalization of the queen from political power may have made her a better intercessor in the eyes of her husband's subjects, just as Mary's identity as a "nonlegalistic form" of the church made her a popular intercessor in the view of Christian supplicants.[26]

The supplicant queen "regrounds her authority on the very fact of exclusion," in the words of Paul Strohm.[27] Distanced from participation in royal government, the queen speaks as an outsider; it is her exclusion from direct authority that defines the influence of her position as an intercessor. In a study of Froissart's portrayal of the pregnant Queen Philippa's intervention to save six burghers of Calais from Edward III's condemnation to death, Strohm shows how the queen takes the position of a "prophetic outsider." He also notes the centrality of the queen's femininity and her pregnancy in the successful petition to her husband.[28]

While the queen's power as intercessor is defined in part by her exclusion from government, her authority to intercede is grounded in her position as the sexual partner of the king and as the mother of his children. This position was emphasized in the staging of intercessory pleas, as Parsons has shown. Eleanor of Castile is known to have received at least one petitioner in her bedchamber, in an explicit reminder of the conjugal relations of the king and the queen, and the births of Eleanor's children provided the occasion for petitions to the queen, reinforcing and emphasizing the privileged status accorded by royal maternity.[29]

The queen's influence as an intercessor was more prominent as a ritual practice in England than in France, but the formulation of this privilege in English rituals acknowledges the influence of any royal wife on her husband. As Sharon Farmer has discussed, clerical writers recognized the persuasive power of a wife's intimacy with her husband, and the implications of this influence for royal wives is codified in rituals of intercession that construct the queen as a mediator between the king and his subjects, but not as a counselor in her own right.[30]

The queen's power in the royal court was not limited to her influence over her husband. As mother of the king's heir, the queen gained authority at the court and could play an important role in guaranteeing her son's succession to his father's throne, particularly before succession rules became fixed. Through her intervention in succession politics the queen could earn the gratitude of a son and, if her son were still a minor, she might rule for him.[31] Regencies provided queens with an opportunity to govern, and this powerful position was occupied by several medieval queens, most notably in France by Blanche of Castile whose activities as regent included legislating, dealing with foreign powers, waging war, and arranging marriages.[32] Not just regents but also queens consort could exercise considerable influence in marriage negotiations, and Parsons's study of the role of royal women in arranging marriage alliances and in preparing daughters to be royal brides demonstrates the extent to which the queen's participation in matrimonial politics afforded her opportunities to claim power.[33]

While a medieval queen consort might exercise influence on several fronts—as intercessor, as mother, as regent, as marriage broker—any authority claimed by the queen was based on her position as wife of the king and mother of his children. In both roles, the queen's chastity was of paramount importance. Efforts to emphasize the imperative of chastity are found alongside acknowledgments of the necessity of childbirth in didactic and religious books prepared for the queen. In her study of the illustrations in Jeanne d'Evreux's *Hours*, Caviness finds the exhortation to curb sexuality alongside scenes of veiled sexual intercourse and seduction, and she suggests that many of the scenes in the prayer book may have frightened the young queen and "warned her to keep her mind on her prayers and to avoid adultery."[34] Exortations to chastity and the praise of motherhood also feature prominently in didactic treatises like the *Speculum dominarum*, written for Jeanne de Navarre, wife of Philip IV of France, and translated into Old French as *Le miroir des dames*.[35] While the *Speculum dominarum* and the *Hours* of Jeanne d'Evreux postdate the romances and the medieval queens under consideration in this study, they build on well-established coventions for women's advice literature, and both fictional and nonfictional accusations of adultery against queens demonstrate the importance of their lessons in chastity for twelfth- and thirteenth-century queens.

At the same time that the queen gained stature and influence in the court through her sexual relationship with the king and through maternity, she was left vulnerable to accusations of sexual transgression and responsible for the failure to produce heirs. Stafford emphasizes the dangerous privilege of queenship in a description of royal women's precarious access to power:

Power itself, or more correctly, authority and power, had its own language which was not entirely gender specific. Women in general and queens in particular enjoyed little of that "magisterial" authority that was considered legitimate, though they derived some accepted authority from the role of mother and mistress of the household. On the other hand, they exercised much power through influence and counsel. These latter, whether exercised by men or women, were fraught and debatable areas throughout the Middle Ages, open to accusations of abuse and of covert use. Women were especially open to accusations of the abuse of sexual power, of secret murder, witchcraft, and scheming. Their activity in the spheres of court and family politics encouraged suspicion, but also encouraged these types of activities.[36]

Queens consort were inevitably dependent on their husbands, their families, or their allies for status and privilege in the royal court.[37] This vulnerability could be exploited in an attempt to weaken or displace a queen, particularly through the accusation of adultery. Bührer-Thierry's suggestion that the early prominence of this form of attack coincides with the queen's newly increased prominence in the ninth-century Carolingian court demonstrates that during this period the most certain way to weaken a queen and her powerful allies in the court was to accuse the queen of adultery.[38]

A charge of adultery could also be used by a king to justify divorce or the repudiation of his wife. In such cases the accusation against the queen was usually linked to a succession dispute or crisis: a king might attempt to repudiate a childless or barren wife in order to take another, presumably more fertile, wife or to marry a mistress and legitimize his children with her. The history of medieval queenship records several such accusations, as in the charge of adultery used by Charles the Fat in an attempt to repudiate his childless wife Richardis so that he could legitimize his bastard son.[39]

While barren queens might also be accused of witchcraft to justify repudiation, adultery seems to dominate in trials of queens.[40] Indeed, it is tempting to suggest that by the twelfth century the association of a barren queen and the accusation of adultery had become something of a narrative convention. Two stories of queens accused of adultery may illustrate this claim. The first, the *Life of Cunegonde*, is a twelfth-century hagiographical narrative that recounts the formal accusation of adultery against a tenth-century queen. The second is the story of the adulterous liaison of Queen Eleanor of Aquitaine with her uncle, Raymond of Antioch, with which I began this chapter.

Queen Cunegonde, wife of Emperor Henry II, died in 1033. Henry was canonized in 1146, Cunegonde in 1200. St. Cunegonde was revered for her conjugal chastity and, perhaps to illustrate her virtue, her story includes a false accusation of adultery made by her husband's advisors. The queen went to the ordeal to prove her innocence, and at a trial presided over by her husband Cunegonde walked barefoot over twelve hot plowshares and was not burned.[41] It is likely that the accusation of adultery and the subsequent trial by ordeal were added to Cunegonde's story with a view to her canonization,[42] and Dyan Elliott has suggested that the trial story suggests a hostility toward chaste wives that is part of "masculine efforts to monopolize chastity—this former bastion of female virtuosity."[43] Indeed, the form of Cunegonde's story may bear the marks of a contest between the chaste husband and the chaste wife. If Cunegonde's con-

tinence were to be challenged in her story, it could not be through an
accusation that she had sexual relations with her husband, since that
would impugn Henry's chastity. The accusation, though it would be
proved false, could not emphasize Cunegonde's virtue by implicat-
ing Henry's. The accusation of adultery was then the most logical
charge for Cunegonde to disprove. Whatever the hagiographer's mo-
tives may have been in adding adultery to Cunegonde's story, the association of a queen and the accusation of sexual transgression has a
long history, and during the century in which Cunegonde's *Life* was
composed, it also became a prominent subject of fictional narratives.

It may be possible to read behind the accounts of Eleanor of
Aquitaine's liaison with her uncle, Raymond of Antioch, in order to
explore further the association of queens and adultery. Most chroniclers who recount Eleanor's story do not identify the rumors of the
queen's adultery as the reason for the royal couple's later divorce.
The discovery of their relationship within proscribed degrees of consanguinity was the ostensible reason for the divorce, although it was
probably strongly motivated by the growing mutual antipathy of the
queen and king.[44] It hard to imagine that succession concerns had no
role in the king's desire to end the marriage. Although Louis "loved
the queen almost beyond reason," in the words of John of Salisbury,[45]
the couple had only two daughters after fifteen years of marriage.
As Jane Martindale has suggested, "for dynastic reasons King Louis
needed the separation rather more than Eleanor."[46] This is certainly
the retrospective view of the incident, held by a thirteenth-century
chronicler who used the rumors about Eleanor's adultery as the basis
for his account of her story in the *Récits d'un ménestrel de Reims*. In
this very free adaptation of the rumored events, the queen's failure
to produce an heir displaces the adultery as the motivating reason to
divorce the queen, and the king's counselors advise him to end the
marriage with Eleanor because the queen is barren: "The best advice
that we can give you is that you let her go," the vassals counsel, "for
she is a demon, and if you keep her for a long time we fear that she
will kill you. And above all, you don't have any children with her."[47]
In this account even Eleanor's two daughters disappear, again suggesting that the link between the lack of children and the accusations

of adultery and witchcraft demonstrated in the lives of earlier queens may have become a literary commonplace.

More importantly, perhaps, the *Récits d'un ménestrel de Reims* illustrates the link between succession and adultery that structures accusations against queens. In the thirteenth-century narrative Eleanor's barrenness substitutes for her adultery as the reason the king must divorce her. In Cunegonde's story the queen's lack of children is a sign of her marital continence, of course, but the royal couple's virtue is at odds with the demands of medieval monarchy, and the accusation of adultery against the queen suggests the extent to which the entire court has a stake in the queen's maternity. These narratives about queens and adultery demonstrate the importance of the queen's sexual purity and of her fertility. They also demonstrate the precarious status of the barren queen in the royal court.

While Eleanor of Aquitaine had only daughters with Louis VII, she had five sons with her second husband, Henry II of England, and she was a powerful queen consort in the English court. Using Aquitaine as a power base, she actively plotted with and against her husband. Ultimately, however, Eleanor's power as queen consort and as a mother could not challenge her husband's sovereignty. In 1174 Henry imprisoned her and kept her captive for a decade.

Eleanor's period of active political intrigue may have marked the beginning of a decline in the power of medieval queens. The main effect of the evolving construction of royal sovereignty in twelfth- and thirteenth-century Europe was to distance the queen from the exercise of royal authority in her own right. Although queens retained some influential roles in the court, those powers were circumscribed by ritual and by their mediatory nature, as in the queen's role as intercessor. Strohm has noted the *limits* inherent in the queen's intercessory powers, which he describes as a "power premised on exceptional vulnerability."[48] That the queen's power was always limited and based on her exclusion from legitimate, regular decision-making processes in the court did not mean that these rituals and symbols were not available for manipulation, as Parsons has shown, but it does mean that the queen's power is defined as secondary, derived from private, rather than public interventions.[49]

Changes in medieval queenship were part of complex and multi-faceted definitions of royal authority and royal sovereignty, and the importance of gender in the evolution of sovereignty is a disputed one. Over the course of the twelfth century several king's daughters claimed their fathers' thrones, and although these successions were challenged, gender was not explicitly used to justify a daughter's exclusion from succession. Urraca, daughter of Alfonso VI of Castile and León, inherited her father's crown and exercised full royal authority before the majority of her own son (1109–1126).[50] Melisende, daughter of Baldwin II of Jerusalem, was crowned after her father died in 1131 and ruled with her husband until his death in 1143, when she was crowned again with her thirteen-year-old son, Baldwin III. The kingdom was subsequently divided between Melisende and her son, and Baldwin gained sovereignty over the entire kingdom only after a brief civil war in 1152.[51] In England, Matilda, daughter of Henry I, was supplanted by her cousin Stephen of Blois, but she assured that the succession of the English crown would go not to Stephen's son, but to her own son, Henry II.[52] In the deliberations and disputes surrounding the successions of Melisende and Urraca, gender was not cited as a reason to prevent the king's daughter from inheriting his throne, nor was gender an issue in the successful challenge of Stephen of Blois that excluded Matilda from the English throne.[53] However, as Huneycutt notes, the silence about Matilda's gender does not mean that contemporary chroniclers did not recognize that a female candidate to the throne posed special problems, and Henry himself seems to have expected that his daughter's accession might not be readily accepted.[54]

Matilda had allies in powerful vassals, as did Baldwin's daughter Melisende, and these kings' daughters' claims may have been more acceptable to their supporters because they could be assimilated to the model of the regent. Both queens were married and had young sons at the time of their fathers' deaths, and Huneycutt has suggested that they were accepted as queens regnant in the model of regents, mothers who would rule until their sons' majorities.[55] Yet the successful accession of Melisende and Urraca did not mean that queens regnant were invulnerable to the kind of attacks sometimes used to undermine the power and authority of queens consort. Both Queen

Urraca and Queen Melisende were rumored to have had adulterous affairs during their reigns, and in the case of Melisende the stories seem to have been encouraged by her husband, who wished to remove her from their shared throne.[56]

Queenship was an evolving institution in the Middle Ages, as was kingship. This study focuses on one period of that evolution, beginning with the changes in the role of queens consort in the twelfth century and ending with the exclusion of women from royal succession in France in the early fourteenth century. This is also the period in which Old French romances about adulterous queens appeared and became popular. Changes in medieval queenship take place largely in practice; they are not extensively debated in philosophical or political treatises. Yet the sources for the study of medieval queenship are rich and varied, as a number of historians and art historians have recently shown: records of queens' coronations, financial records of queens' households, chroniclers' accounts of queens' conduct, and religious and didactic books owned by queens have all been used to explore various aspects of particular queens' lives.[57] This study attempts to extend the sources for the study of medieval queenship to include fictional queens, in particular the adulterous queens of twelfth- and thirteenth-century French romances. My intention is not to assimilate romance representations of queenship to their contemporary counterparts in European courts; romances are not disguised records of contemporary events. However, I will contend that romance narratives respond, sometimes indirectly, to issues raised by the evolving shape of queenship during the period of their production: the role of the queen in government, the importance of childbirth and succession in the royal family, and the importance of the queen's chastity in the rituals and symbolic structures of the royal court.

Romancing the Queen

Romances about adulterous queens and their lovers are some of the best-known examples of medieval French romance narratives. Stories about Guenevere and Lancelot and Iseut and Tristan were trans-

lated, rewritten, and retold throughout most of the European Middle
Ages; they continue to be a popular narrative subject even today.

The *Tristan* romances were probably the first stories about a
courtly queen's enduring love for a knight, and several scholars have
suggested that the introduction of the queen's courtly adultery in the
Lancelot tradition was originally a rewriting of the *Tristan* legend.[58]
The oldest extant versions of the Tristan stories date from the late
twelfth century and include fragments in Anglo-Norman verse by Béroul (around 1190) and by Thomas of England (around 1170–75), and
in Middle High German by Eilhart von Oberg (between 1170 and
1190). Shorter versions of the story appear in other twelfth-century
texts and textual fragments like Marie de France's *Lai de Chevrefeuil*
and the two anonymous *Folie* texts that recount tales of Tristan's
madness. In the early thirteenth century Gottfried von Strassburg
wrote a Middle High German verse adaptation of Thomas's *Tristan*.
Gottfried's text is unfinished, and the earliest extant complete *Tristan* romance is a thirteenth-century Old Norse version of the story
based on Thomas. In the thirteenth century the Tristan stories receive a long prose elaboration in which the Tristan material merges
into the story of King Arthur and his court.[59]

The *Tristan* story has Celtic origins, though scholars have also
identified Hellenic, Persian, and Arabic influences.[60] It is usually assumed that the twelfth-century versions of the Tristan story were
based on oral versions of the legend. The story receives different emphases in all of the twelfth- and thirteenth-century rewritings. The
verse romances have traditionally been classified in two categories:
Béroul and Eilhart represent the *version commune*, the common or
primitive version; the romances of Thomas and Gottfried represent
a *version courtoise*, a courtly version of the story, influenced by French
and German court cultures of the late twelfth and early thirteenth
centuries. This distinction has been the subject of debate, discredited
by some critics and defended by others.[61]

A more precise distinction between the two narrative traditions
in the verse romances has been offered by Tony Hunt and Joan Tasker
Grimbert. These critics identify a moralizing attitude in Thomas's
Tristan that is absent in Béroul; Thomas recounts the adulterous love

as a negative exemplum, a tragic story that condemns rather than celebrates the liaison between the queen and her lover.[62] This view is not shared by all critics. Douglas Kelly, for example, claims that "constancy characterizes *fine amor* as Thomas uses the expression. . . . [L]ove in his romance is, as an ideal, a constant love."[63] The authors of the *Prose Tristan*, composed in the mid- to late thirteenth century, bring yet another perspective to the story. This long elaboration of the Tristan material features the link between love and chivalry and suggests the potential benefits of even adulterous love for the court society protected by the knight's chivalric prowess, which is inspired by love.[64]

The adulterous love of Queen Iseut and Tristan does not have a static representation in twelfth- and thirteenth-century romances. Its pre-Christian elements and motifs are incorporated into a Christian value system and imbued with some of the values of court society in the so-called "courtly" versions of the story; it may be censored by Thomas and Gottfried in moralizing representations and authorial interventions; it is appropriated as an inspiration for chivalric prowess and potential good in the *Prose Tristan*. Yet despite the various authorial stances and treatments of the story, the portrayal of the adulterous queen and her position in the hierarchy of power and in the symbolic structure of the romance feudal court remain remarkably stable. Iseut is vulnerable to accusation and adept at dissimulation in all the stories. She has influence over the king but she is subject to his justice. Her adultery may be implicitly accepted or explicitly condemned by romance authors, but her position as a queen and the definition of her function in the political structure of the court do not change in the various narratives.

Representations of Guenevere demonstrate the same consistency. Both Guenevere and Arthur appear in early chronicles and in Celtic tales, and while Guenevere is an adulterous wife in some of these narratives, it is only with Chrétien de Troyes's *Chevalier de la charrete* (around 1177) that Guenevere is linked with Lancelot.[65] Chrétien's romance provides a model for later medieval developments of the story. The early thirteenth-century *Prose Lancelot* incorporates the *Charrete* in a long prose compilation that includes the quest for the holy grail and the story of the downfall of Arthur's kingdom. The addition of the grail material brings an explicit condemnation of the queen's adultery: Lancelot will not find the grail because he has sinned with the queen—but as in the *Tristan* stories, this attitude does not significantly change the position of the queen in court hierarchies of power and influence, nor does it alter the function of the queen in the political structure of the court.[66]

Twelfth- and thirteenth-century French romances about Iseut and Guenevere present an ambiguous portrait of the adulterous queen, a woman of exemplary beauty and courtesy who betrays her marriage vows to pursue a liaison with a lover. These queens are morally complex characters, neither wholly good nor entirely evil. The constancy of their devotion to their lovers stands in uneasy juxtaposition to their disregard for marital fidelity, and their apparent lack of regret for the betrayal of their husbands is set against the all-consuming nature of their passion for the knights who return their love.

In romance narratives, adultery is a transgression against the king. To be sure, the king is not always a faithful husband and the queen may suffer the consequences of the king's infidelity, but the status of the queen's adultery is different from that of the king's infidelity. First of all, the queen's conception of an illegitimate child threatens the proper succession of the throne in a way that the birth of a king's bastard does not. The queen's child is born into the royal family, whether or not her husband is the father. Second, in romance narratives, the queen's adultery is featured more prominently than the king's sexual infidelities. Guenevere's liaison with Lancelot, although occasionally interrupted, lasts her entire life; Arthur's adulterous relationships are recounted as brief episodes. And finally, although the queen is the transgressor, a woman who deliberately betrays her husband to pursue an adulterous love relationship, she also occupies the place of the victim, as does her lover, because they are ruled by an impossible love and by a passion beyond their control. They are guilty of a crime against the king, but they are also the subjects of a love that is rendered exemplary, even praiseworthy, by its selfless dedication and inescapable force. This passion is given an external source in the *Tristan* romances, where it is caused by a love potion the lovers drink together.[67] The queen's adultery is simultaneously a sin, a crime against the king, and the form of true love in medieval romances about Guenevere and Iseut. The reception of these stories by other romance authors and by poets reflects the ambivalent status of adultery in the two queens' stories. Both Guenevere and Iseut are standards of comparison in descriptions of feminine beauty and of love; Chrétien de Troyes claims that one of his beautiful heroines is more lovely than "Isolz la blonde."[68] But while the queen is praised as an exemplary beauty and an exemplary lover in some texts, in others the queen's love is condemned for its adulterous nature. In Chrétien's *Cligés*, the empress Fenice condemns Iseut as a woman who was willing to share her body between two men: "Love debased himself too much in her, for her heart belonged to one man and her body was the property of two lords." ("Amors en li trop vilena, / Que ses cuers fu a un entiers, / Et ses cors fu a deus rentiers." *Cligés*, vv. 3112–14; Chrétien, 125.)

Alongside romances that represent the courtly adultery of Guenevere and Iseut or that critique that tradition, there is a group of romance narratives about adulterous queens that is not directly linked to the examples of Guenevere or Iseut. Several twelfth- and thirteenth-century narratives recount the story of the queen who attempts to seduce one of her husband's vassals and then tries to destroy him when he refuses her advances. Romances like *Le roman des sept sages* or *Le roman de Silence* eliminate the reciprocal love that characterizes the adultery of Guenevere and Iseut, and they explicitly represent the queen's betrayal of the king as an act motivated by the queen's evil intentions. Seductress queens are not compared to courtly queens like Iseut and Guenevere, but even though their stories take different trajectories, all these queens share a position of dependency upon the king that is highlighted in accusations of adultery, in tests and judgments of the queen, and in the precarious status of the queen's authority in the court.

The romance queen's vulnerability to accusations of sexual transgression resembles the position of medieval queens like Eleanor of Aquitaine. However, medieval French romances about adulterous

queens do not directly address the issues at stake in the evolving definition of medieval queenship in the twelfth and thirteenth centuries;
if anything, they seem to reverse the values promoted in medieval
monarchies. While medieval queens accused of adultery defended
their innocence through oaths or the ordeal, romance queens use
tests and ordeals not to disprove a false accusation but to falsify the
proof of a true accusation. Yet even though romance representations
of queenship do not correspond precisely to the experiences of medieval queens, they nonetheless represent some of the issues at stake in
the debated relationship between women and power.

Reading Adultery

It is the claim of this book that romance representations of adulterous queens are part of a debate about queenship in medieval culture.
Representations of nonfictional queens, whether by the chroniclers
who recorded their actions, the clerics who scripted their piety and
performance of rituals, or the autorepresentations that might be reconstructed from the queen's participation in royal documents, teach
us much about the queen's sphere of action and influence, as recent
work by historians of queenship has shown. Romance representations of queenship cannot provide this kind of evidence about the
lives of individual queens, but they may tell us something about the
anxieties hidden in more "objective" accounts of medieval queenship.
    Literary historians have long proposed that courtly literature
may reveal the concerns and aspirations of aristocratic society. Erich
Köhler, Georges Duby, and, more recently, R. Howard Bloch and
Sandra Hindman have suggested ways in which medieval romances
might speak the concerns and anxieties of a medieval aristocracy in a
changing society.[69] This study attempts to extend the work of these
scholars by providing an account of how romances about adulterous
queens might represent some of the cultural attitudes that contributed to the definition of queenship in medieval France. Although it
does not focus precisely on the question of how romances may represent the interests of an aristocratic class, it assumes that the evolving

definition of queenship in the twelfth and thirteenth centuries is relevant to the nobility in at least two important ways. First, the queen's position in the royal household is a model for all wives, as Duby notes:

> In the ninth century the clergy had described the perfect order of the royal household. In the center was the sovereign, but at his side a woman, his own. She was adorned with the king's title, but in the feminine form, *regina*; she was his associate, *consors*. Although assuredly inferior to him, she dominated the rest of the household. Deputed to the "economy," in the etymological sense of this term, she had the task of maintaining domestic life in good order and, in particular, of supervising its reserves of wealth. Finally and above all, whatever power she enjoyed was bound to the obligation that was hers only, the obligation of maternity. It was as *mater regis*, mother of the future king and of all his progeny to the end of time, that she was celebrated.
>
> This model left its mark first on the princely houses, then on those of all holders of *potestas*. In the twelfth century a man, himself alone, headed these houses, as in the royal house. Beside him a woman, herself alone, his wife. For in these houses there was only one conjugal bed, only one place of licit, legitimate, manifest copulation.[70]

The concerns of the royal household—the wife's role in reproduction, the sphere of her influence and power—were the concerns of the noble household.

Second, apart from the model of domestic organization that the queen's marriage offered, queenship also represented a potential access to government that could be of concern to noblemen in twelfth- and thirteenth-century Europe. Although Capetian queens were queens consort, they could act as regents for underage sons or for absent husbands, as did Blanche of Castile. And although only sons inherited the Capetian throne, women were not officially excluded from royal succession until 1316.

That romances about adulterous queens may speak about some of these issues may at first glance seem unlikely. Although they may repeat the association of adultery and queenship that surfaced occasionally in the history of European queenship, they present adultery as either a courtly love relationship that is widely condoned or as the desire of an evil queen that is widely condemned. And the question of how the representation of adultery might have been understood by its public is a contested one. As Simon Gaunt has noted, "Sexuality is a powerful regulating force in romance, but it has the potential to destroy social cohesion. . . . The hero of romance is a divided self, split between an impulse towards social integration and a counter-impulse towards socially alienating, but privately fulfilling desires."[71] In what follows I start from Gaunt's suggestion of the relationship between sexuality and social cohesion and I argue that, in stories about queens, adultery becomes a narrative structure rather than a moral problem.[72] In a move that may be suspect to some readers, I will avoid attempting to read a moral attitude about adultery in these narratives. Moral judgment is never completely eliminated from the story of the adulterous queen, but it is appropriated as an enabling background for the queen's transgression: adversity defines true love for the queen and her knight. Rather than suggesting that romances offer adultery as an exemplary conduct, or—at the other extreme—that they perform a didactic function in condemning sexual trans-gression, I will try to show that romance narratives about adulterous queens appropriate a moral framework to represent a lesson about status and legitimacy.

This study of medieval French romances about adulterous queens is framed by the accusation of adultery against Eleanor of Aquitaine in 1148 and the adultery scandal involving the daughters-in-law of Philip IV in 1316 that announced the end of the Capetian royal dynasty. It is not strictly chronological in the sense that I do not attempt to trace evolutions in romance representations of adul-terous queens, although I do focus on differences between particular representations. These narratives are highly intertextual—the *Tristan* legend structures almost all of them to some extent—but more im-portant for this study, the *function* of the queen's adultery remains remarkably stable in all of these stories. In what follows, I attempt to show how the queen's adultery is part of the political structure of the romance feudal court and to demonstrate the symbolic function of the queen's sexual transgression within that structure. I suggest that romance representations of adulterous queens, characterized by an ambiguous attitude toward the queen's adultery, correspond to a precise period of narrative possibility created in part by changes in medieval queenship. This project, then, attempts to situate twelfth-and thirteenth-century French romances about adulterous queens in the context of the evolving definition of queenship during the same period. It attempts to show how a narrative structure is also a political structure, and it examines the function of the queen's adultery within that structure.

I begin with an examination of the symbolic uses of the queen's body in the romance feudal court. Chapter 1 focuses on Chrétien de Troyes's *Cligés* and on the way that the heroine, an empress, debates the rhetorical definition of her body in relation to succession, love, and bodily integrity. In Chapter 2 I examine a number of narratives in which chastity tests and trials by ordeal figure a challenge to royal authority that is overcome when the adulterous queen proves that she is innocent of adultery. In these stories the queen's duplicitous proof not only restores a troubled royal sovereignty but exposes the process by which the queen's body is invested with anxieties about royal sovereignty.

If the queen's body is constructed as a symbol of the king's authority in power struggles in the romance court, it is further objectified in the rumors and accusations of adultery whose goal is to displace not the queen, but her lover from a privileged position in the court. The often-evoked threat that adultery poses to political stability is a fiction of the text, spoken by characters who wish to remove the queen's lover from the court. As I show in Chapter 3 with reference to Béroul's *Tristan*, the political stability of the fictitious feudal court is shown to depend on a hidden structure of triangulated relationships defined by the queen's transgressive sexuality; social stability and narrative order depend ironically upon the queen's adultery.

The queen's body is always a barren body in these narratives, and in Chapter 4 I turn to several romances that may explain the necessary absence of children in narratives where the queen's adultery is a pretext for political contests and a source of political stability. Accusations of adultery against the queen and the symbolic equation of the integrity of the queen's body and the integrity of the king's rule locate political stability in the proof of the queen's sexual purity.

They also reveal an anxiety about a political system that depends on women's sexual integrity for its stability. Although in most romances about adulterous queens the queen has no children, in their representation of the duplicitous equation of the queen's body and royal sovereignty, these narratives implicitly speak a fear of illegitimacy and of improper succession that applies not only to the king's throne but to any aristocratic household.

In a final chapter I explore representations of queens whose desire for pleasure and power is explicitly connected. Stories about a queen who attempts to seduce one of her husband's vassals provide the most prominent representations of women's political influence and ambition to be found in medieval romance. The queen actively intervenes in her husband's government of his court, influencing his relationship with a vassal and the judicial procedures of his court. The queen who fails in her seduction is an evil character, however, and her story implicitly identifies a danger in according power to women. I will suggest that what I have identified as an anxiety about illegitimacy in stories of adulterous queens is ultimately an anxiety about women and power: about women's power to hide paternity, about women's power to subvert succession, and about women's illegitimate access to power. In a short conclusion I suggest that after the adultery scandal late in the reign of Philip IV the representation of the courtly adulterous queen is no longer a viable way to represent anxieties about queenship. First, at this period the shape of romance is changed by the addition of the grail quest to the stories of Guenevere and Lancelot and by the growing popularity of allegorical romances. Second, the appearance of adultery and the suspicion of illegitimacy in the royal family realizes the scenario that is consistently avoided in romances and makes the oblique representation of this very crisis irrelevant. Finally, and most importantly, the adultery scandal corresponds to a succession crisis. In 1316 for the first time in France, females are excluded from royal succession. The question of women and power receives a definitive answer, at least on one front: a woman may not rule in France. At least not directly. But that story escapes the scope of this project.

I

Royal Succession
and the Queen's Two Bodies

IN ONE OF THE EARLIEST versions of the story of Queen Guenevere, the Anglo-Norman poet Wace notes that "she had many graces
and she had a noble bearing, she was very generous and spoke well.
Arthur loved and cherished her greatly, but they had no heir and were
unable to have any child" (*Le roman de Brut*, vv. 9653–58).[1] Wace's
reference to Queen Guenevere's inability to produce children is the
only explanation of the queen's barrenness in medieval literature.
It is not found in Wace's source, Geoffrey of Monmouth's *Historia
Regum Britanniae*, and the twelfth- and thirteenth-century romances
that make Guenevere into a celebrated lover and adulteress do not
attempt to explain why the queen has no children.

In around 1155 Wace's *Brut* was presented to the new queen
of England, Eleanor of Aquitaine, a few years after her marriage to
Henry II, according to Layamon, who translated the *Brut* into English.[2] In a recent biographical study of Eleanor, D. D. R. Owen
has suggested that Wace may have been aware of the possible similarities between the lives of Guenevere and Eleanor. Owen further
suggests that Wace's explanation of the queen's lack of children with
Arthur may have been intended to justify her subsequent adultery
with Mordred. With reference to the text's association with Eleanor
of Aquitaine he speculates that Guenevere's relationship with Arthur
may remind readers of Eleanor's relationship with her first husband,
Louis VII, with whom she had no sons.[3] While Henry might have
had some interest in seeing himself represented as a once and future

king, it is hard to imagine that Eleanor would have welcomed the association with an adulteress, particularly since only a few years earlier Eleanor herself was rumored to have had an adulterous liaison with her uncle, Raymond of Antioch.

The speculative equation of Guenevere and Eleanor of Aquitaine may demonstrate the difficulty and, ultimately, the futility of the search for nonfictional models behind fictional representations of adulterous queens. This is not to say that there is no relationship between medieval queens and romance representations of queenship; this book attempts to identify just such a relationship. But I will suggest that the relationship between fictional and nonfictional queens is to be discovered not in biographical imitation, but in the representation of the queen's changing and contested position in the royal court. One important factor in the definition of the status and influence of medieval queens is maternity.

Wace's explanation of Guenevere's barrenness leads Owen to suggest that the queen's lack of children may have provided a partial justification for her adultery.[4] Lancelot does not appear in this early narrative about King Arthur's court, but Guenevere has an adulterous liaision with Mordred, who is not identified as Arthur's illegitimate son in this text.[5] In the French romance tradition the treasonous adultery with Mordred is displaced by the courtly adultery with Lancelot. Although Guenevere is still barren in later retellings and elaborations of her story, her inability to have children is not explained and it is not cited as a reason or a justification for adultery by romance authors. Owen's suggestion of a causal link between the queen's lack of children and her adultery in the *Brut* cannot be applied to later romance narratives about Queen Guenevere, but Owen identifies a link between barrenness and adultery that finds a persistent representation in French romances.

In almost all twelfth- and thirteenth-century medieval French romances, adulterous queens are barren.[6] Iseut has no children and Guenevere is usually childless. In one thirteenth-century grail romance Guenevere has a son with Arthur called Loholt, but he appears only briefly and his primary role in the story seems to be to die young.[7] Moreover, Loholt's paternity is never disputed within the romance, even though the adulterous relationship of Lancelot and Guenevere is recounted in the story.[8] *Le livre de Caradoc* provides the one example in twelfth- and thirteenth-century romance of an adulterous queen who conceives an illegitimate son with her lover. The representation of the relationship between succession and sexual transgression in *Caradoc* is rather different from the barren courtly adultery that characterizes the liaisons of Queen Guenevere and Queen Iseut, and I will discuss it in detail in Chapter 4. But despite the unusual form that the queen's adultery takes in this story—her lover is a magician—*Caradoc* demonstrates that the illegitimate child of an adulterous queen and her lover is a possible subject of romance narratives, and it underscores the repression of reproduction—both legitimate and illegitimate—in other stories about adulterous queens.

Christiane Marchello-Nizia has suggested that the queen's lack of children with either her lover or her husband figures the sterility of the most important relationship in the adulterous love triangle, the relationship of the knight and the king.[9] That is, the adulterous queen's lack of children is a figural representation of the sterile homosocial relationship between the two men who are her lovers. I wish to extend Marchello-Nizia's reading with a deliberately literal examination of the queen's lack of children in medieval romances. Within the context of medieval monarchy, what might motivate the representation of the adulterous queen as barren?

One possible reason for the adulterous queen's lack of children is the threat of illegitimacy. Georges Duby has noted that "adultery, though consummated, was barren. Bastardy was too serious a matter to be treated lightly, even in literature. People were too afraid of it to use it as a subject for a tale."[10] Duby refers, of course, to "bastardy" located within an aristocratic marriage. Many romances represent kings who father children outside of marriage, but the separation of marriage and childbirth is impossible for the queen. Any child of the queen is a child of her marriage, and an illegitimate child in the royal family subverts the proper succession of the crown and opens the possibility of political chaos.

Illegitimacy is certainly not absent in medieval literature, but children born outside of wedlock are not necessarily conceived in adulterous unions.[11] Lancelot's son, Galahad; Bors's son, Hélain le Blanc; and the son that Gauvain conceives with the demoiselle de Lis are all illegitimate, but in each case neither parent is married when the child is conceived. Succession and inheritance issues are absent in these stories of illegitimacy, and even in the case of a romance narrative about a king's son conceived in adultery, illegitimacy is hidden by other kinship ties when succession is at stake. In *La mort le roi Artu*, Mordred, the son of King Arthur and his sister, gains proximity to the throne and to the queen through his recognized kinship with the king, who is his uncle. His claim to the throne is an usurpation, not an illegitimate succession.

The possibility of uncertain succession is resolutely suppressed in medieval romances about adulterous queens. The adulterous queen has no children, legitimate or illegitimate, and her failure to produce children is not a subject of discussion in the romance that recounts her story. Succession concerns may explain the king's decision to marry, as in one version of the Tristan story, where Marc's barons urge him to marry in order to produce an heir, but when Iseut does not have a child, the barons do not again mention their desire for royal progeny.[12] Nor does the queen herself usually acknowledge her own lack of children or the importance of succession in the royal family.

A notable exception to the queen's silence about reproduction is found in the twelfth-century *Cligés* by Chrétien de Troyes. In Chrétien's romance the heroine, Fenice, newly married to the emperor of Constantinople but in love with his nephew, Cligés, wishes to disrupt the succession that she is intended to assure. As long as the emperor has no children, his nephew will be his heir, and the empress claims that she does not want to produce a child who would disinherit Cligés: "Ja de moi ne puisse anfes nestre / Par cui il soit desheritez." ("May I never be able to bear a child and so bring about his disinheritance." *Cligés*, vv. 3152–53; Chrétien, 125–26.) Chrétien's *Cligés* is the story of a disputed succession that extends over two generations. Roughly the first half of the romance recounts the story of Alexander, eldest son of the emperor of Constantinople. Alexander goes to

King Arthur's court to prove his chivalric skills and marries Arthur's niece, Soredamors, with whom he has a son named Cligés. When the emperor of Constantinople dies, Alexander's younger brother, Alis, believes that Alexander is dead and he has himself crowned emperor. Alexander returns to Constantinople to claim his throne, and in order to avoid a civil war the brothers are persuaded to agree on a compromise. Alis will wear the crown, but Alexander will govern. Furthermore, Alis agrees never to marry so that the throne will pass to its rightful heir, Alexander's son, Cligés. The second half of the romance recounts the emperor's betrayal of his promise to his brother, his marriage to the daughter of the emperor of Germany, the love of Fenice and Cligés, the ruses they use to deceive the emperor, and finally, the death of the emperor, the reinstatement of the rightful heir, Cligés, and his marriage to Fenice.

In *Cligés* Chrétien rewrites the celebrated story of Queen Iseut, Tristan, and King Marc. Chrétien does not state that the *Tristan* stories provided a model for *Cligés*, but he certainly knew the *Tristan* romance in some form since in the prologue to *Cligés* he claims to have written a version of the story, now lost, and his heroine, Fenice, makes explicit references to the adulterous love of Tristan and Iseut.[13] The parallels between *Cligés* and *Tristan* are obvious. Both romances recount the story of a knight who loves his uncle's wife. In *Cligés* Alis is an emperor, not a king like Marc, but the imperial throne is clearly hereditary, and the emperor's relationship with the nobles in his court closely resembles King Marc's relationship with his barons. The empress Fenice occupies the same position in the royal family as Queen Iseut: she is married to a sovereign and loves his nephew. Unlike the queen and her lover in the *Tristan* stories, however, Fenice and Cligés do not pursue an adulterous liaison under the eyes of the royal husband. Fenice repeatedly states her desire to avoid the example of Queen Iseut.

Cligés is often called an anti-*Tristan* story, written to revise and refute the legend of Queen Iseut and her two lovers, which Chrétien and his audience would have found distasteful.[14] In what follows I will question the extent to which Chrétien's story really rewrites the story of the adulterous queen, but here I wish to emphasize the way in which *Cligés* acknowledges the succession concerns that are suppressed in the *Tristan* stories and in other romances about adulterous queens.

When Fenice explicitly speaks her desire not to conceive a child who would displace her lover in the succession of the emperor's throne ("Ja de moi ne puisse anfes nestre / Par cui il soit desheritez," vv. 3152–53), the empress recognizes the royal wife's role in dynastic succession and she acknowledges that pregnancy is a logical result of marriage. Fenice does not dwell on the relationship between sexual intercourse and pregnancy; such a discourse would be out of place in a courtly romance, and the fact that the empress is married to a man she does not love may explain why there is any discussion of pregnancy at all.[15] When Fenice states that she does not want to play a role in the usurpation of Cligés's throne, her motivation for saving her virginity is not only to save Cligés's inheritance but also to justify her refusal to open her body to a man she does not love.[16] Even though she offers competing explanations for her desire to avoid a sexual relationship with her husband, Fenice's acknowledgment of the queen's role in succession makes visible the link between chastity, childbirth, and royal succession that is suppressed in other narratives about adulterous queens.

In medieval monarchies, a queen gained influence and status in the royal court through reproduction. Historians have shown that the queen's maternity was promoted in the symbolism of coronation rites and that the ritualization of the queen's intercession with the king included maternal imagery that symbolized the queen's sexual intimacy with her husband and her privileged and important status as mother of the king's children.[17] In medieval romances about royal adultery the queen has no children, and there are few explicit reminders of the importance of royal childbirth in these narratives. One consequence of the disassociation of the adulterous queen from succession in medieval romance is that the queen's barren body becomes the subject of secrets and rumors, of tests and judgments, and of reconciliations and renunciations. While the importance of the queen's physical integrity may be associated implicitly with the importance of royal succession, in romances the queen's chastity comes to have an importance that is independent of the role of the queen's maternity in assuring the continuation of a dynasty. The question of the queen's fidelity subsumes the goal of proper succession, the reproductive body is displaced by an adulterous body, and the concerns about succession and legitimacy that might logically be raised by a knowledge of the queen's adultery are suppressed and displaced in the scrutiny of the queen's sexual body. The narrative and political ends served by this displacement are the subject of what follows.[18]

The Signifying Body

In an analysis of rituals of pollution and taboo that take the human body as their object, Mary Douglas has suggested that the body functions as a symbol of society, "a model which can stand for any bounded system."[19] In its particular configuration of interior and exterior, the body may represent the containments and exclusions that define the margins of a social system, and ritual enactments of concepts of pollution and taboo work to keep the limits of society intact through their symbolic assimilation to the boundaries of the body: "the symbolism of the body's boundaries is used . . . to express danger to community boundaries."[20]

Douglas's study of the way that bodies function symbolically to represent social integrity provides a useful framework through which to read medieval romance. One of the best-known characteristics of this genre is the way in which the virtues and vices of characters may be reflected in their physical appearance: good and brave knights are always beautiful, and physical deformity often reflects moral degradation.[21] Thus, on one obvious level the body is associated with a symbolic system since physical perfection may reflect moral superiority. More pertinent to a reading of the body in the context of the court society represented in medieval romances is the way in which threats to the political stability of the court and to the boundaries that establish and maintain it take as their focus the disputed integrity of the queen's body.

In romances about adulterous queens, the king's political authority at court is often shown to be compromised by his (un)knowing complicity in the adulterous relationship between his wife and her lover. This relationship is represented most clearly in the *Tristan* romances, where King Marc is shown to waver between the certainty that Tristan and Iseut are lovers and the belief in their innocence. Marc's feudal vassals, enemies of Tristan, repeatedly reproach the king for his hesitation and urge him to act against the lovers. In Béroul's *Tristan* they accuse the king of weakness because he tolerates the adultery of his wife and nephew and they demand that he banish Tristan from the kingdom.

"Alon au ro et si li dimes,
Ou il nos aint ou il nos hast,
Nos volon son nevo en chast." . . .
"Rois," ce dïent li troi felon,
"Par foi, mais nu consentiron;
Qar bien savon de verité
Que tu consenz lor cruauté,
Et tu sez bien ceste mervelle.
Q'en feras tu? Or t'en conselle!
Se ton nevo n'ostes de cort,
Si que jamais il ne retort,
Ne nos tenron a vos jamez,
Si ne vos tendron nule pez.
De nos voisins feron partir
De cort, que nel poon soufrir." (Béroul, vv. 600–624)

("Let us go to the king and tell him that whatever he may think of us, we want him to banish his nephew." . . . "King," said the three barons, "by our faith, we will not permit this any longer, because we know for a fact that you are fully aware of their crime and that you condone it. What will you do about it? Consider it carefully: If you do not banish your nephew from court so that he never returns, you will never have our allegiance, and we will never leave you in peace. We will also have others leave the court, for we cannot tolerate this." [Lacy, 31])

Although Marc's barons implicitly invoke the violation of a restricted access to the queen's body in their accusation against Tristan, they do not openly address the question of disputed paternity for the king's future heirs. Their demand that King Marc separate Tristan and the queen may be linked to a desire for a royal heir of undisputed paternity, but this imperative, like any warning of an anticipated challenge to the succession, remains unspoken. In romance narratives accusations of adultery focus on the sexual rather than the dynastic, and despite the fact that accusations of adultery like the one in *Tristan* concern the queen and her lover equally, the separation suggested as a solution to the social and political dilemma focuses on the queen: her monogamy must be restored by re-restricting the access to her body that she granted to her lover. Tristan must be banished.[22]

In the barons' accusation the integrity of the queen's body symbolizes the integrity of the king's sovereignty. Marc can restore both by separating Tristan and Iseut. The equation of the queen's sexual purity and the king's sovereign authority is not the only meaning of the queen's adulterous body in medieval romances. Stories about queens and their lovers are not just narratives about political structures, they are also love stories, and the representation of the queen's body is structured by its relationship to unshared marital love and reciprocal adulterous passion, and to the obligations of marriage and the desire for forbidden pleasure. The adulterous queen's barren body circulates in several symbolic systems in medieval romances and it is shaped by its position in the political hierarchy of the feudal court, by its significance in a system of dynastic reproduction, and by its circulation between marital duty and adulterous passion. The body's meaning is negotiated and contested in relation to various networks of signification.

In her study of pollution and abjection in *Powers of Horror*, Julia Kristeva reconsiders Douglas's work on the symbolic significances of the human body in taboo rituals. Kristeva observes a distinction in Douglas's analysis between the body in a symbolic system and the body as a prototype of the society or of a symbolic system. She categorizes this split in terms of *syntax* (pollution as an element related to the limits or margins of a social order) and *semantics* (the *meaning* of this element of limit in other systems).[23] For Kristeva the split between the syntax and the semantics of the body can only be resolved by placing it in the symbolic order (as opposed to a symbolic system), that is, in its relationship to language.[24] The location of the body in a symbolic order suggests a useful critical perspective on the way that the adulterous queen's barren body acquires meaning in medieval romances. The syntactic view of the romance queen's adulterous body that defines the queen's body as a symbol of political order may be supplemented by an investigation of the adulterous, royal body's *semantic* value, of how it is invested with meaning. Rather than assuming—like Marc's barons—that the state of the queen's body indicates a truth about the king's authority, we might ask how the adulterous queen's body acquires value in the various symbolic systems of medieval romance.

Cligés recounts the way that the queen's adulterous body gains meaning through rhetorical constructions of integrity and dismemberment. When Fenice cites the adultery of her literary predecessor, Queen Iseut, as an example she refuses to follow, she focuses on the metaphorical definition of the queen's body. According to the empress, when Iseut became the lover of her husband's nephew, she split her body between two men:

Mialz voldroie estre desmanbree
Que de nos deus fust remanbree
L'amors d'Ysolt et de Tristan,
Don mainte folie dit an,
Et honte en est a reconter.
Ja ne m'i porroie acorder
A la vie qu'Isolz mena.
Amors en li trop vilena,
Que ses cuers fu a un entiers,
Et ses cors fu a deus rentiers.
Ensi tote sa vie usa
N'onques les deus ne refusa.
Ceste amors ne fu pas resnable,
Mes la moie iert toz jorz estable,
Car de mon cors et de mon cuer
N'iert ja fet partie a nul fuer.
Ja mes cors n'iert voir garçoniers,
N'il n'i avra deus parçoniers.
Qui a le cuer, cil a le cors,
Toz les autres an met defors. (*Cligés*, vv. 3105–24)

(I would rather be torn limb from limb than have the two of us be reminiscent of the love of Tristan and Iseult. Many madnesses, shameful to recount, were spoken of them. I could never reconcile myself to the life Iseult led. Love debased himself too much in her, for her heart belonged to one man and her body was the property of two lords. Thus she passed all her life, never refusing the two. Unreasonable was that love. But mine will always be stable, for under no circumstance will my heart and my body ever be divided. My body will never be prostituted. It will never be possessed by two partners. The man who has the heart has the body too; I exclude all others. [Chrétien, 125])

Fenice claims that she would rather her body be mutilated than to have it split between two lovers, as Iseut's was. The empress identifies the division of the body—the heart and body possessed by one man while another possesses only the body—as an abasement of love and as a prostitution of the body that she describes with metaphors of fragmentation. She rejects the unreasonable, dismembering love enjoyed by Iseut in favor of a "stable" (*estable*) love symbolized by the physical integrity of her body.[25] Fenice defines monogamy as a bodily integrity that counters the psychological fragmentation of adultery.

Fenice's metaphors of dismemberment and integrity are part of a conventional love rhetoric. In the empress's discourse, the separation of the body and the heart represents the alienation of adultery, but it may also simply describe the experience of falling in love. In a study of *Cligés* Michelle Freeman has noted the important "development of metaphors that call to one another throughout the text and which draw the attention of the reader ever deeper into the inward dynamics of the poem."[26] Metaphors of body and heart feature prominently in Cligés, and an examination of their uses may suggest the role played by figural language in defining the significance of the queen's body. Before she states her refusal to follow Iseut's example and separate her body and her heart, Fenice claims that Cligés has stolen her heart, which now disdains its lodging in her body: "Mes cuers de son ostel s'estrenge, / Ne ne vialt o moi remenoir, / Tant het et moi et mon menoir" (vv. 4416–18). And when Cligés returns from England, the knight claims that his body is an empty shell, "like bark without timber" ("com escorce sanz fust," v. 5120) because his heart

stayed with Fenice while his body traveled to King Arthur's court.
Fenice uses the same metaphor to describe her love for Cligés: "En
moi n'a mes fors que l'escorce, / Car sanz cuer vif et sanz cuer sui."
("In me is nothing but the bark, for I live without a heart and exist
without a heart." *Cligés*, vv. 5144–45; Chrétien, 150.)

Although the metaphor of the separation of the heart from the
body is used a number of times in the love story of Fenice and Cligés,
particularly in the passage where the knight and the empress reveal
their love to each other, in other passages there is an adamant rejection of the figurative mutilation of the body. The metaphor receives
a literal reading that emphasizes the violence to the body inherent
in the separation of the body and the heart, as when Fenice claims
that Iseut split her body between two men. The literalization of the
metaphor of the heart that leaves the body is not limited to Fenice's
interpretation of Iseut's adultery. The narrator, too, denies the possibility of the figurative theft of the heart:

Ne dirai pas si com cil dïent
Qui an un cors deus cuers alïent,
Qu'il n'est voirs, n'estre ne le sanble
Qu'an un cors ait deus cuers ansanble;
Et s'il pooient assanbler,
Ne porroit il voir resanbler.
Mes s'il vos pleisoit a entandre,
Bien vos ferai le voir antandre,
Comant dui cuer a un se tienent,
Sanz ce qu'ansanble ne parvienent.
Seul de tant se tienent a un
Que la volanté de chascun
De l'un a l'autre s'an trespasse;
Si vuelent une chose a masse,
Et por tant c'une chose veulent,
I a de tiex qui dire seulent
Que chascuns a le cuer as deus;
Mes uns cuers n'est pas an deus leus.
Bien pueent lor voloir estre uns,
Et s'a adés son cuer chascuns,
Ausi com maint home divers
Pueent an chançons et an vers

Chanter a une concordance.
Si vos pruis par ceste sanblance
C'uns cors ne puet deus cuers avoir,
Ce sachiez vos trestot de voir;
Ne por ce que se li uns set
Quanqu'il covoite et quanqu'il het,
Ne plus que les voiz qui assanblent
Si que tote une chose sanblent
Et si ne pueent estre a un,
Ne puet cors avoir cuer que un. (*Cligés*, vv. 2783–814)

(I shall not talk as do people who speak of uniting two hearts in one body. That two hearts can lodge together in one body is not true, nor does it appear true. And if indeed they could come together, it would not seem to resemble truth. But if it be your pleasure to listen, I shall explain to you the true sense in which two hearts are one without coming together. They become one only insofar as the desire of each passes to the other. They have like desires, and because their desires are identical, some people are accustomed to saying that each possesses two hearts. But one heart is not in two places. Their desires may well be the same, but each has his own heart, just as many different men may sing verses and songs in unison. From this simile I present to you proof that one body is incapable of having two hearts. You may be absolutely certain of this, because even if one does know another's desires and loathings, a body can have but one heart, just as voices in unison that seem a single voice cannot come from one mouth. But there is no need to dwell on this, for another urgent task presses on me. [Chrétien, 121])

The narrator dwells on the logical impossibility of one body possessing two hearts. If Fenice stresses the violent separation of a heart from its body, the narrator stresses the impossible excess of a body with two hearts. Both make a literal interpretation of the metaphor that describes love as the possession of the beloved's heart.

A similarly literal interpretation of a figurative embodiment characterizes the solution Fenice finds to the dilemma that provokes the comparison to Iseut. In an effort to remain faithful to Cligés and to avoid separating the possession of her body from the possession of her heart, the empress uses the drugs prepared by her nurse to double her body through pharmacological illusions.[27] A first potion, administered during the wedding feast, makes the emperor Alis dream that he has sexual intercourse with his wife even though he never touches her. The nurse concocts a second drug when Fenice learns that Cligés returns her love. The empress drinks a potion that gives her a death-like appearance, the emperor believes she is dead, she is placed in her tomb, then rescued by Cligés and revived by her nurse. In Chrétien's romance the fragmented body of the adulterous queen claimed by two men is displaced by the illusion of a doubled body as Fenice creates the fiction of two bodies possessed by two men.[28]

Following Douglas's observation that the body may symbolically contain social anxieties, it might be suggested that Fenice's adulterous and illusory doubled body reflects the doubled claim to the throne by Cligés and Alis. The first claim, by Cligés, is a legitimate one agreed on by Cligés's father and uncle: Alis, a younger brother who claimed the throne based on false rumors of his older brother's death, will hold the title of emperor until his own death, but he will not marry, so that the throne will pass to Cligés in a rightful succession to the elder brother's son. The second claim to the throne, by Alis, is fraudulent and contrary to the agreement that established Cligés's succession, that Alis would never marry and produce heirs (vv. 2531–38).[29] Fenice figures in the conflict since her role as empress is to guarantee the succession of the throne through Alis, and the tricks the empress uses to dupe her husband might be seen as part of an effort to rectify the potential exclusion of Cligés from his inheritance. Fenice herself claims this justification for her deception of Alis: "Garder cuide son pucelage / Por lui sauver son heritage." ("She thought to preserve her virginity in order to save his inheritance for him." *Cligés*, vv. 3185–86; Chrétien, 126.)

The empress's deception acknowledges the importance of the reproductive female body in the succession of a dynastic throne, even an usurped throne. At the same time, it suggests that the significance of the queen's body is not limited to its role in reproducing dynastic continuity, but that its meaning may be contested. In Fenice's references to Iseut the queen's body is defined through metaphors, and the empress's refusal to imitate Iseut moves her motivation for doubling her body from inside the recounted political dilemma that her doubled body might reflect to an intertextual space in which the empress's concern for the metaphoric description of her own body seems to replace political considerations. Fenice's claim that her betrayal of the emperor is motivated by a concern for the proper succession of the crown is undermined by her repeatedly stated fears about how her adultery with Cligés would be described if it were discovered.[30]

When the empress learns that Cligés returns her love, she contemplates how the two of them might live together and share their love. Once again she states her repugnance for the example of Iseut. As in the earlier passage where she condemned the fragmenting effect of Iseut's pursuit of an adulterous liaison with Tristan while married to King Marc, Fenice refuses to follow Iseut's example of corporeal disintegration. Here, however, the focus of Fenice's condemnation of Iseut has shifted from the adulterous queen's willingness to split her body to Iseut's reputation as a woman with two lovers, and the importance of the body's integrity has become secondary to the importance of the body's reputation. Fenice states her willingness to open her body to Cligés, but only if she can avoid being known as an adulteress like Iseut.

Vostre est mes cuers, vostre est mes cors,
Ne ja nus par mon essanplaire
N'aprendra vilenie a faire;
Car quant mes cuers an vos se mist,
Le cors vos dona et promist,
Si qu'autres ja part n'i avra. . . .
Se je vos aim, et vos m'amez,
Ja n'en seroiz Tristanz clamez,
Ne je n'an serai ja Yseuz,
Car puis ne seroit l'amors preuz,
Qu'il i avroit blasme ne vice.
Ja de mon cors n'avroiz delice
Autre que vos or en avez,
Se apanser ne vos poez
Comant je poïsse estre anblee
A vostre oncle et desasanblee,
Si que ja mes ne me retruisse,
Ne moi ne vos blasmer ne puisse,
Ne ja ne s'an sache a cui prandre. (*Cligés*, vv. 5190–211)

(My heart is yours. My body is yours. No one will ever learn base behavior from my example, for when my heart surrendered to you, it promised and gave you the body so that no one else would ever have part of it. . . . If I love you and you love me, you will never be called Tristan and I shall never be Iseult, for then the love would be not honorable but base and subject to reproach. The pleasure you now derive from my body is all you will ever know unless you can contrive the seizure and theft of my person from your uncle in such a way that he can never again find me, nor be able to blame you or me, nor know anything to use in accusation. [Chrétien, 151])

Fenice's explanation of the conditions under which she will become Cligés's lover focus on the rhetorical definition of the body. Her concern for her reputation emphasizes not only that the body figures social anxieties but that it is constructed by and within a symbolic order. The royal female body's simultaneous participation in a sexual system, in a political system, and in a system of amorous exchange and transgression defines how it acquires meaning in the symbolic order of medieval romance.

The alternative Fenice finds to splitting her body between two men does not significantly change the terms of the political and amorous appropriation of her body. Her advice to Cligés to "contrive the seizure and theft of my person from your uncle" echoes the kidnapping by the Duke of Saxony's men that almost prevented her marriage to Alis. The integrity of the empress's body and the integrity of her love depend on the unshared possession of her body by Cligés, a possession that can only be effected through deceit and secret seizure.

The plan that Cligés proposes to accomplish the undisputed possession of Fenice is hardly worthy of the empress's impassioned plea for seizure and theft. Cligés suggests that the lovers flee together to King Arthur's court. The empress refuses, repeating her fear of being compared to Queen Iseut, a woman with two lovers:

Ja avoec vos ensi n'irai,
Car lors seroit par tot le monde
Ausi come d'Ysolt la Blonde
Et de Tristant de nos parlé;
Quant nos an serïens alé,
Et ci, et la, totes et tuit

Blasmeroient nostre deduit.
Nus ne diroit, ne devroit croirre
La chose si com ele est voire.
De vostre oncle qui crerroit dons
Que je si li fusse an pardons
Pucele estorse et eschapee?
Por trop baude et top estapee
Me tendroit l'en, et vos por fol. (*Cligés*, vv. 5250–63)

(I shall never go away with you in this fashion, for then the entire world would talk of us the way people do of the blond Iseult and Tristan. After we had gone, men and women all over would censure our happiness. No one would tell the story as it is, and none would accept it as true. Who would then believe that I evaded your uncle and preserved my virginity? People would consider me most shameless and dissolute, and consider you a fool. [Chrétien, 151–52])

Preoccupied with the preservation of her good reputation, Fenice rejects the possible identification with Iseut, a woman who split her body between two men. The empress insists on the metaphoric integrity of her body and she attempts to control the meaning of her body through the invention of a monogamous adultery.

If a story is told about the adulterous body, the adulterous body also tells a story: it functions symbolically in the narrative. Fenice's attempt to redefine Queen Iseut's sexual transgression by creating a monogamous adultery and her specific focus on the rhetorical construction of her body through the use of metaphors of fragmentation and doubling point to the way that the meaning of the queen's sexual body is negotiated in the romance narratives through rhetoric: rumors, accusations, and defenses all claim to define the queen's body and its relationship to royal sovereignty. The queen's body is not the only body that circulates between various systems of significance in medieval romances. The knight's body moves between chivalric contests, love relationships, and kinship networks, and the body may symbolize or stand for different qualities or values in each context. Yet the queen's position is unique in the royal courts of medieval romance. No matter what other networks of loyalties or desires may be shown to define her body, she is still the king's wife and, as Fenice emphasizes, she is still responsible for royal succession.

Fenice's invention of the monogamous adulterous body in opposition to Iseut's fragmented body invites an interrogation of how the conflation of sovereignty and adulterous passion contributes to the definition of the queen's body and of how metaphors that describe the adulterous queen's body construct meaning within romance. Perhaps more importantly, it interrogates the possible forms of the story of royal adultery, questioning the extent to which Fenice's story can ever be any different from Iseut's. For despite the repeated justifications of her desire not to repeat Iseut's example and split her body between two men, and despite the complicated ruses she uses to try to avoid her husband's embraces, Fenice's body does not escape physical mutilation or rhetorical condemnation.

The Queen's Two Bodies

Through the use of pharmacological tricks and rhetorical figures that double the queen's body with empty illusions and emptied tombs, Fenice attempts to remove her body from a dynastic structure that defines it as a maternal body and from a discursive network in which it would be constructed as a body fragmented by its possession by two men at the same time. Ultimately, she is unsuccessful in both attempts. Through the use of pharmacological ruses, the empress attempts to create a distinction between the corporeal, sexual body, and the symbolic, royal body. Her failure demonstrates that this is an impossible distinction for a queen, although it is a prominent metaphor used to describe the king in medieval political theory. The immortal yet human nature of the royal sovereign is represented by the king's two bodies, one undying and transcendent, the other mortal and human.[31] The rhetorical doubling of the sovereign's body does not apply to the king's consort; since her official function is not to govern, it is absent from theoretical formulations that attempt to explain the sovereign's relationship to his office, his state, or his subjects.

In contrast to the perceived gap between the enduring nature of the king's office and his human, mortal body, the queen consort's political role in the medieval court was located entirely in her physical body. Unlike the king, whose corporeal body may be separate from the transcendent, immortal body of sovereign, the queen's role is uniquely corporeal and any symbolic use of her office depends precisely on the maternal body that Fenice seeks to redefine as a virginal body. Unlike kings, queens consort have only one body, a reproductive body. The symbolic body of the queen is defined by the products and transgressions of the material body.

John Carmi Parsons has suggested that the queen's intercessory role in medieval courts might allow the conceptualization of the queen's two bodies, though he emphasizes that the model does not correspond to the one Ernst Kantorowicz identifies for kingship:

A queen did not enter her office in the same manner as a king, nor did one consort succeed another as a king succeeds his predecessor. Thus there is a sense in which a queen "dies" while the king does not, but certain of her attributes and duties could be seen to adhere to her office, not her person: if her biological maternity was limited in time by natural physiological processes, her role as a nurturing mediator was not and could be identified with her official self. Long after her natural body ceased to manifest the king's physical powers, intercession allowed her to continue a maternal function and reveal his ideal paternal magnanimity.[32]

Parsons's suggestion is a provocative one, and I cite it here to underline the notable absence both of the queen's maternity in *Cligés* and other romances about adulterous queens and of the influence and authority that maternity might offer a queen. To push Parsons's suggestion to its limit (and to risk distorting it), the queen produces her own official body along with royal children; it is, paradoxically, through maternity that the queen might transcend the uniquely corporeal nature of her position.

In *Cligés* Fenice's efforts to create a second body ultimately fail to guarantee her body's integrity. She successfully avoids her husband's embraces using the pharmacological skills of her nurse, but the drugs intended to prevent the fragmentation of adultery do not spare her body from mutilation. In preparation for the pharmacologically induced "death" that will free her from her marriage, Fenice pretends to be ill and she forbids the court doctors to examine her

(vv. 5598–99, 5627–33). Confronted with the contrived evidence of a fatal disease, these doctors believe that the empress is gravely ill, and after she drinks the potion that gives her a death-like appearance, they pronounce her dead. The success of Fenice's deception is threatened only by the arrival of three physicians from Salerno who demand to see and inspect the "dead" body. When they learn that the empress had not allowed her body to be examined by the court doctors, the physicians are immediately reminded of the ruse undertaken by a legendary adulterous woman—the wife of Solomon, who feigned death to escape her marriage so that she could live with her lover.

> Lors lor sovint de Salemon,
> Que sa fame tant le haï
> Que come morte le trahi.
> Espoir autel a ceste fet,
> Mes se il pueent par nul plet
> Feire tant que il la santissent,
> Il n'est hom nez por qu'an mantissent,
> Se barat i pueent veoir,
> Que il n'en dïent tot le voir. (*Cligés*, vv. 5802–10)

(The physicians then recalled Solomon, whose wife hated him so much that she deceived him by feigning death. Perhaps this lady had done the same. If they could somehow manage to examine her closely, no man alive could make them utter falsehood or prevent them from telling the entire truth, should they find deception operating there. [Chrétien, 158])

The physicians go to examine the empress's body, and when they can discern her pulse, they are sure she is still alive and has feigned death in order to escape her marriage. They promise the emperor that they will revive her, and in their attempt to make her confess her deception they entreat the empress to speak. When she remains silent, they threaten her, strip off her shroud, beat her, and torture her.

Fenice becomes caught in the very narrative tradition that she sought to escape. In her effort to avoid the example of Iseut, Fenice inadvertently follows the example of Solomon's wife, and the doctors who arrive at court are familiar with the story of this famous adulterous queen. The empress does not feign death through the strength of her will, as did Solomon's wife; her death-like state has been induced by drugs, and she cannot speak to confess her deception as the physicians repeatedly urge her to do. The Salernitans are determined to expose the empress's trick, and Fenice is saved from death only by the intervention of the women of the court, who see that the physicians are preparing to roast the empress's body in a final effort to elicit a confession. The women break into the locked room and throw the physicians out a window to end the torture of the empress's lifeless body. Fenice's deception is successful, but it provokes comparison with yet another adulterous queen, and the empress's ability to avoid the mutilating effect of adultery is subverted as her carefully laid plans for the restriction of her body fail to protect her from the violent examination of the Salernitan physicians.

The empress's desire for a monogamous adultery corresponds to her concern for secrecy. Both should ensure that she will never be known as a woman who split her body between two men. Yet although Iseut is the only adulteress that Fenice names in her claim to preserve a reputation for physical integrity, several famous adulterous queens are featured in the narrative. The Salernitan physicians judge Fenice according to the example of Solomon's wife; Fenice fears being remembered as another Iseut; even Cligés offers the example of a famous adulteress as an incentive for the lovers to flee to Arthur's court, where, he claims, they would be welcomed as warmly as was Helen when Paris brought her from Troy: "C'onques ne fu a si grant joie / Eleinne reçeüe a Troie, / Quant Paris li ot amenee" (vv. 5239–41). The accumulation of Fenice's literary predecessors in the narrative suggests that adultery—even monogamous adultery— cannot remain hidden.

Fenice's body is ultimately defined by exactly the kind of story she wished to avoid in her attempt to rewrite the story of her literary predecessors. When the empress claims that she will not flee to Arthur's court with Cligés because "then the entire world would speak of [the lovers] the way people do of the blond Iseult and Tristan,"[33] she recognizes the inescapable public scrutiny of the queen's sexual body. The inevitable story of her adultery, told by men and women everywhere ("Et ci, et la, et totes et tuit," v. 5255) could never be revised by claims to the secret integrity of her body. Fenice's deception of her royal husband is unbelieveable because of its magical nature, but also because it allows the queen's body to escape the very system that defines it: royal marriage, the royal marriage bed, and implicitly, royal maternity. If the queen's body is invested with meaning by her position in a hierarchy of privilege and power, once she leaves the symbolic system that defines her body as a site of royal privilege and the source of dynastic continuity, the symbolic significance of her body is undefined. As the narrator suggests in a passage describing the effect of the first potion that Fenice and her nurse give to the emperor, the royal female body that shuns the marriage bed is "nothing."

Tenir la cuide, n'an tient mie,
Mes de neant est a grant eise,
Car neant tient, et neant beise,
Neant tient, a neant parole,
Neant voit, et neant acole,
A neant tance, a neant luite. (*Cligés*, vv. 3316–21)

(He believed that he held her and he held her not. But he took much pleasure from nothing, for he received nothing, kissed nothing, held nothing, saw nothing, embraced nothing, quarreled with nothing, struggled with nothing. [Chrétien, 128])

The drug-induced dream of possession replaces the empress's body with an imaginary presence, and Fenice's absent body is doubled by a "nothing" that questions the nature of its absent model. In the play of substitution and illusion and in the alternation of presence and absence, the "nothing" that is the double of Fenice's body puts into question the nature of the original: if "nothing" can stand as its substitute, where is the body itself located and of what does it consist?

The Body's Story

If the body's meaning derives from its place in a symbolic system, *Cligés* recounts the negotiation of the body's meaning between two competing systems. The royal sovereignty that depends on dynastic continuation constructs the queen's body as chaste and maternal; mutual love and sexual pleasure define the queen's body as transgressive, and as a threat to the king's authority and position. In Fenice's refusal to produce an heir for Alis and in her repeated rejection of the example of Queen Iseut, *Cligés* also suggests that there are only two stories to tell about the royal female body: a tale of maternity or a story of adultery. Fenice attempts to write a new narrative of queenship and sexual pleasure through the invention of a monogamous adultery, but the pretended death that did not save Solomon's wife from a reputation as an adulteress cannot preserve Fenice's body from stories of sexual transgression. By the time that Cligés rescues Fenice from her tomb, the empress's ability to maintain the story of her body's integrity has been rhetorically compromised on several levels. Its metaphoric equation with absence and lack, its mutilation by the Salernitan physicians, and its association with yet another adulterous queen, the wife of Solomon, suggest that Fenice's body cannot escape the reputation she has repeatedly tried to avoid. The empress is definitively inscribed in the narrative tradition of adulterous queens when she is discovered alive and living with Cligés. After Cligés rescues Fenice from her tomb, the lovers live together in a sealed tower that has no visible entrance and whose architectural integrity would seem to figure the intact body.[34] One day when Fenice and Cligés go into their hidden garden, a hunter leaps into the enclosure in pursuit of his prey and discovers the lovers lying together naked. This scene rewrites the discovery of Tristan and Iseut sleeping side by side, clothed, with Tristan's sword between them. In the *Tristan* stories, the discovery reinforces King Marc's ambivalence about the lovers' guilt; in *Cligés* ambiguity is absent. The lovers' transgression is revealed, and Fenice's adulterous body gains the reputation that the doubled body was intended to help her to avoid.

Fenice ultimately fails to revise the story told of Queen Iseut. Like Iseut, the empress Fenice is remembered as a legendary adulteress whose example must be avoided. Because of her example, the empresses who succeed her are firmly removed from the public and confined to private spaces, a displacement that is designed to maintain the integrity of the royal wife's body.

Einz puis n'i ot empereor
N'eüst de sa fame peor
Qu'ele nel deüst decevoir,
Se il oï ramantevoir
Comant Fenice Alis deçut,
Primes par la poison qu'il but,
Et puis par l'autre traïson.
Por ce einsi com an prison
Est gardee an Costantinoble,
Ja n'iert tant haute ne tant noble,
L'empererriz, quex qu'ele soit:
L'empereres point ne s'i croit,
Tant con de celi li remanbre. (*Cligés*, vv. 6645–57)

(Since then there has been no emperor who did not fear being deceived by
his wife after hearing the story of Fenice deceiving Alis, first with the potion
he drank, and then with the other treachery. For this reason every empress,
no matter who she was, no matter how highborn or noble, was guarded in
Constantinople as though imprisoned. The emperor had no trust in her so
long as he remembered Fenice. [Chrétien, 169])

If Fenice is remembered as an exemplary adulteress, she is also
remembered as an exemplary lover. In the thirteenth-century *Roman
de la poire*, Cligés and Fenice appear as the first pair in a series of celebrated lovers, followed by Tristan and Iseut, Pyramus and Thisbe,
and Paris and Helen. Cligés speaks to praise Love and the amorous
wounds he inflicts and then, in the passage that follows, to condemn
enemies of love who inflict a different kind of wound:

Par traïteurs defaut, ce ne puet nus repondre,
tote amor. Ne lur chaut fors des amanz confondre.
Le plon firent tot chaut es mains Fenice fondre.
Dieu pri de la en haut qu'en enfer les effondre.[35]

(All love is destroyed by traitors, no one can deny it. They care only about
destroying lovers. They melted hot lead in Fenice's hands. I pray to God on
high to send them to hell.)

The empress's tortured body is represented in an illumination
in the earliest complete manuscript of *Le roman de la poire*, which

may have been copied as little as twenty years after the romance was written around 1250 (Figure 1).[36] The manuscript painting illustrates Cligés's claim that Fenice is a victim of the enemies of love as she suffers the tortures inflicted by the "traïteurs," those who oppose true love, the Salernitan physicians. The illumination is one of what Sylvia Huot has labeled "tableaux vivants" in this manuscript, and she suggests that, as a reference to a nearly tragic episode in a story that ultimately has a happy ending, the representation of the false death serves to negate the tragedy of the stories of Tristan and Pyramus, the lovers who follow Cligés in the recitation of love histories to the aspiring lover who is their interlocuteur. In Huot's reading, the double representation of the scene of the false death—in the text and in the illumination—offers a narrative "undoing" of the negative aspects of the next two figures and "contributes to the overall optimistic tone of the poem."[37]

Although Cligés invokes love service to his sovereign lady ("Dame a qui sui sougiez et a qui ge me rent," v. 89) in Le Roman de la poire, he does not mention Fenice's royal status, nor does he mention her husband, the emperor. Cligés also leaves out his marriage to Fenice and his coronation, which are recounted at the end of Chrétien's poem. R. Howard Bloch has suggested that Cligés "comes down on the side of reconciliation between the claims of lineage and desire."[38] Le roman de la poire certainly recognizes the romance's happy ending, as Huot shows, but the account of the empress's reputation at the end of Cligés may reveal unresolved tensions in the reconciliation between lineage and desire that Bloch identifies. In Cligés the empress's body moves between competing systems of signification. Royal marriage defines her body as the source of dynastic continuation, and mutual passion constructs the empress's body as the site of sexual pleasure. Fenice's ruse represents an attempt to embody both systems, but Cligés suggests that the queen's sexual body is always defined by its political significance. Although she manages to escape her marriage to Alis, Fenice does not escape the system that locates political integrity and legitimacy in the body of the queen. She merely relocates the site of legitimacy from the uncle's fraudulent claim to the nephew's rightful possession of the empress and

Figure 1. Cligés and Fenice (top); the Salernian physicians pour hot lead into Fenice's hands (bottom). *Roman de la poire*. BN fr. 2186, fol. 3 v. Photograph: Bibliothèque Nationale, Paris.

the throne. However, even though Fenice is ultimately subsumed back into the system as a symbolic support of dynastic royal succession, her escape—however brief—demonstrates the anxiety that might be provoked by the perceived vulnerability of a political stability grounded on women's sexual integrity.

If Fenice has a place in the memory of generations of emperors in Constantinople who lock up their wives because of her example, it is not only because she tricked Alis but, perhaps more important, because through her ruses she revealed the illusory nature of symbolic integrity. *Cligés* suggests that the meaning of the queen's body is never self-evident, but always contested and negotiated. The symbolic system that equates the integrity of the queen's body with the state of the kingdom defines the queen's adulterous body as the site of royal legitimacy and of contests for political power, but Fenice's deliberations about the rhetorical construction of her body suggest that the integrity that guarantees political stability is always illusory and that the recognition of the king's legitimate sovereignty depends on the queen's ruse. In the chapter that follows I examine the king's investment in the queen's deception and in the public display of an innocent adulterous body.

2

Royal Sovereignty
and the Test of the Queen's Body

IN 830 JUDITH, wife of the Carolingian emperor Louis the Pious, was accused of adultery. She was said to have dishonored her family, her husband, and her country by carrying on a sexual relationship with Bernard of Septimania, the emperor's chamberlain. Chroniclers loyal to Louis's eldest son, Lothar, condemned the queen's adultery as a threat to the entire political system, blaming all disruption and instability at court on the queen's sexual transgression, as Geneviève Bührer-Thierry has emphasized.[1] Agobard of Lyons, a supporter of Lothar, claimed that the queen's adultery caused a political disorder that forced Louis's sons to act against her: "This is why the emperor's sons acted, moved by a reasonable zeal, when they saw the paternal bed soiled, the palace tainted, the kingdom in confusion, and blackened the name of the Franks, previously illustrious throughout the world."[2] The queen's adultery was characterized as both the cause and the emblem of a crisis in sovereignty.

As Bührer-Thierry and others have noted, threats to the king's sovereignty often take the form of accusations against the queen.[3] The charge against Judith was part of an attempt by her three stepsons to remove their father from the influence of his powerful second wife and to discredit the factions that supported the empress, but as a political move its results were not those intended by the empress's accusors.[4] Judith cleared herself of the charge of adultery with a purgatory oath taken before a council assembled to judge her. The exculpation took place after her husband had reconciled with his sons and had imprisoned the leaders of the rebellion who initiated the accusation against the empress;[5] the public vow of marital chastity thus coincided with a restoration of political integrity. Judith's oath demonstrated a truth about the empress's body that was seen to reflect a truth about the emperor's corporate body, and the emperor's undisputed sovereignty was restored along with his wife's undisputed chastity.

The symbolic equation of the queen's sexual integrity and the king's sovereignty is one exploited in many medieval narratives. Tests of the queen's chastity make visible a hidden truth about the body, and the public demonstration of the state of the queen's body reaffirms the king's sovereignty and the unity of his court. The accusation against the empress Judith demonstrates both the emperor's vulnerability to accusations against his wife and the empress's vulnerability to attacks against her husband that take her chastity as their pretext. The double focus of attacks on the queen's chastity is a defining feature of the representations of the queen's adultery in twelfth- and thirteenth-century romances. Royal authority is challenged and reaffirmed through accusations of the queen's infidelity and proofs of her sexual integrity.

When the three physicians from Salerno unsuccessfully torture Fenice's body in order to expose the deception of the false death, they intend to uncover the empress's betrayal of her husband. Their tortures are but one example of the many tests of the royal female body in medieval romances. Most are intended to discover a truth about the queen's sexual integrity; most are subverted by the adulterous queen's ruses. Romance representations of chastity tests extend the play between illusion and truth that characterizes the representation of the empress's body in *Cligés* and suggest that any truth about the body is subject to tricks, to subversions, and to reinterpretations.

While in the case of Judith and other queens accused of adultery in medieval monarchies the charge of sexual transgression may be based on contrived evidence, the queen's innocence is not established through the simple proof of her integrity. Rather, the truth about her body is subject to political negotiations. By the time Judith

swore an oath of innocence, her accusers had been exiled or imprisoned, Louis had reconciled with his sons, and there was no one
left in the court to challenge the empress's vow.[6] The truth of about
Judith's sexual integrity, like the accusation of adultery, was at least
in part defined by political contests and their resolutions. In contrast to what happened when nonfictional queens were accused of
sexual transgression, when a romance queen is accused of adultery
the evidence is usually true and the proof of innocence is contrived.
The queen is tested, and she usually escapes a judgment of guilt: the
proof of her guilt is disregarded or negated by the circumstances of
the trial, the queen uses verbal tricks to avoid condemnation, or she
is saved by her champion. The accusation against the queen is, however, no less political in romance representations than it is in the
records of accusations against late Carolingian queens like Judith.
The charge of adultery may come from outside the court, as part of
an attempt to dishonor the king through a proof about the disloyalty of the women in his court; or the charge may come from inside
the court, as a challenge to the king's authority. In both cases, the
queen's body becomes a symbol of royal sovereignty, and a proof of
her chastity guarantees her husband's authority while a proof of guilt
would indicate his weakness. The ways in which tests are subverted
and negated in romance accounts of accusations against the queen
suggest that the privileging of the woman's body as the site on which
authority and power are made visible depends on the paradoxical invention of the queen as an innocent adulteress.

The Guilty Queen

In medieval romances tests of women's bodies generally reveal a
truth about chastity; tests of knights' bodies usually prove chivalric prowess.[7] Knights leave the court to pursue adventures, or they
participate in tournaments organized at court to test their skills in
combats with each other. The king is outside this system of chivalric
proof; he does not usually pursue adventure or participate in tournaments.[8] His is a symbolic body, constituted by the kingdom of which

he is the head,[9] and tests of the king are tests of his sovereignty that arrive from outside the court to challenge the prowess of his knights or the fidelity of his wife.

Chastity tests are the subject of a number of medieval narratives. They take two forms: a coat that will properly fit only a woman faithful to her lover, as in the fabliau *Du mantel mautaillié* and in the romance *La vengeance Raguidel*; and a drinking horn that spills on the drinker to indicate transgression, as in the short fabliau-like narrative *Le lai du corn*, in the *Livre de Caradoc* section of the *First Continuation of the Old French Perceval*, and in the *Prose Tristan*. Each of these stories takes place in a royal court and begins with the unexpected arrival of a messenger with a magic test of chastity. The queen is first to be tested and she is proved guilty; subsequently each woman at court must take a turn at the test and all but one fail. The outline of the story remains fairly constant from text to text, and while I will examine the different forms of the story, I will not attempt to situate my reading with respect to the narrative evolution of the tale.[10] Rather, I will explore the ways in which the chastity test defines the king's status in his court with respect to the state of his wife's body in all these stories.

The magic drinking horn marks the female body guilty of sexual transgression: when an unfaithful woman drinks from the horn the wine will spill and stain her clothes, as the messenger who brings the drinking horn to King Marc's court explains in the *Prose Tristan*:

"Faites en cest palés venir totes les dames de vostre cort, povres et riches, et la roïne meesmes veigne. Quant eles seront venues, faites cest cor emplir de vin. Et cele qui mesfait avra vers son seignor et qui avra fait ami par dejoste le mariaige ne porra boire a cest cor que li vins n'espande sor li; mes cele qui lealment se sera tenue i porra boire seürement que ja li vins sor li ne respendra." (Curtis, 2: 131)

("Have all the ladies of your court, both rich and poor, come to this palace, and have the queen come, too. When they arrive, have the horn filled with wine. And any woman who has betrayed her husband and who has had a lover outside of marriage will not be able to drink from this horn without the wine spilling on her. But she who has maintained her loyalty will be able to drink with the certainty that the wine will not spill on her.")

The stained clothing of the guilty women visibly figures the body marked by the sexual transgression. The drinking horn test demonstrates a truth that cannot be read directly on the body and must be represented figurally.

The second form of the chastity test, the ill-fitting coat, also figures the guilty body. A marvelous coat, made by a fairy, is constructed so that it will conform to the shape of the faithful woman. When worn by a woman who has been unfaithful to her lover, the coat does not fit and exposes the body guilty of transgression in love, as the narrator of *Du mantel mautaillié* explains:

La fée fist el drap une oevre
Qui les fausses dames descuevre;
Ja feme qui l'ait afublé,
Se ele a de rien meserré
Vers son seignor, se ele l'a,
Ja puis à droit ne li serra,
Ne aus puceles autressi,
Se ele vers son bon ami
Avoit mespris en nul endroit
Ja plus ne li serroit à droit
Que ne soit trop lonc ou trop cort. (*Mantel*, p. 8)

(The fairy made from cloth a work that exposes unfaithful women; no woman who tried it on, if she had betrayed her lord in any way, would find it a fit. Nor could any maiden who had betrayed her lover in any way find it a good fit; it would be too long or too short.)

The marvelous character of the coat is reflected in its beauty which is impossible to describe ("Nul n'en saveroit le portret / Ne l'uevre du drap aconter." *Mantel*, 8); it is a garment without equal ("Il n'a son per en tout le mont," *Mantel*, 10). Its extraordinary beauty figures the extraordinary character of the woman it will fit, and the changing shape of the coat that is alternately too long or too short when tried by each of the ladies of the court reflects the metaphorically misshapen body of the adulteress, split between two men, dismembered by the competing sexual claims of her husband and lover.

R. Howard Bloch has suggested that the fabliau speaks its own inadequacy as a representation, that it shows the scandalous inadequacy of representation itself. In this discussion of chastity tests, I extend Bloch's analysis of the lack of distinction between "the ill-fitting garment of of fiction ('le mantel mautaillié') and that which lies beyond it" in order to examine the lack of distinction between a truth about the king's court and a truth about the queen's body in these stories. In romance representations of chastity tests, that double truth is defined through the queen's duplicitous performance and through the king's desire for a demonstration of her innocence.[11]

When the magic coat is brought to Arthur's court in *Du mantel mautaillié*, the queen is called into the king's presence, where she tries on the coat without knowing its magic properties. When it does not fit, the queen passes the coat to another lady, who tries it on and finds it too short. When the meaning of the test is explained to the queen, she decides not to dispute its result, but to turn the test into a joke: "Si l'a en jenglois atorné" (*Mantel*, 12). The queen then calls for all the ladies of the court to try on the coat, but after the queen's guilty body is exposed by the ill-fitting garment, the other ladies of the court do not wish to try it on. Keu confidently brings his own lady forward to continue the test: "Damoisele, venez avant; / Oiant ces chevaliers, me vant / Que vous estes leaus part tout." ("Demoiselle, come forward. Before these knights I claim that you are completely loyal." *Mantel*, 14.) The lady protests, Keu commands her to try on the coat, the coat does not fit her, and Keu becomes the object of the other knights' ridicule. As each woman is tested it becomes increasingly apparent that all are at fault, and the knights lose their enthusiasm for the proof and become reluctant to see their ladies tested. However, the discovery of universal unfaithfulness among the women leads not to discord but to harmony. Keu ceremoniously seats each lady with her equals after she fails the test. No knight's lady is more virtuous than any other knight's, and their collective guilt seems to make the women all the more worthy of love:

Et Kex li seneschaus a dit:
"Seignor, ne vous corouciez pas.
Igaument sont partis li gas

Quant chascune en porte son fès.
Bien doivent estre dès or mès
Par nous chieries et amées;
Quar bien se sont hui acuitées.
Ce nous doit molt reconforter
Li uns ne puet l'autre gaber." (*Mantel*, 24)

(And Keu the seneschal said, "Lords, do not be angry. The joke is shared equally since each woman carries its mark. From now on we should love and cherish them, for they have acted well today. It should comfort us that no one can mock anyone else.")

When Gauvain protests that knights should not find comfort in dishonor, Keu responds that it is not a dishonor for a knight if his lady loves another because all the knights are equal in betrayal. For although the coat performs a test on women's bodies, revealing a hidden truth about the female body's sexual integrity, the chastity test is represented as a competition between men. In all the stories that recount the tests of the ill-fitting coat and the drinking horn, the women who undergo the test are anonymous but the knights to whom they should have been faithful are named.

In *Du mantel mautaillié* the competition between men played out on the bodies of women seems to have no winner, and the test of the ill-fitting coat shifts from its appropriation by the individual knights as a contest between themselves back to its original purpose, which is to test the reputation of the court itself. As the messenger who brings the coat to Arthur's court explains to the king, if no faithful woman is found in his court, it will be blamed in many lands and adventures will no longer arrive there.[12] The court's reputation is saved when one lady is found whom the coat will fit, thus disrupting the solidarity established by the guilt of the other women.

The discovery of the faithful lady preserves the honor of Arthur's court, but the extraordinary status of this woman is emphasized in the narrative: the valet who carries the horn from court to court has tested more that a thousand women and none of them proved herself innocent of misdeed or bad intention (*Mantel*, 29). The faithful lady, Galeta, wins the marvelously beautiful coat as a reward, but the unity of the betrayed men and the unfaithful women dominates at the end of the tale. The knights and their ladies wish for the coat simply to disappear, and although they dare not say anything but good of Galeta's success at the proof, their rancor is soon revealed and has the effect of excluding Galeta from the group of unfaithful ladies and their cuckolded knights. Just as she is one among a thousand, Galeta remains isolated as one against a thousand.

This isolation results in exile in *Le livre de Caradoc*. Like *Le lai du corn* and the *Prose Tristan* this version of the chastity test story uses a drinking horn as a physical proof. The test is also defined more explicitly as a contest between men since here, as in *Le lai du corn*, it is the knights and not their ladies who drink from the horn, and the woman's chastity is proved in a test that marks the male body. In *Le livre de Caradoc* King Caradoc is the only knight who succeeds in drinking from the horn, and Emmanuèle Baumgartner has discussed how the test proves not only the lady's fidelity but the knight's powers of seduction.[13] All the women of the court who have been proved unfaithful hate Guignier, Caradoc's chaste wife. Arthur retains Caradoc at his court, but Caradoc sends Guignier back to his own lands, for he knows that she has incurred the queen's anger along with the enmity of the other women.[14] The elimination of the disruptive presence of the chaste wife restores tranquility to the court, and the king and his knights bask in the honor and reputation retained by Guignier's chastity as the episode ends with an emphasis on the unity and fame of Arthur's court:

S'avint qu'ensi fu puis maint jor
En grant repos et en sejor
Li rois et la bone maisnie
Qui par le mont ert tant proisie. (*Caradoc*, vv. 3265–68)

(And then the king and his household, so praised throughout the world, spent many days there resting.)

In stories about chastity tests extraordinary status is awarded not to the queen, but to the single chaste woman in the court. Yet although the faithful woman demonstrates exemplary virtue, she is not represented as a model to be imitated in these stories. Rather,

she is a disruptive presence that reinforces the unity of those implicated in transgression.[15] No one knight can speak badly of any other
since they have all been betrayed and no lady can accuse any other
since they have all betrayed their lovers. The equilibrium established
by the shared experience of dishonor establishes men as the victims
of women, and women as ruled by their natures: if men are all alike
it is because women are all alike, and in this contest the queen and
the king are like all the other women and men at court.

Louise Fradenburg has discussed the "privileged site" of kingship as a threat to boundaries: "The king cannot be too much like
his subjects, in part because this would reveal that sovereignty is an
artifact. . . . But the king also cannot be too much different from
his subjects. . . . [H]e will seem to be too much, not like us, and
therefore foreign."[16] If the king's relationship to his subjects, and
particularly to his vassals, as I will argue in Chapter 3, is negotiated
through a scrutiny of the queen's body, that negotation equates the
state of the queen's body with the state of the king's rule. In stories
about chastity tests, the dangerous discovery of the queen's adultery
is diluted by the universal guilt of all the women at court. The king is
a cuckold, but so are all the other men. In every version of this story,
the queen is proven guilty of adultery only to have her guilt effaced
by the proof of universal transgression.[17]

Although narratives that recount the test of the queen's chastity
assume that the queen has a lover, the test does not usually appear
in romances that give a prominent place to the story of the queen's
liaison with her knight. The test is recounted without prior contextualization in short narratives like *Du mantel mautaillié* and *Le lai du
corn*, or it may be inserted into longer narratives that do not focus
primarily on the relationship between the queen and her lover, like
Le livre de Caradoc or *La vengeance Raguidel*. Only the *Prose Tristan*
includes the episode of the chastity test as part of a continuing series
of discoveries of the queen's adultery and their subsequent cover-
ups. In this version of the drinking horn test, the unity that the test
establishes among unfaithful women and among betrayed men is not
enough to counter the dangerous consequences of discovery. In the
Prose Tristan the queen is not like other women, even though other

women may be like the queen; the transgression of the king's wife cannot be dismissed or hidden by the collective guilt of all women in the court.

The testing episode in the *Prose Tristan* begins with the diversion of the magic drinking horn test from King Arthur's court to King Marc's. Initially sent to Arthur by his sister, Morgan, as a test intended to reveal Guenevere's adultery, the drinking horn is intercepted and rerouted to King Marc's court. The test of chastity is not an adventure that arrives mysteriously—or even randomly—at court as in *Le lai du corn* and *Le livre de Caradoc*, nor is it sent by an unidentified lady to Arthur's court and to many others as in *Du mantel mautaillié*. It is not a general test of the fidelity of the women at Arthur's court and therefore of the worth of the knights who love them. This test, unlike its analogues, is aimed specifically at married women. As Morgan's messenger explains to Lamorat de Gales, who encounters him on his way to Arthur's court: "nule dame qui ait geü avec autre que avec son mari n'i puet boire que li vins ne s'espande sor lui." ("No woman who has slept with a man other than her husband will be able to drink from it without the wine spilling all over her." Curtis, 2: 129.) The knight immediately recognizes the possible result of the test:

"Coment!" fait Lamoraz, "et s'il avenoit que madame la roïne Genevre, qui est ores la plus haute dame dou monde, se fust joee par aventure a aucun chevalier de son ostel, si covendroit que li rois en seüst la verité por l'espreve de cesti cor?" (Curtis, 2: 129)

("What?!" says Lamorat, "and if it were that case that Queen Guenevere, who is now the highest lady in the world, had by chance amused herself with some knight in her household, should the king find out about it through the test of this horn?")

Lamorat seems to think that it is perfectly possible that Guenevere could have had a lover in her husband's court, but when he learns that the horn was sent by Morgan, he also suggests that the king's sister may intend to use her magical powers to turn Arthur against his wife.

"[P]ar sa delealté a ele maintes foiz pourchacié honte a madame la roïne Genevre. Et je sai bien que ceste merveille de cest cor a ele ensi establi par son

enchantement por metre mortel haine entre le roi Artus et la roïne Genevre."
(Curtis, 2: 130)

("Many times she has disloyally sought to shame Queen Guenevere. And I
know well that she created this marvelous horn through her magic in order
to put a mortal hate between King Arthur and Queen Guenevere.")

This is exactly the claim that Queen Iseut will make when she is
proved guilty of adultery through the drinking horn test—that magi-
cians sent the horn to create discord between the king and the queen.
Here, as in Iseut's protest, exactly which part of the proof is an enchantment remains ambiguous: does the magic result in a false proof
or does the magic create the possibility of proof?

Lamorat recognizes that Morgan's drinking horn test is a demonstration of her enmity toward the queen. The chastity test is part
of a contest between women, Guenevere and Morgan, that Lamorat
appropriates as a test between men, himself and Tristan, as he re-
directs Morgan's messenger to King Marc's court:

"[T]u t'en iras droit en l'ostel le roi Marc, et li diras que li chevaliers qui
point ne l'aime li envoie cest cor por esprover la bonté des dames de Cornoaille, car la bonté des chevaliers fu ja bien esprovee sor la marine devant les
paveillons, la ou Tristanz, li biaus mauvés, refusa la bataille del chevalier es-
trange. Et bien sache Tristanz que por haine et por male volenté de li est cil
cors envoiez en Cornoaille." (Curtis, 2: 130)

("You will go directly to the court of King Marc, and tell him that the knight
who does not love him sends him this horn to test the worth of the ladies of
Cornwall, for the worth of the knights has already been tested on the shore
in front of the tents where Tristan, the fair unworthy one, refused to do
battle with an unknown knight. And let Tristan know that this horn is sent
to Cornwall because of his hate and ill-will.")

The contest that Tristan refused to undertake in battle will be played
out on the bodies of the women of Cornwall.

Although Lamorat seems to suspect that Guenevere would have
failed the test, his rerouting of the drinking horn adventure from
Arthur's court to Marc's is not explicitly aimed at provoking discord between Marc and Iseut, but rather at exposing a general shame

among Marc's knights. In this it corresponds to its analogues: the horn arrives mysteriously at Arthur's court to test the reputation of the court through the loyalty of its women. However, in the *Prose Tristan* the test has the unintended effect of exposing the queen's adultery and of provoking the king's wrath. Iseut is the first to submit to the test. A fourteenth-century manuscript illumination suggests the division between the knights and their wives that the test will provoke (Figure 2). The men seem to confer quietly behind the king's throne while the women incline toward each other in a suggestion of whispered anticipation.

All of the women fail to drink from the horn (in Marc's court the one exception provided by Caradoc's wife is absent), but in this narrative Iseut is not assimilated into an anonymous sisterhood of guilt. The queen remains an exemplary figure, and the revelation of her disloyalty provokes the promise of exemplary punishment from her husband: a disloyal queen must be burned to death: "Dame, malement va. Or est vostre deleauté tote aperte! Vos avez deservie mort. Le jugement est tel que roïne qui vers son seignor se mesfait de tel chose com je vos di, doit estre destruite et arse." ("Lady, this goes badly. Now your disloyalty is exposed! You have earned your death. I tell you that the judgment is that a queen who does such a thing to her husband must be destroyed and burned." Curtis, 2: 132.)

In medieval law the punishment for adultery may be death, but only under very precisely defined definitions of proof.[18] The *Prose Tristan* provides its own legal history in which the punishment for adultery is defined as death by burning. This penalty is established by legal precedent in a judgment first pronounced by a queen:

Un jor avint que cil de leanz pristrent une dame avec un chevalier. Et amenerent adonc la dame devant le roi, et distrent: "Sire, nos avons pris ceste dame avec un chevalier. Que vos plest il que l'en en face?" "Et que est devenuz li chevaliers?" fait li rois. "Sire, il se deffendi et par tel eschapa. La dame nos remest, si la vos avons amenee."
La roïne estoit adonce devant le roi quant cest parole fu esmeüe. Li rois li demande: "Dame, que vos est avis que l'en doie faire de ceste dame que l'en a prise en avoutire?" La roïne pense un petit, et puis respont: "Sire, je jugeroie qu'ele deüst estre arse." Et li rois respont: "Cist jugemenz est bons."

Figure 2. Queen Iseut and the magic horn. *Tristan.* BN fr. 100, fol. 95 v.
Photograph: Bibliothèque Nationale, Paris.

Lors comande que de la dame fust fait ce que la roïne en avoit dit; et cil le
firent maintenant.

Si sachiez que la premiere dame qui fist cest jugement que feme esposee
prise en avoutire deüst estre arse, si fu ceste roïne. Si dura puis cest jugement
par tote Gaule et par tote la Grant Bretaigne et par moutes autres terres
grant tens dusques aprés l'aaige le roi Artus. (Curtis, 1: 115–16)

(One day the men of the court took a lady with a knight. And they brought
the lady before the king and said, "Sire, we took this lady with a knight.

What do you wish us to do with her?" "What happened to the knight?" asked the king. "Sire, he defended himself so well that he escaped. The lady was left behind, and we have brought her to you."

The queen was beside the king when the accusation was made. The king asks her, "Lady, what do you think we should do with this lady who was taken in adultery?" The queen thinks for a moment and then says, "Sire, I judge that she should be burned." And the king says, "This is a good judgment." Then he commands that the lady should be dealt with according to the queen's command, and they did it right away.

And so you should know that this queen was the first lady to make the judgment that a married woman taken in adultery should be burned. This judgment endured throughout Gaul and throughout Great Britain and in many other lands for a long time after the age of King Arthur.)

Despite the claims of the *Prose Tristan*'s narrator, death by fire as a punishment for adultery does not seem to have had a long history in the medieval judicial record; its use seems mainly limited to romances.[19] This story about an unnamed adulteress repeats a familiar motif from the Tristan and Lancelot romances: the queen and her lover are found together, the knight escapes, and the queen is led away to be burned. The illumination of the adulterous woman's punishment in a fourteenth-century French manuscript suggests its voyeuristic character (Figure 3). The woman is naked and the silhouettes of the men assembled to watch her burning are visible in the background. The scrutiny of the female body by those who witness the punishment are elements in the judgment of adultery that are fully exploited in romance representations of trials of adulterous queens, as I will suggest below.

A magic drinking horn test is not one of the standards of proof admitted in medieval law, but in the *Prose Tristan* King Marc accepts its results as a valid demonstration of the queen's guilt. And when Marc cites burning as an appropriate punishment for a queen, Iseut extends the penalty to all the women of the court who fail to drink from the horn.[20] In this version of the chastity test the queen's failure to prove her innocence is not diffused by the shared guilt of the other women, but rather the other women are considered to share the guilt of the queen.

Iseut manages to escape her death sentence by objecting that the

Figure 3. Adulterous woman burned at the stake. *Tristan*. BN fr. 102, fol. 22. Photograph: Bibliothèque Nationale, Paris.

horn is enchanted and by offering to prove her innocence through judicial battle. Marc's barons second her objection to the test on the grounds that it is a marvelous deception, and when they refuse to judge their wives, the king dismisses the evidence of adultery offered by the drinking horn:

Et li baron de Cornoaille, qui amoient lor femes autant com aus meesmes et qui ne vosissent en nule maniere lor destruction, et d'autre part il ne creoient mie que cele espreve fust vraie, dient au roi: "Sire, sire, vos feroiz destruire ce que vos voudroiz, mes que que vos facez de la roïne qui vostre est, nos retendrons nos moilliers. Diex nos deffende que nos ne les faciens destruire por si povre achoison com ceste nos semble!" "Non? fait li rois. Vos veez bien qu'eles vos ont honiz, et n'en osez prendre vengence." "Sire, font il, sauve vostre grace, nos nel veons ne ne savons. Por ce se vos volez a la roïne mal, nel volons nos pas a nos moilliers." Et li rois est auques liez de ceste novele, car tot deïst il ce por chastier la roïne, ne vosist il pas sa mort, s'il ne veïst plus apertement son mesfet qu'il ne l'avoit veü. (Curtis, 2: 133)

(And the barons of Cornwall, who loved their wives as much as themselves and who had no wish to execute them and who did not believe that the proof was true either, said to the king: "Sire, sire, you may destroy what you wish, but no matter what you do to the queen who belongs to you, we will keep our wives. God forbid that we have them executed for such a poor cause as this!" "No?" says the king. "It is obvious that they have shamed you, and you do not dare take vengeance." "Sire," they say, "by your grace we do not see it, and we do not know it. For this reason, even if you wish to hold it against the queen we do not hold it against our wives." And the king is happy at this, for he made these threats to chastise the queen, but he did not wish for her death unless he could see her guilt demonstrated more clearly than he had seen it here.)

This episode offers another example of King Marc's famous ambivalence toward knowledge about his wife's adultery. In spite of Marc's desire to take revenge on his nephew—he is delighted to note Tristan's discomfort when the test is explained before the assembled barons—he hesitates to condemn the queen and he justifies his hesitation by accepting the claim introduced by Iseut and repeated by his vassals, that the proof is unreliable. Marc refuses to punish his wife unless he sees the proof demonstrated more clearly ("plus apertement").

In the *Prose Tristan* the drinking horn test functions as one of the many examples of the revelation of the queen's adultery and its subsequent cover-up. However, as a test whose truth is disputed, the drinking horn episode questions the status of proofs and of judicial procedure in the royal court. Iseut claims that the test is invalid, that it is part of a plot by enchanters from Great Britain who wish to destroy honest noblewomen and to sow discord in Cornwall.[21] The queen's objection is dismissed by Marc as a far-fetched attempt to avoid condemnation, but it is close to the truth: the horn was sent by an enchantress, Morgan, to create conflict between a king and a queen, as Lamorat recognized when he encountered Morgan's messenger. Iseut's claim of a plot against Cornwall is also accurate, but the plot does not originate with the enchantress, it is the idea of the knight who diverted the adventure from its original destination and sent it to King Marc's court.

In her questioning of the validity of the proof the queen reverses the equivalence between women's chastity and the court's reputation that usually structures the drinking horn tale. She redefines the proof of the court's reputation as a test of the king's justice; Marc will act unjustly if he bases a judgment on a truth proved with magic. "Surely, sire," says the queen, "if because of the test of the horn which was made by enchantment you wish to destroy me, your felony, your betrayal and your cruelty will be better known than my disloyalty." ("Certes, sire, ce dit la roïne, se vos por l'espreve del cor qui est faiz par enchantement me volez destruire, vostre felonie et vostre delealté et vostre crealté i seroit mout apertement coneüe plus que ci n'est ma delealté." Curtis, 2: 132.) But when the queen claims that she will prove her innocence through judicial battle against any knight who will accuse her, the king scoffs at her offer because everyone knows that Iseut's champion is the best knight in Cornwall and none will dare to oppose him: "Dame, fait [Marc], vos avez par devers vos tel champion qu'il n'a chevalier en tote Cornoaille qui encontre li osast bataille emprendre." ("Lady," said [Marc], "you have on your side such a champion that there is no knight in all Cornwall who dares to undertake a battle with him." Curtis, 2: 133.)

The queen does not renew her demand to prove her innocence through judicial battle because Marc follows the example of his barons and dismisses the evidence of the drinking horn. Yet the brief mention of the inevitable result of the battle if Tristan is the queen's champion—Tristan is the best knight in Cornwall, he will conquer any challenger—announces a crisis in judicial procedure that is provoked not by magic but by might. This crisis is explored more explicitly later in the romance when King Marc himself unjustly wins a judicial battle. Accused of the murder of Bertholais by the victim's brother, Armant, Marc falsely proves his innocence in battle:

Chelui jour se combati il a Armant et l'ochist sans faille, voiant le roi Artu meïsmes et voiant tous chiaus qui la estoient. Et ja fust il ensi toutesvoies que Armans se combatist pour loiale querele et pour droituriere, car bien estoit verités que li rois March avoit ochis Bertholais, et mauvaisement, si fu Armans vaincus de chele bataille. Et puis fu il recordé que cele bataille fu la premiere ki onques fust vaincue par tort en la maison le roi Artu, et fu dit a chelui point que desloiautés avoit mis loiauté au dessous; par coi li sairement des batailles furent adonc mis avant premierement, ki encore sont maintemant. Ne devant ce n'estoient sairement fait de nule bataille, s'il ne lour plaisoit. (*Prose Tristan* 4: 163)

(That day he engaged Armant and killed him without hesitation before King Arthur himself and before all those present. And this in spite of the fact that Armant undertook the battle with right and loyalty, for it was certainly true that King Marc had killed Bertholais, and in treason, but Armant was defeated in this battle. And afterwards it was recorded that this battle was the first that was ever won unjustly in the court of King Arthur, and it was said then that disloyalty had overcome loyalty. For this reason the oath was put first in battles, as it still is today. Before there was no oath sworn in battle if the combatants did not wish it.)

The narrative makes a history lesson of Marc's unjust victory, and the battle becomes the catalyst for a change in the system of judicial battle. The evolution of judicial procedure is an invention of the *Prose Tristan*—oaths were always part of the ritualized proof in the medieval use of judicial battle—but the problem that the scene of Marc's victory locates within the proof and tries to solve is the same one that arose in the drinking horn episode when Iseut claimed her right to prove her innocence in battle. A crisis of faith in the functioning of the proof is manifested in the fear that the strongest knight will win any battle he undertakes, regardless of whether or not he defends a just cause. This representation of judicial battles is very different from the idealized battle described in *La chanson de Roland*, where the small, weak Thierry defeats the strong, valiant Pinabel to prove Ganelon's treason. The faith in immanent justice, that God will intervene in the physical world to demonstrate truth, is shaken; judgments are no longer determined by superior right, but by superior strength.[22]

Whether by an explicit questioning of the nature of the proof or by a dismissal of guilt as part of "women's nature," the results of magic tests of chastity are consistently negated when the queen is proved guilty of sexual transgression. When the queen's transgression is ignored, her relative innocence is reinstated. The ultimate effect of the magic tests is not to reveal the queen's adultery but to hide it— to obscure the queen's guilt by representing her as one unfaithful woman among many, or to negate the queen's guilt by questioning the validity of the proof.

The threats to the unity of the court that arrive from the outside in the form of magic tests are meant to reveal a truth about the court that will affect its reputation. The discovery of one faithful woman saves the court's fame; the discovery of many unfaithful women dilutes the crime and the importance of the proof. As tests imposed from the outside, the magic drinking horn and the ill-fitting coat represent attacks on Arthur's court that take women's bodies as a site of political contest. Although initially the chastity test may provoke a competition between the knights over whose lady is most faithful, magic tests not are intended to create discord within the king's court, they are intended to damage the court's reputation abroad. And they do not create lasting disharmony among the knights. Competition is quickly abandoned as all the women are shown to be at fault, and the test ultimately has the effect of promoting solidarity among the cuckolded knights and among the unfaithful women. However, when a direct accusation of sexual transgression against the queen comes from inside the court, proofs are not so easily dismissed as faulty or irrelevant. When the queen alone is accused of adultery, the king alone is shamed; his authority is challenged and can be restored only through a judicially sanctioned proof of the queen's innocence.

The Queen's Ordeal

The medieval *iudicum Dei* was based on a concept of immanent justice, on the idea that God would intervene in the physical world to manifest his judgment in trials that oppose truth and perjury, innocence and guilt.[23] God ensures victory for the champion of truth in judicial battles; God guarantees that a true oath will be proved through a physical test in a trial by ordeal. In unilateral ordeals divine judgment was revealed through a corporeal sign. During the hot iron ordeal the accused carried a heated iron a specified number of paces, the burn was bandaged, and after three days it was uncovered. An infected wound indicated guilt, a cleanly healing wound affirmed the innocence of the accused. The examination of a burn was also used to determine truth in the hot water ordeal, in which the accused was required to retrieve an object—a ring or a stone, for example—from the bottom of a boiling cauldron. In the ordeal of cold water, the accused was thrown into water and would sink if innocent, float if guilty.

The use of judicial ordeal was abolished by the Fourth Lateran Council in 1215. This date is at the center of a historiographical debate about the end of ordeal. Most studies have concluded that the Lateran Council merely put an official end to an already declining practice.[24] In this view, the end of ordeal represents a triumph of rationality and results from a lack of belief in its efficacy among lay people and from a serious questioning of the canonicity of ordeal by the clergy. The learned objections to the practice were based on the lack of Biblical sanctions for ordeals and on the idea that it is wrong to tempt God, since to demand that God intervene in earthly affairs is equal to testing God. These objections to the practice of ordeal were voiced from the very first recorded discussions of its legitimacy in the ninth century; they have a long history and were not new in the twelfth century.[25]

Taking issue with the assumption that a decline in the use of ordeal must precede and thus explain its abandonment in 1215, some historians have claimed that ordeal survived as a thriving practice that unified clerical and secular interests right up to the moment of its interdiction by the Lateran Council. The end of ordeal was thus due to the coincidence at a particular time—the early thirteenth century—of a renewed questioning of the legitimacy of ordeal by a powerful intellectual elite within the church and of the increased unilateral power of the church to impose law. From this perspective, it is a mistake to think of ordeal as an irrational practice that was gradually abolished through a growing rationalization of the law during the twelfth century and finally interdicted by the church in 1215.[26] Rather, ordeal should be seen in the context of the various forms of proof in medieval society and medieval law; it was a practice abolished not because of an increasing doubt about its efficacy or appropriateness—those doubts were always in evidence—but because in 1215 these views were held by an influential faction of a body capable of incorporating them into the law.[27]

Like the practice of ordeal, literary representations of trials by ordeal continue well into the thirteenth century: examples include Queen Isolde's famous hot-iron ordeal recounted by Gottfried von Strassburg, based on Thomas's twelfth-century French romance, and the water ordeal trial of the senechal in Guillaume de Dole's *Roman de la rose*. In a recent study of the survival of judicial ordeal up to its interdiction, Robert Bartlett claims that the continued practice of judicial ordeals can in part be explained by the interests served by the ordeal. Priests received gratuities and churches received income when designated as officially sanctioned sites for the ritual. Local forces may have promoted the practice of ordeal while the church administration moved toward its prohibition.[28] Rather than examining literary representations of the *iudicum Dei* for how well they reflect a growing distrust or a continued faith in the effectiveness of physical proofs, it may be more fruitful, following Bartlett, to ask whose interests are served by the representation of the ritual of ordeal. In the literary trials of adulterous queens, who profits, not just from the outcome of the test, but from the ritualized performance that constitutes the proof?

The ordeal provides a visible judgment inscribed on or by the body: the burned hand, the floating body. Like magic tests of chastity, the unilateral ordeal is a spectacle in which the body is displayed and scrutinized, and in which a truth about that body is revealed. In what is perhaps the best-known trial in medieval romance, Queen Iseut's exculpation at the hot iron ordeal, truth is simultaneously proclaimed and hidden, displayed and covered up.[29] In this fictional representation of a judicial ordeal, as in the marvelous tests of chastity, the ostensible display of truth is enacted in terms of clothing and status.

In Béroul's version of the episode, Queen Iseut agrees to perform an exculpatory oath when King Marc's vassals demand proof of her fidelity to the king after her return from the sojourn in the Morrois forest with Tristan. The queen has been reconciled with the king after she and Tristan were discovered in the forest sleeping with Tristan's sword lying between them as a sign of chastity, in King Marc's reading of the scene. After the queen's return to court the barons demand that she prove her innocence of adultery with Tristan with an oath. No physical ordeal accompanies Iseut's oath, but it is sworn on relics, and the logic of unilateral ordeals also pertains to this kind of test: God will not allow a false oath to go unpunished.[30] Iseut's exculpation (*desreisne*) is a result of an implicit lack of faith in judicial battle. When Iseut returns from the Morrois to be reconciled with King Marc, Tristan offers to prove her chastity in battle against any man who would challenge it. Marc's barons refuse this occasion to demand proof of the queen's innocence of adultery, but after Iseut has been reinstated in Marc's court and Tristan has agreed to leave the country, they insist that the queen undergo a unilateral proof of her chastity.[31] Distrustful of the outcome of a judicial battle, the barons prefer to demonstrate Tristan's disloyalty to his uncle through a test whose results are displayed on the queen's body.

While the barons' rivalry with the king's nephew motivates many accusations against the queen and her lover—and I will discuss these further in the following chapter—here their enmity with Tristan is secondary. Tristan is implicated in the demand for the proof of the queen's innocence of adultery, but at this point in the story the barons think that he has already left Cornwall. It is not the knight's loyalty but the king's authority that must be demonstrated in the queen's exculpation, as Marc explains to Iseut:

"J'ai trois felons, d'ancesorie,
Qui heent mon amendement;
Mais se encor nes en desment,
Que nes enchaz for de ma terre,
Li fel ne crient mais ma gerre." (Béroul, 3186–90)

("[F]or a long time three evil men have been jealous of my accomplishments. Unless I do something about it now, unless I drive them out of my land, the villains will no longer fear my power." [Lacy, 151])

In this episode of accusation, the queen's exculpation is no longer a scene played out for the wavering king's eyes in order to persuade him to believe in the innocence of the lovers, as in the staged tryst beneath the pine tree observed by Marc earlier in Béroul's version of the story. It is a public trial that implicates the king's sovereignty. Georges Duby claims that trials of adultery demonstrate that "infractions of the marriage laws were viewed as matters of secular justice, and did not fall within the jurisdiction of the church," and he goes on to conclude that such trials "were more than secular: they were private and domestic. It was for the members of the household involved to observe the effect of the red-hot iron and to hear the wife swear her innocence, taking God as her witness and laying her hand on the Gospels or some holy relic."[32] The location of the transgression in the king's household blurs distinctions of private and public. When the king's wife goes to the ordeal, the spectators include not only the king's personal household but his larger *maisne*, his court, and also his feudal lord, King Arthur, and members of Arthur's court. In the exculpation episode, unlike other episodes of accusation against the queen, the barons' suspicion of the queen does not unleash Marc's doubts about his wife's loyalty. Rather, it provokes his anger at the assault on his sovereignty.[33] Iseut responds to precisely this affront, staging the exculpation as a display of royal authority.

E. Jane Burns has noted the importance of visual truth in Iseut's trial, and the repeated challenges to visible truth in Béroul's romance.[34] Her study of the relationship between seeing and truth (*voir* and *li voirs*) might be extended to Iseut's manipulation of the spectacle of her body. The queen arrives at the site of her exculpation clothed according to her royal status. Closely scrutinized, watched by all, the queen—and her clothes—inspire awe among all those who watch her:

La roïne out molt grant esgart
De ceus qui sont de l'autre part.
Li roi prisié s'en esbahirent,
Et tuit li autre qui le virent.
La roïne out de soie dras:

Aporté furent de Baudas,
Forré furent de blanc hermine.
Mantel, bliaut, tot li traïne.
Sor ses espaules sont si crin,
Bendé a ligne sor or fin.
Un cercle d'or out sor son chief,
Qui empare de chief en chief,
Color rosine, fresche et blanche. (Béroul, vv. 3899–911)

(The queen had been watched closely by those on the other side. The great kings marveled at her, as did all the others who saw her. The queen was wearing garments of silk, brought from Bagdad; they were trimmed in white ermine. Her mantel and tunic formed a train behind her. Her hair fell to her shoulders and was tied in linen ribbons over a fine gold net. She wore on her head a golden band that encircled it entirely, and her face was rosy, fresh, and fair. [Lacy, 185])

As Burns has noted, clothing plays an important role in the ordeal episode, highlighting Iseut's status in the judgment of the queen.[35] I want to emphasize how the relationships figured by clothing are part of the negotiation of the king's authority. When Queen Iseut arrives at the ford, her dress is a sign of her status as queen— and as the innocent wife of the king. The significance of Iseut's dress is all the more evident when her rich attire in the scene of exculpation is compared with her dress at her condemnation to the fire earlier in the story. After evidence of the queen's adultery is discovered in the blood drops from Tristan's wound that fell between the knight's bed and the queen's bed as Tristan leaped from one to the other, King Marc refuses to grant the lovers a trial, and in an abuse of royal power, he condemns them to be burned. Iseut is led to the pyre in rich but simple dress. Her hands are bound, and tears run down her face. The queen's loss of royal status is emphasized in the contrast between her rich clothing and the abjection of her body:

En un bliaut de paile bis
Estoit la dame estroit vestue
Et d'un fil d'or menu cosue.
Si chevel hurtent a ses piez,

D'un filet d'or les ot trechiez.
Qui voit son cors et sa faaction,
Trop par avroit le cuer felon
Qui n'en avroit de lié pitié.
Molt sont li braz estroit lïé. (Béroul, 1146–54)

(The lady was dressed in a fitted tunic of dark silk, finely stitched with gold thread. Her hair reached to her feet and was held by a gold net. Anyone who saw her face and figure would have to have a very cruel heart not to feel pity for her. Her arms were tied very tightly. [Lacy, 55, 57])

The spectacle of the queen's body evokes pity; the gold threads of her dress suggest royal status, its simple cut and dark color echo the subjugation demonstrated by her bound hands. As she is led away to be burned the queen is portrayed as the victim of royal command, not as a participant in royal sovereignty.

In this episode Iseut is saved from death by Tristan, who has escaped his executioners. The lovers flee to the Morrois forest, where they live in exile until they are discovered sleeping with the sword between them. When Marc agrees to a reconciliation with the queen, Iseut prepares for her return to court by procuring clothes that indicate the status she will reassume: Iseut dresses as a queen.

Li hermites en vet au Mont,
Por les richeces qui la sont.
Aprés achate ver et gris,
Dras de soie et de porpre bis,
Escarlates et blanc chainsil,
Asez plus blanc que flor de lil,
Et palefroi souef anblant,
Bien atornez d'or flanboiant.
Ogrins l'ermite tant achate
Et tant acroit et tant barate
Pailes, vairs et gris et hermine
Que richement vest la roïne. (Béroul, 2733–44)

(The hermit went to the Mount because of the rich market held there. He bought gray and white furs, silk and rich purple fabrics, fine wool and linen far whiter than lilies; and he bought a gentle riding-horse with a harness of brightest gold. The hermit Ogrin bought and bartered and acquired by credit enough precious cloth and gray furs and ermine to dress the queen richly. [Lacy, 129])

The queen reclaims her royal status through her sumptuous dress; her clothing is a sign of her noble body: "Riche ert la robe et gent le cors" (v. 2887).[36]

At the scene of her exculpation the queen's garments of silk trimmed with white ermine echo the earlier resumption of royal status through clothing, but here her attire does more than simply represent royal privilege and authority. In this episode clothing symbolizes hidden relationships and dependencies, both political and sexual. Indeed, the narrator seems obsessed with descriptions of clothing in the story of the queen's trial. The episode opens with a detailed description of the rough clothes that Tristan uses in his disguise as a leper (vv. 3567–74), and Tristan begs for alms and for clothes as he sits by the treacherous ford that leads to the site of Iseut's exculpation.[37] King Arthur passes and Tristan claims his leggings, King Marc gives him his fur bonnet, and the leper receives many fine clothes ("Fin dras en a a grant plenté," v. 3738).[38]

Queen Iseut is the last to arrive at the marsh. All the other members of the two royal courts have passed across the ford and watch her from the other side. The queen is a spectacle and she knows it ("Bien savoit que cil l'esgardoient / Qui outre le Mal Pas estoient," vv. 3883–84). The kings and all those who observe the queen marvel at her. She is dressed sumptuously and regally as befits her station. When the queen was taken to be burned she wore a simple dark-colored silk tunic; when she was reconciled with King Marc she wore scarlet and purple silk. When she arrives at Mal Pas, the only color mentioned in the description of her clothes is white, and the queen states her refusal to dirty her clothing: "Ne vuel mes dras enpaluer" (v. 3917). The unsoiled white robe symbolizes the chastity of the body it covers at the same time that the queen's professed desire to prevent her robe from being soiled permits her to get the leper between her legs; she calls on the disguised Tristan to carry her across the muddy ford. Although the ordeal ceremony will not take place until the following day, through her deliberate actions and her studied self-presentation Queen Iseut performs a ritual of exculpation that is merely confirmed by her subsequent formal oath.

Iseut's performance with the leper is reenacted in her oath at the ordeal. The well-known conflation of her husband and her lover permits her to profess her innocence while confessing her adultery: ". . . entre mes cuises n'entra home, / Fors le ladre qui fist soi some, / Qui me porta outre les guez, / Et li rois Marc mes esposez" (". . . no man has ever been between my thighs except the leper who made himself a beast of burden and carried me over the ford and my husband King Mark," Béroul, vv. 4205–8; Lacy, 197, 199). As Burns suggests, Iseut reverses the position she held between the two men by putting the two men between her thighs.

[Iseut's] anatomy, now sexualized by her own definition, by her own devising, can include *both* husband *and* leper, as the categories used previously to distinguish them break down. The leper in this scene is the leper/lover/knight that the disguised Tristan plays; the husband is the naive cuckold falsely represented by this trial as a potent king and proper spouse. As the space between Iseut's thighs expands in her definition to include *both* lover *and* husband, her body becomes a map for a new legal coding and the site for a redefinition of heterosexual and homosocial bonding.[39]

Burns shows that Iseut's oath offers "a thorough redefinition of the terms by which truth is established," that "Against [the baron's] assertions that Marc must establish the lovers' guilt *or* innocence, and prove himself thereby *either* virile *or* cuckolded, Iseut's convincing lies provide the alternative of a nuanced truth that escapes the logic of binary opposition."[40]

Burns's analysis of how Iseut's oath breaks down the binary logic that defines her as either wife or mistress is part of a broad-ranging and challenging study of how female characters might be heard to speak "both within and against" the conventions that define them in Old French narratives.[41] Burns's reading may also be extended to show how the queen speaks "both within and against" the *political* structure that defines her relationship to her husband, to the court, and to the power contests that appropriate her sexuality as a symbol of sovereign authority. When Iseut claims that no man has been between her legs but her husband, the king, and the leper who carried her across the ford, she successfully proves her innocence by changing the terms of the proof. Through the display of her innocent sovereign body, Iseut demonstrates the unsullied authority of the king. But she also exposes the fragility of an authority based on the illusory truth of the body.

Fradenburg offers a perceptive analysis of the relationship between the queen's beauty, virtue, and sovereignty:

The queen's beauty signifies that she is set-apart, peerless; at the same time, her beauty keeps her in the realm of the senses. Thus the association, in turn, of beauty and queenship with a discourse of virtue is also essential to the art of queenship. Insofar as virtue provides a hidden, inaccessible interior for the magnificent surface of beauty, the question of whether the queen is both beautiful and virtuous is a way of posing the question of queenship: how is it to make accessible the body of sovereignty, so that it may be "loved in the flesh," while limiting its circulation, preserving its rare, indeed its extraordinary character?[42]

Fradenburg's equation of the question of the queen's beauty and virtue to the question of queenship might be extended to encompass the question of kingship and of the king's sovereign body. When Iseut dresses herself with clothing that symbolizes innocence and royal sovereignty, she promotes the definition of the queen's body as symbol of the political integrity of her husband's kingdom and she locates the confirmation of the king's sovereign authority in the queen's manipulation of that definition. The queen's successful ordeal is a ritual that functions like the public execution that Foucault describes as "a ceremonial in which a momentarily injured sovereignty is reconstituted."[43] But the queen's manipulation of the ritual proof depends on deception: she embodies what Burns calls "the paradox of the innocent adulteress."[44] The ambiguity of Iseut's oath—simultaneously a confession of guilt and a claim of innocence—is echoed throughout the ordeal episode. Tristan tells King Marc that his lover dresses just like Iseut, and the queen admits her infidelity when she says the leper has been between her legs. The veiled articulation of the relationship between Tristan and Iseut names a hidden truth about the king's sovereignty. When Tristan claims to have been infected with leprosy by his lover who passed it to him from her husband, he alludes to a sickness in the king's corporate body that is covered up by the queen's clever oath and her magnificent white clothes: the king's weakness is masked by the queen's display of sovereignty. The leper who wears the king's clothes, the king who shares a lover with a leper, and doubled meanings that contain both exculpation and confession—all these contradictions work to define the queen as an innocent adulteress and as a well-dressed emblem of royal power.

Béroul's representation of Queen Iseut's exculpation at the hot iron ordeal as a spectacle of royal sovereignty is particularly striking when compared with Gottfried's (and presumably Thomas's) version of the episode. In Gottfried's *Tristan* the queen's exculpation is not explicitly linked to a challenge of the king's authority, as in Béroul's romance. The queen's oath follows the discovery of the bloody sheets in the lovers' beds that are taken to demonstrate their guilt. King Mark does not immediately and unlawfully condemn the lovers to be burned, as in Béroul's romance, but he defers to his nobles, who advise him to have Isolde prove her innocence through the hot iron ordeal. King Mark sees his vassals as his allies, rather than as his enemies, and he turns to them for counsel. Queen Isolde's arrival at the site of the ordeal is also markedly different from the ostentatious display provided by Béroul's Iseut. The queen is dressed simply and piously:

[S]he wore a rough hair-shirt next her skin and above it a short woollen robe which failed to reach her slender ankles by more than a hand's breadth. Her sleeves were folded back right to the elbow; her arms and feet were bare. Many eyes observed her, many hearts felt sorrow and pity for her. Her garment and figure attracted much attention. (Gottfried, 247)

The uncovered royal body is perhaps all the more royal because of the unaccustomed exposure that demonstrates its unaccustomed abjection. The almost naked body signifies humility and piety, but only in relation to its usual covering, the rich clothes that the queen normally wears and that she has given away along with her silver, gold, jewels, and horses in order to win God's favor.

In Gottfried's *Tristan* the interpretation of Queen Isolde's successful ordeal by the king and by the narrator is notably different from the oath's reinstatement of royal power in Béroul's romance. Gottfried recounts the queen's exculpation as one in a series of episodes that represent the discovery and subsequent cover-up of the queen's adultery. And if King Mark and the other witnesses to the ordeal are duped, it is because of God's ambivalence toward the truth, according to the narrator. God's justice, like clothes, can be changed at will, claims the narrator in his description of God's fickle judgment.

Thus it was made manifest and confirmed to all the world that Christ in His great virtue is pliant as a windblown sleeve. He falls into place and clings, whichever way you try Him, closely and smoothly, as He is bound to do. He is at the beck of every heart for honest deeds or fraud. Be it deadly earnest or a game, He is just as you would have Him. This was amply revealed in the facile Queen. She was saved by her guile and by the doctored oath that went flying up to God, with the result that she redeemed her honour and was again much beloved of her lord Mark, and was praised, lauded, and esteemed among the people. (Gottfried, 248)

Gottfried's condemnation of the *iudicum Dei* ("Christ in His great virtue is pliant as a windblown sleeve . . . at the beck of every heart for honest deeds or fraud") questions the utility of the ordeal as a proof of innocence and emphasizes King Mark's own ambivalence toward knowledge of his wife's adultery. The king seems to wish for a proof of his wife's innocence despite his doubts: he does not immediately condemn the queen to burn when her adultery is discovered and he rejoices at the result of the ordeal. Mark's love for Isolde is emphasized in the text and the exculpation provides yet further justification for his familiar wavering between confidence in his wife's fidelity and doubts about her liaison with his nephew.[45]

In Gottfried's *Tristan* the political function of the queen's exculpation is much less explicit than in Béroul's, where the stakes of the judgment are stated by the king himself: "[F]or a long time three evil men have been jealous of my accomplishments. Unless I do something about it now, unless I drive them out of my land, the villains will no longer fear my power."[46] In Béroul's romance Iseut's exculpation accomplishes exactly what King Marc needs it to do. The ritualized proof of her richly dressed innocent, adulterous body re-establishes royal authority: "Li rois a Cornoualle en pes, / Tuit le crie-ment et luin et pres." ("The king now had peace in Cornwall, and he was feared by all, from far and near." Béroul, vv. 4267–68; Lacy, 201.) King Marc needs the proof of the queen's innocence as much—per-haps more—than Iseut does because his authority as king has been put into question by the barons' challenge. In Béroul's romance, the test of the queen is not so much a confrontation between Marc, Iseut, and, indirectly, Tristan, but the display of their interdependence and of their common investment in the proof of Iseut's innocence.

It has been suggested that the ordeal functioned in medieval societies as a ritual of reconciliation, that the public ceremony of proof served to eliminate tensions and to promote community.[47] Iseut's exculpatory oath in Béroul's version of the story may be seen to function in this way: the reconciliation of the queen and the king is reconfirmed with the proof of the queen's chastity, and the king's authority is demonstrated when his wife is proved innocent of adul-tery. The empress Judith's exculpatory oath, with which I began this chapter, may have served a similar function. The empress was not ultimately required to undergo a formal ordeal: she swore an oath before a council convened to judge her. After Louis had reconciled with his sons and exiled his enemies, there was no one left at court to formally accuse the queen and demand that her innocence be proved on her body: "And since there was no one present who accused her of any evil, she purified herself according to the judgment of the Franks, of all that she had been accused."[48] The empress's oath was not chal-lenged and may have served as both an acknowledgment of her re-instatement and a recognition of a restored peace in the kingdom.

The truth of the royal female body is interpreted according to its significance in a political system, as Empress Judith's unchallenged oath suggests. Foucault has described the political appropriation of bodies as follows:

[T]he body is also directly involved in a political field; power relations have an immediate hold on it; they invest it, mark it, train it, torture it, force it to carry out tasks, to perform ceremonies, to emit signs. This political investment of the body is bound up, in accordance with complex reciprocal relations, with its economic use; it is largely as a force of production that the body is invested with relations of power and domination; but, on the other hand, its constitution as labour power is possible only if it is caught up in a system of subjection. . . . [T]he body becomes a useful force only if it is both a productive body and a subjected body. . . . [T]here may be a "knowledge" of the body that is not exactly the science of its functioning, and a mastery of its forces that is more than the ability to conquer them: this knowledge and this mastery constitute what might be called the political technology of the body.[49]

Foucault's definition of "the political technology of the body" does not acknowledge gender difference, and when he speaks of labor, he speaks of work, not of childbirth. As I emphasized in Chapter 1, the story of the adulterous queen does not include maternity, either, at least not explicitly. But if we extend Foucault's definition to include the labor of childbirth, his formulation of a "political technology of the body" that takes knowledge as its field of operation may be a useful one for reading the function of the queen's adulterous body in medieval romances. In the absence of children, what is produced by the queen's body? And in light of the deceptive proofs offered by the test of the queen's body, what knowledge of the royal barren body is possible? In Chapter 3 I explore how the rhetorical exchange of the queen between men through claims of knowledge about her body may produce political stability in the royal court.

3

Rumors, Rivalries, and the Queen's Secret Adultery

WHEN KING MARC'S BARONS demand that the queen prove that she remained chaste during her sojourn in the Morrois forest with Tristan, they equate the state of the queen's body with the state of the king's sovereign status, and they speak as vassals of the king concerned about a disorder that undermines the king's control of his household and his court. In an earlier episode of Béroul's *Tristan*, the barons claim already to know the truth about the queen's adultery. They assert that Tristan and Iseut are lovers, and they accuse King Marc of complicity in the crime. Here they speak as the king's vassals, but also as rivals of the king's nephew, Tristan, with whom they compete for influence over the king.

A la cort avoit trois barons,
Ainz ne veïstes plus felons.
Par soirement s'estoient pris
Que, se li rois de son païs
N'en faisot son nevo partir,
Il nu voudroient mais soufrir:
A lor chasteaus sus s'en trairoient
Et au roi Marc gerre feroient.
Qar, en un gardin, soz une ente,
Virent l'autrier Yseut la gente
Ovoc Tristran en tel endroit
Que nus hon consentir ne doit;
Et plusors foiz les ont veüz
El lit roi Marc gesir toz nus;

Quar, quant li rois en vet el bois,
Et Tristran dit: "Sir, g'en vois,"
Puis se remaint, entre en la chanbre,
Iluec grant piece sont ensenble. . . .
A une part ont le roi trait:
"Sire," font il, "malement vet.
Tes niés s'entraiment et Yseut,
Savoir le puet qui c'onques veut;
Et nos nu volon mais sofrir." (Béroul, vv. 581–609)

(There were at the court three barons, and never have you seen such evil men! They had taken an oath that, if the king did not banish his nephew from his land, they would tolerate it no longer; rather, they would withdraw to their castles and wage war against King Mark. For the other day they had seen the fair Iseut with Tristran, in a garden, under a grafted tree, in a situation that no one should tolerate. And several times they had seen them lying completely naked in King Mark's bed. For whenever the king went into the forest, Tristran would say: "Sir, I am leaving." But then he would stay behind and enter the chamber, and they would remain together a long time. . . .They drew the king aside: "Sir," they said, "there is trouble. Your nephew and Iseut love each other. It is obvious to anyone who cares to look, and we will no longer tolerate it!" [Lacy, 30–31])

The barons' accusation takes the not-so-secret adultery as an instrument of political conflict. Knowledge of the secret can be used against the queen, undermining any influence she might have over her husband. More important, knowledge of the secret can be used to subvert the powerful position of the queen's lover in the royal court. The political rivalry that motivates the accusation of adultery has long been acknowledged by readers of the romance.[1] In this chapter I argue that the inadequacy of the secrecy surrounding the queen's adultery and the ambiguity that characterizes refutations of the baron's accusations are also part of a political structure.

The queen's close bond with her knight is openly acknowledged in the best-known romances about royal adultery even while the adultery itself is ostensibly hidden. Lancelot is known as Guenevere's knight, and Tristan's close relationship to Iseut is explained by the service he owes to the wife of his lord, who is also his kinswoman through marriage to his uncle, and by his part in winning her for

King Marc and bringing her to Cornwall to marry the king. Loyalty to the queen represents the knight's service to a lady idealized by all the court because of her beauty and courtesy, and esteemed above all other women because she is the wife of the king. In an important study of what she calls "courtly adultery" (*adultère courtois*), Christiane Marchello-Nizia discusses the various seductions at work in the triangular relationship between the queen, the king, and the knight. She suggests that the knight's love for the lady is a displaced desire to occupy the lady's position in proximity to a powerful lord. It is no coincidence that the beloved lady is a queen in stories of courtly adultery; the queen is a symbol of the sovereign power of her husband, the true object of the knight's desire.[2] Marchello-Nizia suggests that romances about adulterous queens transform a potentially conflicted feudal relationship between an aspiring vassal and a powerful lord into a sexually pleasurable relationship with the wife of the lord. These stories hide the knight's resentment and jealousy of the king's power behind the figural representation of a power to which the knight submits willingly. Love service to the queen is a displaced form of attraction to, rivalry with, and submission to the king's power.[3]

In what follows I use Marchello-Nizia's description of the mediating function of the queen to examine how sexual transgression itself is constructed as a mediating act in medieval romances about adulterous queens. Just as the possession of the queen substitutes for the possession of the king's power, the possession of knowledge about the queen's adultery can be seen to substitute for the possession of the queen. If the queen mediates a relationship between the knight and the lord, she also mediates relationships between the knight and his rivals in the royal court. And if courtly adultery hides an antagonistic relationship between the knight and the king, as Marchello-Nizia suggests, rivalries are more overt in contests between the king's vassals and the queen's lover, but power struggles are still displaced onto the queen. They take the form not of the seduction of the queen, but of threats to the king. When the barons tell King Marc that they will withdraw from court and make war on him if he does not banish Tristan from the court, they define a relationship of power and authority that is based on knowledge of the queen's adultery.

The Queen's Secret

Although the possession of the queen by the knight may establish a desired relationship between the king and the knight, the adulterous liaison between the queen and her lover must remain secret in medieval romances. As Karma Lochrie has suggested, secrecy is essential to the power relationships structured by the exchange of women's bodies:

"Secrecy is crucial to the operations of this exchange system and to the mystification of woman so that the power relationships among men are concealed and preserved. At the same time, woman's own desire, sexuality, and body become a secret to her through this conversion into what Irigaray calls a "social value." Both forms of secrecy are essential to the functioning of patriarchal relations of power, to the masking of homosocial relations created and enjoyed through such exchanges, and to masculine control of female sexuality.[4]

Lochrie examines how fabliau-like narratives humorously exploit the formulaic aspect of this structure; its representation is less humorous in romances about courtly adultery, but secrecy is no less crucial to the operations of the exchange system in these narratives. The king must not learn of his wife's adultery, and the danger of discovery is only apparently diluted by the king's repeated demonstrations of ambivalence toward knowledge of his wife's sexual transgression. In stories about Tristan and Iseut and Lancelot and Guenevere, once the king is confronted with evidence of betrayal, he acts quickly to condemn the lovers to die for their crime. The importance of secrecy is fully recognized by the queen. In the *Prose Tristan* the narrator suggests that Iseut's participation in the masquerade of her marriage is motivated by the fear that Marc will learn of her liaison with Tristan if he suspects that she does not love her husband:

Figure 4. The queen is taken prisoner. *Lancelot*. BN fr. 342, fol. 184 v. Photograph: Bibliothèque Nationale, Paris.

[E]t coment qu'[Iseut] face joie au roi Marc et en son lit et defors, ele nel fait fors por dotance qu'ele a de li qu'il ne s'aperçoeve de l'amor qu'ele a a Tristan. Et ele set bien se il s'en apercevoit qu'il les feroit endeus destruire. Por ceste chose se coevre quanqu'ele puet. (Curtis, 2: 94)

(And however much [Iseut] gave King Marc joy in his bed and outside of it, she did it only because of her fear that he would perceive her love for Tristan. And she was sure that if he perceived it he would have both of them destroyed. For this reason she pretended as best she could.)

The knight's adulterous liaison with the queen is an act of treason against the king, who could execute both of the lovers if he found them together.[5] The queen accused of adultery is particularly vulnerable to the king's vengeance when her dependency on her husband and lover is complete. Both Iseut and Guenevere live far from kinsmen who might protect them or defend them (justly or unjustly) against the king's accusation. While the queen's lover might escape the king's judgment and go to live in another land and serve some other king, the dishonored queen would have only two choices: to remain with her husband and face the consequences of discovery, or to flee with her lover. Queen Guenevere suggests the particular vulnerability of her position when she claims that, if the king found her with her lover, Lancelot would be shamed, but the queen would be destroyed: "si ne voldroie, fait ele, por riens que nos fussions trové ensamble, car j'en seroie destruite et vos honniz" (*Lancelot*, 4: 381). An illustration of the queen's capture in a thirteenth-century *Lancelot* manuscript emphasizes the vulnerability of the queen in its portrayal of the unarmed woman surrounded by knights in what is surely an exaggerated show of force, since Lancelot has already fled (Figure 4).

The potential consequences of discovery are explicit and they are specifically dictated by the lovers' position within a political structure. When Lancelot and Guenevere are discovered alone together in the queen's bedchamber in *La mort le roi Artu*, Agravain and his brothers claim that a queen who lets another man lie in the place of the king must be burned, and the narrator adds that because of her high office, a queen who betrays can only be punished by burning:

Et li baron se trestrent a un conseill, si le demandent a Agravain, que l'en en devoit fere, et aus autres deus freres; et il distrent qu'il esgardoient par droit qu'ele en devoit morir a honte, car trop avoit fet grant desloiauté, quant ele en leu del roi qui tant estoit preudom avoit lessié gesir un autre chevalier. . . . Et li rois commande a ses sergenz qu'il feïssent en la praerie de Kamaalot un feu grant et merveillex, ou la reïne sera mise; car autrement ne doit reïne morir qui desloiauté fet, puis que ele est sacree. (*La mort*, 121–22)

(And the barons went into counsel, and they asked Agravain and his two brothers what should be done, and they said that they thought she should die with shame because she had acted with great disloyalty when she let another knight lie in the place of the king, who was a very noble man. . . . And the king commanded his sergeants to build a great and marvelous fire on the prairie of Camaalot, where the queen would be burned; for a queen who commits a disloyalty should not die any other way, because she is sacred.)

Arthur's explanation of the queen's consecration as the reason for the execution by fire disputes the *Prose Tristan*'s claim that all adulterous women should be burned.[6] Neither fictional account corresponds to penalties in medieval law codes, although the discovery of Lancelot and Guenevere alone together does correspond to a situation that, according to Philippe de Beaumanoir, justifies the husband's execution of both wife and lover.[7] This law would also dictate King Marc's actions when he discovers Tristan and Iseut sleeping side by side in the forest with Tristan's sword lying between them. R. Howard Bloch has discussed Béroul's account of Marc's hesitation to kill Tristan and Iseut, and Bloch shows that the king's actions are part of a changing culture of government in which contractual obligation becomes internalized.[8] Bloch sees the second half of Béroul's romance as characterized by a "growing emphasis on the subjectivity of personal vision as opposed to the commonly acknowledged vision of the group," and he suggests that this shift is particularly evident in a changed relationship between the king and his vassals.[9] When Marc initially resists his barons' demand that Iseut prove her chastity with an exculpatory oath, he inaugurates a new idea of kingship, a "notion of active kingship in which power descends from above through the monarch to the community and in which the king is at once above positive but below natural law."[10]

While Béroul's *Roman de Tristan* points to an evolution in kingship, as Bloch's analysis suggests, the role of the queen does not change. The queen's body continues to be exchanged between men, both literally in the sexual possession by husband and lover and rhetorically in the rumors of adultery that structure the competition between Tristan and the barons. Although romance narratives may recount changes in the theory and practice of kingship, the role of the queen as a symbol of her husband's authority remains remarkably constant in twelfth- and thirteenth-century romances that recount stories of the queen's "courtly adultery."

If the queen's position as wife of the king defines the knight's desire for her, as Marchello-Nizia suggests, it also defines the danger of discovery for both the queen and her lover, although the knight is not subject to the king's justice in the same way that the queen is. As a woman without kinship alliances at the court, without children through whom she might gain status and influence, and without recourse to flight or battle, the queen is completely vulnerable to the king's definition of how or whether she should be judged. Moreover, when the queen's sexual betrayal becomes public, it is seen to challenge the king's authority, as Marc suggests when he interprets the barons' demand that Iseut prove her chastity at the hot iron ordeal as an attack on his sovereignty. It is precisely this politicization of the adultery that defines its function in the story of the queen's adultery. The tension between secret love and the knowledge of transgression is located not only in the triangle formed by the king, the queen, and the knight but in the relationship of all three parties to the court and, especially, to the king's vassals.[11]

Secrecy protects the adulterous lovers from discovery and its consequences. Yet complete discretion in love proves difficult, even impossible, because true love cannot be hidden. Lovers who live at court face unavoidable scrutiny and will inevitably reveal their love, explains Béroul:

Ha, Dex! Qui puet amor tenir
Un an ou deus sanz descovrir?
Car amors ne se puet celer:

Sovent cline l'un vers son per,
Sovent vienent a parlement,
Et a celé et voiant gent.
Par tot ne püent aise atendre,
Maint parlement lor estuet prendre. (Béroul, vv. 573–80)

(Oh, God! Who could love for a year or two and still keep it secret? For love
cannot be hidden. Often one lover nods to the other; they often meet to
speak together, both in private and in public. [Lacy, 29])

The necessary link between secrecy and adulterous love is recognized
in other passages of Béroul's romance, but in the lines cited above the
narrator suggests that the sign of true love is indiscretion. This equation of love and indiscretion invites an examination of the place of
the impossible secret of true love in the story of the queen's adultery.

If the feudal court is inhospitable to secrets about love, it is because the secret resists the centralizing organization of the court as
a place where stories are told and adventures are recounted and recorded. Many romances recount the arrival of an unknown lady or
knight at court, the announcement of a quest to be completed or a
mysterious adventure to be pursued, and the subsequent return of
Arthur's knights to court, where they recount their exploits to the
king, who has them recorded. The court is defined by a desire to
discover, accomplish, and recount unknown adventures; it is characterized by a desire to know secrets.

The court is also characterized by a desire to learn about love affairs. The personification of the desire to uncover secrets is found in
the ever-present *lausengiers* evoked in lyric poetry and in narratives.
Descriptions of these court gossips frame the story of a châtelaine
and her lover in *La châtelaine de Vergi*. *Lausengiers* are disloyal, the
narrator warns in the prologue, and the story ends with a warning
about those who "seek to know the loves of others" and take pleasure in destroying a love affair by publicizing it to all the court.[12]
The presence of the *lausengiers* in courtly narratives implicitly asks
a question: is there a hidden love affair? Silence should respond in
the negative according to the narrator of *La châtelaine de Vergi*, who

counsels discretion in order to thwart the curiosity of those who would speak of the affairs of others.

Et par cest example doit l'en
s'amor celer par si grant sen
c'on ait toz jors en remembrance
que li descouvrirs riens n'avance
et li celers en toz poins vaut.
Qui si le fet, ne crient assaut
des faus felons enquereors
qui enquierent autrui amors. (*La châtelaine*, vv. 951–58)

(And according to this example one should always hide his love with great wisdom and always keep in mind that revealing secrets serves no purpose and hiding them is always worthwhile. Whoever acts in this way does not fear the attacks of felonous false gossips who seek to know the loves of others.)

But perfect discretion proves impossible in the fictional courts of medieval romance, as Béroul suggests, and the gossips who wish to learn of a love affair in order to speak of it and thus destroy it are given a prominent role in narratives about adulterous love in which a queen is the heroine. In the twelfth-century French *Tristan* romances, those who wish to uncover the love affair between Tristan and Iseut are the three barons who are Marc's vassals and Tristan's enemies. The barons are never called "lausengiers" in Béroul; they are usually called "félon," a term that, as Jean-Charles Payen has noted, belongs to a feudal, rather than an amorous context and demonstrates the political motivation of their desire to reveal the adultery to Marc.[13]

In stories of Lancelot and Guenevere the kinship roles are reversed and it is the king's nephews who accuse the queen and her lover.[14] Agravain in particular pursues the lovers aggressively. He and his brothers wish to displace Lancelot and his cousins from their prominent position in the king's court. Arthur's nephews are, in theory, his heirs, although he does not specifically name them as his successors, as Marc does Tristan. They seek to discredit an outsider, Lancelot, who has won his place in Arthur's esteem through chivalric prowess and courtliness. The conflict is explicitly described as a political rivalry: Arthur's knights resent the favor shown to Lancelot; they "hated Lancelot forever with a mortal hate, but did not want to show it before his sin with the queen was proved." ("[I]l en haïrent puis touz dis Lancelot de mortel haine, ne onques samblant n'en voldrent faire devant que il mesfez de lui et de la roine fu prouvez." *Lancelot*, 4: 399.)

Discovery is dangerous for the queen and her lover, and the danger is heightened by the presence at court of the knight's enemies, who try to destroy him through accusations of adultery with the queen. Oddly enough, however, the queen and her lover do not seem to try to hide their liaison. This is particularly explicit in the stories of Tristan and Iseut. In the passage I cited at the beginning of this chapter Marc's barons accuse Tristan and Iseut of adultery and of indiscretion: the adultery is "obvious to anyone who cares to look." [15] There are several indications in the *Tristan* stories that the discovery of the queen's secret is not a great surprise to Marc's subjects. When the king finds traces of Tristan's leap into the queen's bed in the flour on the floor episode and condemns the lovers to die, they are led away to be burned and the people of the city assemble along their route to proclaim their sympathy for the lovers. [16]

"A, Las! Tant avon a plorer!
Ahi! Tristran, tant par es ber!
Qel damage qu'en traïson
Vos ont fait prendre cil gloton!
Ha! roïne franche, honoree,
En qel terre sera mais nee
Fille de roi qui ton cors valle? . . ."
Live la noisë et li bruit;
Tuit en corent droit au palés.
Li rois fu molt fel et engrés;
N'i ot baron tant fort ne fier
Qui ost le roi mot araisnier
Qu'i li pardonast cel mesfait. (Béroul, vv. 833–65)

("Alas, we have good reason to weep! Oh Tristran, you are such a worthy knight! What a pity that these villains treacherously trapped you! Oh, noble and honored queen, in what land will there ever be born a princess who is your equal? . . ." The noise and confusion increased, and everyone came running to the palace. The king was in a cruel and violent humor; there was no baron so strong or courageous that he dared urge the king to pardon him for this crime. [Lacy, 41, 43])

The sympathetic protests of the king's treatment of the lovers are made more explicit in the *Prose Tristan*. Many, seeing Iseut and Tristan together, marvel that Tristan has given Iseut to the king, because Tristan and Iseut are a perfect couple.

Toz li regarz des dames et des chevaliers est sor Yselt. Et puis regardent Tristan. Tristanz est dejoste Yselt, et se li uns est biax, encores est li autres plus. Et li plusor quant il les ont assez regardez dient que merveilles a fait Tristanz quant il a Yselt livree a son oncle; mieuz s'acordassent ensemble et par biauté et par aaige, et se Diex eüst sofert que li uns eüst l'autre, onques mes nus plus biax mariaiges n'eüst esté veüz en nule terre com cist fust. Ensi disoient li plusor. (Curtis, 2: 92–93)

(The eyes of the ladies and the knights were completely focused on Iseut. And then they looked at Tristan. Tristan is beside Iseut, and if one is beautiful, the other is even more beautiful. And when they had looked at them for a while many said that Tristan did a marvelous thing when he gave Iseut to his uncle; they were better suited to each other in both beauty and age, and if God had permitted that they have each other, never would a more beautiful marriage be seen anywhere in the world. So said many people.)

Knowledge about the liaison between Tristan and Iseut is not limited to a sympathetic recognition of their suitability for each other. The barons claim that the adultery is "obvious to anyone who cares to look," and knowledge of the queen's sexual relationship with the king's nephew seems to be fairly widespread in Marc's kingdom. In an episode in the *Prose Tristan* King Marc encounters some shepherds who do not recognize the king and who speak freely to him about the state of the kingdom. They claim that Tristan and the queen are lovers and that everyone knows it, even the king himself: "Le fait de monsigneur Tristan et de la roïne est bien seü chertainnement par tout le monde, et li rois March meïsmement le set bien" (*Prose Tristan*, 1: 272).

The love of the adulterous queen and her knight is different from the love relationship described in narratives like *La châtelaine de Vergi* and *Lanval*, where the lady imposes secrecy on her lover and claims that their love will survive only as long as it is hidden from others. The concealed, interiorized desire that is fulfilled away from the court in isolation and in secrecy contrasts with the adulterous passion that cannot be restrained to private, secret demonstrations.[17] But if the lovers cannot restrain their demonstrations of love, if—as Béroul's *Roman de Tristan* suggests—anyone who wished to learn of the adulterous affair could do so, why doesn't the spectacle of their liaison provoke more reaction within the story? The indiscretion of the lovers is evoked a number of times in the narratives that recount the adventures of Tristan and Iseut, but there does not seem to be any general gossip about the queen and her lover, nor are there any explicit accusations against the lovers by anyone other than the three barons and the dwarf who helps them in their schemes to destroy Marc's affection for his nephew.[18] And when Lancelot and Guenevere abandon their usual discretion, many notice the relationship, but only Agravain and his brothers go to the king to reveal the adultery.

Since the queen and her lover cannot hide their relationship, they rely on silence rather than secrecy to protect their liaison. Because of what looks like a general complicity with the adulterous lovers, secrecy remains imperative for the lovers only in relation to the king, whose ambivalence toward knowledge about the two lovers is well known to readers of the romance as well as to the characters in the story, particularly in the case of King Marc. His indecisiveness about how to deal with accusations against the lovers is even broadcast by the king's messenger to Arthur's court: "The king constantly changes his mind, now believing one thing, now another." ("Li rois n'a pas coraige entier, / Senpres est ci et senpres la." Béroul, vv. 3432–33; Lacy, 161, 162.) Marc's willingness to change his mind and to credit uncertainty permits the repeated reinstatement of the secret. He is the witness who must not see and he is the potential knower in relation to whom the secret is defined. Indeed, he seems to be the only spectator of the adultery who must be duped and, apparently, the only spectator that it is possible to dupe.

King Marc is represented slightly differently in the three Old French versions of the Tristan story. The King Marc eager and willing to be duped in the verse romances becomes a suspicious and evil king in the *Prose Tristan*. In Béroul and Thomas, the wavering (or complicitious) king does not see (or refuses to see) the adultery and is easily tricked; in the prose *Tristan* the malevolent king does see the adultery but is thwarted when he wishes to punish it. But even in the *Prose Tristan*, where King Marc becomes an character with expressly evil intentions, he still hesitates when he condemns the guilty lovers.[19] The king's hesitation is made possible by the repeated episodes of accusation and exculpation: the episode under the pine tree that opens Béroul's *Tristan* and the meeting in Iseut's apartment that ends it; the flour on the floor episode; Marc's discovery of the lovers in the Morrois with Tristan's sword lying between them; Iseut's ambiguous exculpatory oath; the discovery of the lovers in the garden recounted by Thomas; and the episode of the *faux trenchantes* in the *Prose Tristan*. It is always possible to explain away compromising evidence of the adultery, and as Matilda Bruckner has suggested, "It is this inherent ambiguity of signs that helps keep the story of Tristan and Iseut moving from episode to episode, as Marc fails to resolve his uncertainty about their secret love once and for all."[20] The lovers' repeated escapes from condemnation seem to diffuse the urgency of hiding the liaison.

The complicitous silence that hides the queen's adultery from the king and the king's ambivalence toward knowledge about the lovers may be related to the knight's importance in preserving the court from outside threats, as in Tristan's defeat of the Morholt and Lancelot's negotiation of peace with Galehot in the *Prose Lancelot*. The knight's role in securing peace is well known within the kingdom: the shepherds who tell King Marc of the general knowledge of the queen's adultery begin their conversation by lamenting Tristan's departure from Cornwall, which has created a situation of political instability (*Prose Tristan*, 1: 271). But the repeated discoveries and cover-ups of the queen's adultery speak a general consent to the affair that may also acknowledge the queen's role in the political equilibrium of the court. Silence about the queen's adultery implicitly constructs the queen's sexual transgression as part of the political structure of the fictional feudal court.

Adultery and Political Stability

The romance representation of the queen's adultery as an open secret makes it possible for the lovers' enemies to use knowledge about the queen's sexual transgression to gain political influence over the king, who is the only person who must not learn of it. In the *Tristan* stories Marc's vassals accuse Tristan and Iseut of adultery in order to eliminate the king's nephew and heir from his position at court and from his influence over the king.[21] Béroul recounts that the barons demand Tristan's exile from Cornwall in their accusation of adultery.

"Alon au ro et si li dimes,
Ou il nos aint ou il nos hast,
Nos volon son nevo en chast." . . .
"Rois," ce dient li troi felon,
"Par foi, mais nu consentiron;
Qar bien savon de verité
Que tu consenz lor cruauté,
Et tu sez bien ceste mervelle.
Q'en feras tu? Or t'en conselle!
Se ton nevo n'ostes de cort,
Si que jamais il ne retort,
Ne nos tenron a vos jamez,
Si ne vos tendron nule pez.
De nos voisins feron partir
De cort, que nel poon soufrir." (Béroul, vv. 600–624)

("Let us go to the king and tell him that whatever he may think of us, we want him to banish his nephew." . . . "King," said the three barons, "by our faith, we will not permit this any longer, because we know for a fact that you are fully aware of their crime and that you condone it. What will you do about it? Consider it carefully: If you do not banish your nephew from court so that he never returns, you will never have our allegiance, and we will never leave you in peace. We will also have others leave the court, for we cannot tolerate this." [Lacy, 31])

The barons accuse Marc of complicity in the open secret of adultery and threaten the dissolution of his feudal court if he does not act to separate the lovers.

The barons never confront Tristan face to face; rather, they focus on knowledge of the queen's adulterous body as the disputed source of power over the king. J. M. Stary sees the barons' accusations as representative of their desire to see a weakened monarch, to decentralize and fragment the power of the king.[22] Stary and many others see the conflict created by the queen's adultery as an instability; Marchello-Nizia's suggestion that courtly adultery may diffuse overt political conflict between the king and his potential challenger, the knight who is the queen's lover, contradicts this view and credits adultery with establishing an equilbrium in the royal court.[23] The stabilizing effect of the queen's adultery is not limited to the relationship between the knight and the king. As I argue below, it also mediates power contests between the king's vassals.

In her analysis of courtly adultery Marchello-Nizia proposes a rereading of the figurative language that describes the love relationship. She suggests that we understand the description of the knight's feudal service to his lady and the chivalric duties it includes not as a metaphorical description of love service, but as a literal description of a power relationship. In Marchello-Nizia's reading of the knight's subjection to his sovereign lady, it is the lady who becomes a figure, a metonymy of her husband, the king.[24] This perceptive analysis of the political relationships structured by the queen's adultery might be extended to account not only for the bond between the knight and the king but also for the relationship between the king and the vassals who wish to replace the queen's lover in his privileged proximity to the king. If the knight loves the queen as a metonymic representation of the king, as Marchello-Nizia has suggested, it is because the possession of the queen figures a possession of the king and his affections. For the barons who wish to replace the knight, the queen holds a different figurative position. Their goal is not to possess the queen, but to isolate her from her lover. In the baron's plots against the queen's lover, the queen is a metaphor for the king. Her adulterous love figures the king's affection for his favorite vassal, and accusations of a transgressive relationship between the queen and her knight are a displaced attack on the relationship between the king and the knight which the barons wish to disrupt.

The queen's adultery is the pretext that the barons use to avoid direct conflict with the king's nephew. If they can succeed in alienating the king from his heir by naming Tristan as the queen's lover, they can eliminate the greatest challenge to their control of the throne. And if Tristan can do away with the barons, Marc will have no reason to question the loyalty of his heir. While the barons act out of a desire for political power, Tristan is motivated by the need to preserve his place in Marc's court in order to be near the queen. His attempts to influence the king, like his claims of faithful service, are aimed at retaining his proximity to Iseut. He uses professions of loyalty to disguise his betrayal of the king; the barons use accusations of betrayal to undermine the king's loyalty to Tristan and to promote their own claims to power.

Ultimately, however, the baron's accusations and the lovers' professions of loyalty create a sort of perverse equilibrium in the royal court, precisely because Marc is a weak king. Confronted with accusations against his nephew and his wife, Marc moves indecisively between feudal loyalty to the barons, familial love for Tristan, and sexual love for Iseut. In the *Prose Tristan* Marc's nephew Audret directly links the king's hesitation to his ineffectual rule: "Vos tenez avec vos celi qui honte vos fait et jor et nuit de la roïne, et quant vos ce sofrez, vos iestes li plus viz rois et li plus recranz qui soit el monde." ("You keep with you one who shames you day and night with the queen, and as long as you permit this you will be the most shameful and cowardly king in the world." Curtis, 2: 117–18.) The king's constantly changing loyalties are a sign of his weakness, but Marc's wavering may also be seen as an effective, though not deliberate strategy for maintaining control of his kingdom. The king's hesitation between faith in his nephew and wife and loyalty to his vassals results in an equilibrium between the opposing forces whose power depends on proximity to the king and whose contests are played out in accusations and defenses of the queen's adultery.

The constantly negotiated status of the secret is what allows

Marc not to take decisive action to punish the lovers or definitively to alienate his vassals. The king's loyalty shifts between the two factions as he debates whether to act on the barons' accusations against Tristan and the queen or to believe the lovers' demonstrations of innocence. As a result of the king's wavering, he never holds a position of excessive dependence on the feudal vassals who wish to control him and he avoids an equally dangerous disregard for their desires and accusations that might destroy the integrity of the kingdom. The king also retains the services of his best knight, who guarantees the safety of the kingdom from outside threats. As long as Marc's court remains split between factions the king retains a semblance of power, and a certain stability is gained in the realm through the equilibrium of competing claims to the king's loyalty. The precarious and constantly negotiated status of the king's power in his kingdom is mediated and maintained by the open secret of adultery.

The appropriation of the queen's secret adultery as an instrument of political intrigue is made possible by the relationships of dependency and desire that unite the king, the queen, and the knight. As Marchello-Nizia has shown, the queen mediates conflicts between the king and the knight, and her role in maintaining their relationship is stressed in stories about Iseut and Guenevere. In the scene under the pine tree that opens Béroul's version of the *Tristan* story, when Tristan perceives that his uncle is present to spy on the lovers, he turns the secret meeting with the queen into an occasion to plead for her help in regaining his uncle's trust.

"Dame, je vos en cri merci:
Tenez moi bien a mon ami.
Quant je vinc ça a lui par mer,
Com a seignor i vol torner." (Béroul, vv. 159–62)

("Lady, I implore your mercy: Reconcile me with my friend. When I came to him here, from across the sea, I did so in order to serve him as my lord." [Lacy, 9])

Tristan's words are a charade dictated by the king's presence, but they refer nonetheless to the queen's influence over her husband

and to the mediating role she might play between Tristan and the king. The queen's role as an intercessor with the king is also stressed in the changing construction of medieval queenship in twelfth- and thirteenth-century Europe, particularly in English courts, where it was formalized in rituals of petition.[25] Romances acknowledge the influential position of the queen as the wife of the sovereign, but they limit the queen's intercessory powers to the protection of her secret adultery.

In the ties of mutual dependence represented by the adulterous love triangle, the king recognizes the queen's influence over his knight and tries to use it to his advantage. When King Arthur is convinced that his queen is an impostor in the False Guenevere episode of the *Prose Lancelot*, he denounces her as a traitor, and Lancelot abandons the king in protest. Arthur calls on the repudiated Guenevere to persuade Lancelot to remain at his court. In this case Guenevere refuses to mediate between the king and the knight, citing Arthur's treachery and openly encouraging Lancelot's loyalty to herself over the king.

"[J]a ne l'en proierai, kar j'avrai plus sovent sa compaignie que la vostre et miels le doi je amer, kar il me rescost par sa grant debonaireté la ou vos me volsistes destruire par vostre felonie." (*Lancelot*, 1: 150–51)

(I will not ask him, for I would rather have his company than yours, and I should love him better than you because he saved me out of his goodness when you wanted to destroy me by felonous intention.)

Like the *Tristan* romances, medieval stories about Lancelot and Guenevere recount the negotiation of political rivalries among the king's knights as a story about the queen's secret adultery. Although Arthur's wife and her lover are not as indiscreet as Tristan and Iseut, and although Arthur is confronted less frequently than Marc with the allegation that his knight loves his queen, the king's attitude toward accusations against Lancelot and Guenevere closely resembles Marc's wavering between a desire to know and a desire not to know. As in the *Tristan* story, the couple's enemies repeatedly seek to destroy them through revelations of their liaison, the lovers successfully disprove the accusation, and the king is reassured.

In an early episode of discovery in the *Prose Lancelot* Morgan kidnaps Lancelot, learns of his liaison with the queen, and sends a messenger to announce the adulterous love of Guenevere and Lancelot to Arthur's court, presenting as proof of the accusation a ring that the queen gave her lover. The queen acknowledges her gift of the ring but not the adultery, and Arthur is easily convinced of the queen's innocence although he does not dismiss the seriousness of the charge. As Arthur explains to Guenevere, Lancelot could do nothing that the king would hate more than to seduce the queen, but Arthur would prefer that Lancelot had *married* the queen if it would mean that the king could avoid losing his knight and could keep him at court:

"[J]ou vaudroie mieus que il vous eust loiaument a feme prise, par si que jou eusse a tous jors s'amor et sa compaignie." (*Lancelot*, 3: 226)

("I would rather he had taken you as wife if it meant that I could always have his love and his company.") [26]

The accusation against the queen and the subsequent proof of her innocence allow the king to name the queen's relationship to the knight without openly acknowledging it, and stories of the queen's adultery represent many of these unknowing testimonies of awareness through which the king's desire not to know is emphasized. In the *Prose Lancelot* Arthur claims that if Guenevere were not the queen, she would do well to love Lancelot:

"[S]e vos estiez une autre dame et vos en aviez envie, ja Diex ne m'aïst se ja vos en blasmoie, car vos porriez bien faire plus grant folie que li amers par amors." (*Lancelot*, 4: 344)

("If you were any other woman and you wished it, God help me if I would blame you, for you could do much worse than to love him.")

Arthur's unacknowledged knowledge of the queen's adultery is emphasized in a fourteenth-century manuscript of the *Prose Lancelot*. In an illustration of the episode where Guenevere kisses Lancelot for the first time, a kiss that takes place far from observers ("loing des autres a une part," *Lancelot* 8: 103), the illuminator has portrayed the

Figure 5. Guenevere kisses Lancelot. *Lancelot*. BN fr. 16999, fol. 88 v. Photograph: Bibliothèque Nationale, Paris.

king observing the scene (Figure 5).[27] Arthur is absent in the textual description of the scene; the illuminator seems to have added the suggestion that Arthur knew about the adulterous liaison from its originating moment.

Guenevere's close relationship to Lancelot is well known at Arthur's court, but the queen's adultery is not represented as an open secret in Arthur's kingdom, as in is in King Marc's. Bors calls Lancelot the most secretive man in the world ("c'est li hons el monde qui plus celeement velt faire ses afaires," *Lancelot*, 5: 187). But the knight and the queen become careless and forget discretion: "se demenerent si folement que li pluseur de leanz le sorent veraiement, et messire Gauvains meïsmes le sot tout apertement, et ausi firent tuit si quatre frere" ("They carried on so foolishly that many learned of it, and Messire Gauvain himself knew it with certainty, as did his four brothers" *La mort*, 107). Agravain wishes to tell the king immediately, as he did earlier in the story when he first suspected the lovers; Gauvain prefers to silence his brothers and to keep the secret from the king. Gauvain is overruled by his brothers, who tell the king that Lancelot "dishonors him with his wife" ("[Lancelot] vos est si loiaus qu'il vos fet desenneur de la reïne vostre fame et qu'il l'a conneüe charnelment." *La mort*, 109). In a thirteenth-century manuscript illumination of the confrontation, the isolation of the queen as the figure furthest from the king illustrates the king's position between the two rivals for his favors—Agravain and his brothers on the left and Lancelot on the right (Figure 6). The discovery of the lovers in the queen's bedroom—and the illumination emphasizes their transgressive isolation in the portrait of the lovers alone in a private place—sets in motion the events that will culminate in the destruction of Arthur's kingdom.

Like King Marc, Arthur does not wish to credit accusations of the lovers' betrayal, but not because he is certain of his wife's loyalty. When Agravain first accuses Lancelot and the queen, Arthur refuses to believe that Lancelot would betray him. Gauvain reassures the king that he is right in his refusal to credit Agravain's charge against the king's best knight, and he claims that Lancelot could not love the queen because he loves the demoiselle d'Escalot and before

Figure 6. Discovery of Guenevere and Lancelot in the queen's bedroom. *Lancelot.* BN 1422, fol. 86. Photograph: Bibliothèque Nationale, Paris.

that he loved the daughter of King Pellas (*La mort*, 28–30). Despite the evidence Gauvain offers of Lancelot's interests outside the court, Arthur bases his faith in Lancelot's innocence not on evidence that the knight loves women other than the queen, but on Lancelot's fealty to the king. Arthur claims that even if Lancelot had loved the queen, he would never have shamed the king:

"[S]'il estoit voirs que Lancelos l'amast tres bien par amors, si nel porroie ge pas croire qu'il eüst cuer de fere si grant desloiauté comme de moi honir de ma fame; car en cuer ou il a si grant proesce ne se porroit enbatre traïsons, se ce n'estoit la greigneur deablie del monde. . . . [S]e touz li monz le m'aloit disant de jor en jor ne ne m'en aperceüsse mieuz que ge m'en sui aperceüz, si nel creroie ge pas." (*La mort*, 30)

("If it was true that Lancelot loved her, I still could not believe that he would have the heart to commit such a great disloyalty as to shame me with my wife; for he has such great prowess in his heart that it could not undertake betrayal, unless it was because of the world's greatest enchantment . . . and even if everyone kept telling me so every day, and even if I perceived it better than I have seen it, I would not believe it.")

Arthur refuses to know the secret of the queen's adultery, he denies that such a secret is possible. There can be no secret adultery between the Lancelot and the queen simply because it is unbelievable that Lancelot would betray the king. Even if Arthur had evidence of the adultery, even if others continued to report it to him, or even if he saw it himself, he would not believe it because Lancelot is too honorable to betray his king. Arthur does not mention his queen's honor, nor does he consider her possible guilt of the charge of adultery. Implicit in Arthur's defense of Lancelot is the suggestion that the queen could not have betrayed him because Lancelot would not have betrayed him.

Although the political equilibrium of Arthur's court is not explicitly maintained by the series of accusations and exculpations that maintain stability in King Marc's court, the queen's adultery is nonetheless an important part of its political structure since it guarantees Lancelot's presence in King Arthur's court. The consequences of discovery are dictated by the fact that it is precisely those who wish to destroy Lancelot who learn of the adulterous liaison, and the war that ultimately destroys Arthur's kingdom is the result of a rivalry that appropriates the queen's adultery in a contest for political power. The revelation of the secret of the queen's adulterous liaison with Lancelot is announced as the outcome of the enmity of Arthur's knights provoked by their resentment of Lancelot's place in the king's affections. Like Iseut's liaison with Tristan, Guenevere's adultery becomes the instrument of political contests between factions that compete for the king's favor, and the secrecy surrounding the queen's transgression allows the king to move between the accusations against the queen and her lover by his nephews and his sister, and the protests of innocence by his wife.

Royal Subjects

When Lancelot and Guenevere are found alone in the queen's bedchamber and King Arthur claims that an adulterous queen must be burned because she has been consecrated, the king acknowledges Guenevere's unique status as a consecrated queen at the same time as he demonstrates her subjection to the judgment of her husband and king.[28] The position of Guenevere as both queen and subject of the king is also demonstrated in narratives where chastity tests prove that the queen is like other women, yet the trial by ordeal demonstrates her unique status as a symbol of the king's sovereignty. She is possessed by the knight as a metonymy of the king and she is defined by the king's vassals as a metaphor of the sovereign in attempts to isolate her from the powerful knight who is her lover. In Marchello-Nizia's reading the queen stands between her husband and her lover; she mediates a relationship between the king and the knight.[29] I have argued that the queen also mediates a relationship between her lover and the king's vassals; knowledge of her adultery becomes the pretext for attacks against the knight and for threats to the king. The stability of the romance court thus seems to depend on contests in which the definition of the queen's sexuality is debated.

Representations of romance queens both do and do not corre-

spond to representations of nonfictional queens in the evolving construction of medieval queenship. Like kings' wives in twelfth- and
thirteenth-century Europe, the romance queen is subject to restrictions intended to guarantee her sexual integrity and the purity of the
king's lineage; unlike nonfictional queens, romance queens do not
produce children who would justify these restrictions, nor do they
benefit from the influence and authority that nonfictional queens
gained from royal maternity. Romance queens, like nonfictional
queens, are assumed to have some influence over their husbands because of the sexual intimacy of marriage. However, in romance narratives, the queen's intimacy with her husband is compromised by
her sexual intimacy with her lover, and while romances that do not
recount the story of the queen's adultery may represent the queen
as a counselor to her husband in a way that benefits the court, in
romances about adulterous queens the king's wife uses her intimacy
with her husband only to conceal her liaison with the knight.[30]

If the figure of the romance queen is defined by transgressive
sexuality in some romance narratives, it is in part because the possession of her body is part of a system of exchange that defines chivalric
honor and status. Just as the judgment of women's bodies reveals
a truth about men's status in the chastity tests that arrive mysteriously at the feudal romance court, the exchange of women between
men is also a form of chivalric competition. This exchange functions
not only as a displaced power struggle between the king and the
knight-lover, as Marchello-Nizia has shown, but also as an indirect
confrontation between the knight and his rivals. In a perceptive and
nuanced reading of this structure of exchange, Roberta Krueger suggests that Chrétien de Troyes's romances both define and expose its
operation.[31] Krueger goes on to examine the exchange of a queen between knights in Chrétien's *Le chevalier de la charrete*. While she does
not examine this narrative structure in terms of queenship, Krueger's
analysis provides a suggestive perspective from which to explore
the political stakes of the exchange of women when the woman exchanged between knights is a queen.

The kidnapping of Guenevere by Méléagant that opens *Le chevalier de la charrete* demonstrates yet again how the queen's body figures

the king's authority. In this case, a knight arrives at Arthur's court and boasts that he has already imprisoned many of Arthur's subjects and that the king is not powerful enough to do anything about it. Arthur agrees ("Li rois respont qu'il li estuet / sofrir, s'amender ne le puet," *Charrete*, vv. 61–62), and the knight claims the possession of the queen as the prize for his challenge to Arthur's sovereignty.

> "Rois, s'a ta cort chevalier a
> nes un an cui tu te fiasses
> que la reïne li osasses
> baillier por mener an ce bois
> aprés moi, la ou ge m'an vois,
> par un covant l'i atandrai
> que les prisons toz te randrai
> qui sont an prison an ma terre,
> se il la puet vers moi conquerre
> et tant face qu'il l'an ramaint." (*Charrete*, vv. 70–79)

("Your Majesty, if your court has a single knight you would dare entrust with the queen to lead her into the forest following me, on my word I will wait there for him; for if he can win her in combat against me and succeed in bringing her back again, I will surrender to you at once all the prisoners I hold captive in my land." [Chrétien, 171])

Keu claims the battle, he is defeated and taken with the captive queen to Gorre, where Lancelot arrives and successfully challenges Méléagant for the queen. When Lancelot goes to greet the queen after the battle, Guenevere disdains his service, "lowering her head, and remaining silent in an appearance of anger" (". . . fet sanblant de correciee, / si s'anbruncha et ne dist mot," *Charrete*, vv. 3940–41; Chrétien, 218). Guenevere's reaction, which she later regrets and characterizes as a joke ("sel cuidai ge feire a gas," v. 4205) and as a sin ("molt s'ancolpe, / del pechié qu'ele fet avoit," vv. 4184–85) has remained a puzzling one for many critics. As Krueger notes, it has been variously explained as a coquettish reaction, as an attempt by the queen to deny her true feelings, or as a mistake.[32] Rather than trying to explain away the contradictory explanations that Guenevere gives for her rejection of Lancelot, Krueger sees the queen's paradoxical disdain for the knight as a challenge to the narrative coherence of Lancelot's quest for the queen: "By refusing to become the automatic prize in the Meleagant/Lancelot combat, Guenevere removes herself from the triangle of exchange defined by the custom of Logres. . . . Her silence and her anger toward the knight who comes forward for her blessing constitute a gesture of feminine resistance to an ideology that circulates women as objects."[33] However, the queen's resistance, often seen as the emblem of the woman's power in the courtly love relationship, is significantly undermined in the narrative, as Krueger goes on to show. The narrator's description of her anger as a pretence and Guenevere's characterization of her refusal as a joke, combine with the definition of women's resistance as a condition of male desire, and the appropriation of Guenevere's pretended "sin" of disdain as a condition of Lancelot's love negates any notion of power in the queen's response: "Women's 'power' is a fiction of the male subject who needs her to resist so that he can desire her." In other words, as Krueger continues, the woman's claim to inaccessibility "marks her displacement from the position of the desiring subject."[34]

Krueger situates her reading of the exchange of women in the *Charrete* with respect to the inscription of the woman reader, Marie de Champagne, whom Chrétien identifies as the patron of his romance in the prologue. Krueger suggests that the position of the resisting queen parallels that of the woman reader, who "is at once privileged within the courtly circle and displaced from its center." But she also suggests that, just as romance narratives may invite women readers to identify with the women exchanged in chivalric proofs of prowess and honor, they also expose the sexual and political tensions of courtly gender ideology.[35]

I have lingered over Krueger's analysis of the *Charrete* because it provides a nuanced reading of just how the exchange of women between knights who compete for the king's sovereignty displaces the queen as a subject of desire. As Krueger shows, even the queen's resistance to the system is part of the system, yet at the same time it may expose the ideological foundations of the exchange. I wish to use Krueger's insights to explore how the queen's resistance to what E. Jane Burns, in her analysis of Iseut's ordeal, has identified

as a binary logic—the queen is either wife or mistress—might constitute a position for the royal female subject that is then displaced
by power negotiations between men. If the queen's resistance to the
wife/mistress dichotomy (which in the *Tristan* romances is also a
court/exile dichotomy) is itself appropriated into a system that makes
it the source of political stability, how might the queen's refusal to
choose also demonstrate the operations of a system that appropriates
the queen's transgressive sexuality as a means to political order?

Guenevere and Iseut are always shown to be aware of the prestige and influence of their position as the king's wife, a privileged
position they are reluctant to give up, even to live with their lovers.
During her exile with Tristan in the Morrois forest Iseut regrets the
loss of her status and of the duties that fell to her as wife of the king.
She grows tired of her rough life in the Morrois, and she wishes to
regain the honor and influence she enjoyed as queen:

Sovent disoit: "Lasse, dolente,
Porquoi eüstes vos jovente?
En bois estes com autre serve,
Petit trovez qui ci vus serve.
Je suis roïne, mais le non
En ai perdu par ma poison
Que nos beümes en la mer. . . .
Les damoiseles des anors,
Les filles as frans vavasors
Deüse ensenble o moi tenir
En mes chanbres, por moi servir,
Et les deüse marïer
Et as seignors por bien doner." (Béroul, vv. 2201–16)

(She kept repeating to herself: "Alas, miserable woman! How you have
wasted your youth! You are living in the forest like a serf, with no one to
serve you here. I am a queen, but I have lost that title because of the potion
we drank at sea. . . . I should have around me well-bred young women, the
daughters of worthy vassals, to serve me in my chambers, and I should arrange their marriages and give them to noble men." [Lacy, 105])

The influence Iseut could have exercised at court by arranging marriages and advising the king is sacrificed to live in hiding with her
lover, and the queen regrets it.[36]

This passage occurs after the love potion begins to wane in Béroul's version of the *Tristan* story. Iseut's regrets for her life at court thus correspond to the waning intensity of the drug that induced their passion. But Iseut's lament does not indicate a desire to abandon Tristan, despite the fading effect of the love philtre, and although the lovers' subsequent agreement with Marc for Iseut's return to court includes the provision that Tristan will leave the country, Iseut asks him to stay near her in hiding until he is sure that Marc will not mistreat her. And of course, Tristan and Iseut meet again after Iseut's reinstatement in Marc's court. In Thomas's version of the story, the waning effect of the potion does not motivate the lovers' decision to leave the forest, and in the *Prose Tristan* once the lovers drink the potion it disappears from the story.[37]

For romance queens, as for all medieval queens, privilege is located in the position as the king's wife, but the queen's status and influence depend on her relationship with her husband. Although that relationship is defined through legal procedure, its form depends on the intimacy of the two partners, as the example of a thirteenth-century Capetian queen consort may demonstrate. Ingeborg of Denmark was married to King Philip Augustus in 1193. The king took an immediate and unexplained aversion to his new bride, sent her to a monastery, and refused to see her for seven years. Philip sought an annulment of the marriage, based on a claim that he and Ingeborg were related within the church's prohibited degrees. The marriage was duly anulled by a council convened at Compiègne, but before it was approved by the pope Philip took a third wife, Agnès of Meran. John W. Baldwin's description of the young Ingeborg, "[s]equestered in a royal monastery, unable to understand French, and deprived of all contact with her countrymen," suggests the isolation and vulnerability of the foreign bride, subject to the king's will, with no influence over the king himself.[38]

Ingeborg was not entirely without resources, however, and with the support of Danish royal envoys she appealed to the pope, who required Philip to remove Agnès from the court and reinstate Ingeborg before presenting the request for an annulment. Philip resisted, but when Agnès died giving birth to the king's second son in 1201, the king's irregular marital situation was resolved, and when Inno-

cent III agreed to legitimize his children with Agnès, giving him
two royal male heirs, the succession of the throne seemed assured.[39]
Philip still did not abandon his efforts to receive an annulment of
his marriage to Ingeborg, however. In 1205, abandoning the claim
of consanguinity, the king made a request for an annulment based
on nonconsummation by sorcery; he claimed that Ingeborg had be-
witched him and he had been unable to consummate the marriage.
Ingeborg denied the charge, of course, and the king withdrew his
petition when faced with the prospect of another lengthy trial.[40] One
year later, in 1213, the king suddenly claimed to be reconciled with
the queen. Baldwin suggests that the decision probably had nothing
to do with any change in the status of the queen's claim and every-
thing to do with the king's desire to reconcile with the church as
he prepared for an English invasion led by King John.[41] As Baldwin notes, Philip's reconciliation consisted of recognizing Ingeborg
as queen, though not as wife, and until his death Philip continued to
refuse a sexual relationship with her.[42]

Ingeborg's experience of royal marriage demonstrates the importance of proximity to the king and of maternity, both denied to
Ingeborg; the king refused to have her in his presence and, of course,
never had any children with her. Romance narratives recognize the
importance of a queen's proximity to her husband as a position of
influence and power. Because adulterous romance queens are not
mothers, proximity to the king is even more important, since it is
their only access to power. The queen's presence at the center of the
court gives her access to the influence and prestige that Iseut longs to
regain after her exile in the forest. In an analysis of Iseut's dream in
the Morrois forest, recounted in Béroul's *Tristan*, Pierre Jonin suggests that, in the dream image of the two lions who each take a hand
of the queen, Iseut reveals the desire for the court and for love before she articulates it in her lament for lost privileges and luxuries.[43]
That is, Iseut longs to regain precisely the split position that Empress Fenice tries to avoid in *Cligés*. Fenice wishes to live secretly
with her lover in a hidden tower, and when Cligés becomes emperor
she ceases to be an active participant in her own story. Fenice's desire
to avoid the fragmented subjectivity of a position between men leads
to a narrative effacement that foreshadows the effective disempow-

erment of the empresses who succeed her. Completely absent from participation in their husbands' courts, Fenice's successors are locked away and guarded to assure that they do not repeat Fenice's adulterous deception of her first husband.

Iseut seems to embrace the position that Fenice rejects; as Burns emphasizes, she refuses to choose between her lover and her husband and she refuses the dichotomy of wife or mistress.[44] For this queen, to choose both positions is to choose not to leave the court. In the *Prose Tristan* Iseut claims that she would be happy to live forever as Marc's wife and Tristan's lover, as long as the adultery could remain secret: "Et quant ele a ceste vie demené bien demi an qu'ele n'ot parole ne novele de s'amor, il li est avis qu'ele porra bien toz jorz mes demener ceste vie, et porra avoir son ami a sa volenté et tost et tart, se ele n'est descoverte" (Curtis, 2: 94). Tristan is not content to share Iseut with her husband and he proposes to Iseut that they escape to Logres, where they could live together openly. Iseut refuses: if they left Marc's court Tristan would be branded a traitor and she would be called a foolish and disloyal queen. Iseut's fear for her reputation echoes Fenice's horror of being identified as an adulteress—as a second Iseut. However, Iseut's fear for her reputation does not mean that she wishes to avoid adultery or even, like Fenice, to create the possibility of a monogamous adultery. Iseut prefers to live at court as long as the lovers can continue their affair undiscovered by the king:

"[S]e nos nos en aliens orandroit ensi com vos l'avez devisié, lors seroit nostre folie coneüe apertement, et vos en seriez apelez traïtor vostre oncle, et je en seroie clamee roïne fole et deleal. Por ce vient il mieuz, ce me semble, que nos nos en alons orandroit au roi Marc, et menrons autretel vie et ausi envoisiee com nos avons dusques ci fait." (Curtis, 2: 116)

("If we go away now as you have suggested our folly would be openly known and you would be called a traitor to your uncle and I would be called a foolish and disloyal queen. Because of this I think it is better that we go back to King Marc now and that we lead the same life as before and with just as much pleasure as we have had up to now.")

When Marc finds the lovers together and forces his nephew into exile, Tristan asks Iseut to go with him because he fears the king will mistreat her. Iseut chooses to stay at court because she is sure that her husband loves her too much to harm her. She counsels Tristan to leave the court while she works to reconcile him with Marc: "Je vos di qu'il m'aime de si grant amor qu'il n'avroit pas cuer de moi mal faire. Mes or vos en alez de ci, et je ferai tant, se je puis, que vostre pes sera bien faite" (Curtis, 2: 119).[45]

Guenevere, too, chooses to occupy a double position as both queen and mistress. When she is accused of being an imposter in the *Prose Lancelot* and King Arthur condemns her to die for her crime, Lancelot undertakes a judicial battle to save her from death and then goes into exile with her. The queen and the knight live together far from court, but the queen demands an even greater attention to secrecy than the lovers had observed up to this point in the story, partly in penance for her adultery but partly in hope of her eventual reinstatement as Arthur's rightful wife. Her reconciliation with her husband must not be hindered by rumors of a liaison with Lancelot.

"Bials amis doz, la chose est issi menee, com vos veés, que je sui departie del roi mon seignor par mon meffet, je le conois bien: non pas por ce que je ne soie sa feme espose et roine coronee et sacree ausi com il fu, et sui fille al roi Leodagan de Tarmelide, mais li pechiés m'a neü de ce que je me cochai o autre qu'a mon seignor. Et neporquant il n'a si preude dame el monde qui ne deust fere un grant meschief por metre a aise un si preude chevalier com vos estes, mais Nostre Sire ne garde mie a la cortoisie del monde, kar cil qui est buens al monde est mals a Dieu. Mais des ore mes vos pri je que vos me doigneis un don que je vos demanderai, kar je sui ore el point ou il me covendroit miels garder que onques mes ne fis: si vos requier por la grant amor que vos avés a moi que vos des ore mes ne me querrois nule compaigie, ne mes de baisier et d'acoler, se il vos plest, que vos ne le faciés por ma priere." (*Lancelot* 1: 151–52)

("Good sweet friend, things have ended, as you see, with my separation from my lord the king because of my misdeed. I know it well. Not because I am not his wedded wife and queen, crowned and consecrated just as he was, or because I am not the daughter of King Leodagnan of Tarmelide, but because of the sin of sleeping with a man other than my husband. Yet there is no worthy woman in all the world who would not have done a great misdeed to satisfy such a worthy knight as you. But our Lord does not judge according to the courtesy of this world, for that which is good in the world is bad in God's view. Now I pray you to give me the gift that I will ask of you, for I am now at the point where I must guard myself better than I ever have before. And so I ask you, for the sake of the great love that you have for me, that from now on you do not ask me for my company, nor for my kisses, nor for my embraces; please do not do this, I beg you.")

Guenevere's desire to regain her position as queen coexists with her desire for the pleasure of her relationship with Lancelot, and she is unwilling to give up her royal status for the pleasures of a life with her lover.

In her discussion of Guenevere in the *Charrete*, Krueger shows how the queen's resistance to the exchange of her body between knights is appropriated by that very system of exchange in the definition of male desire as grounded in female refusal.[46] Krueger's analysis may also apply to the queen's refusal to choose between queenship and exile. If the queen positions herself outside of what Burns identifies as the binary logic that makes her either wife or mistress, the queen's resistance to the choice between court and exile provides the context for negotiations of power between the king and his vassals and between the king's vassals and his best knight. That is, the queen's refusal to choose between the status and authority of queenship and the sexual pleasures of exile with her lover defines the vulnerability of her position, a vulnerability appropriated by the barons in challenges to the king. The repeated discoveries and concealments of the queen's adultery that permit the king to waver between loyalty to his barons and love for his wife and his knight depend on the queen's refusal to choose between royal privilege and transgressive sexual pleasure.

As Krueger notes in her analysis of the *Charrete*, the appropriation of the woman's resistance to exchange is not seamless, but exposes the ideological stakes of its operation and opens them to debate.[47] If the queen's adultery structures a political stability in the romance feudal court, it also exposes the anxious tension provoked by a system that locates political order in the sexual purity of women. Romance representations of the test of the queen's chastity reveal the perceived instability in the equation of the state of the queen's body and the integrity of the king's rule. The exchange of the queen's body in rumors and exculpations of adultery and the repeated negotiations of the secret truth about the queen's sexual acts further suggest the anxiety produced by the foundation of a political system in which men govern as grounded on a truth about women's bodies. In the following chapter I suggest that that anxiety is produced—at least in part—by the fear of illegitimacy.

4

Adultery, Illegitimacy, and Royal Maternity

GEORGES DUBY HAS SUGGESTED that the medieval romance representation of the barren, adulterous queen is a symptom of the anxiety produced by the possibility of illegitimacy. In romances, he suggests, "adultery, though consummated, was barren. Bastardy was too serious a matter to be treated lightly, even in literature. People were too afraid of it to use it as a subject for a tale."[1] Duby's observation is a logical one, particularly in the study of aristocratic marriage in which it appears. "Bastardy" may be seen as particularly threatening in the context of monarchy, where the queen's illegitimate son might subvert the proper succession of the throne.

Medieval romances about adulterous queens demonstrate an ambivalent attitude toward illegitimacy. On the one hand, as Duby suggests, illegitimacy is simply absent; adulterous queens do not usually have any children. On the other hand, the absence of children in the royal family leaves succession unresolved and the need for dynastic continuity unacknowledged. Although the potential succession of the king's nephew motivates Marc's vassals to insist that the king marry and produce an heir, when Iseut does not produce a child, Tristan remains his uncle's heir.[2] Unlike Empress Fenice in *Cligés*, Iseut never deliberately avoids the king's bed with the intention of preserving her lover's inheritance, nor is Tristan's status as his uncle's heir emphasized in the romances that recount his story: Tristan dies far from his uncle's court at the end of Thomas's *Tristan*, Béroul's unfinished romance ends with Tristan in exile, and in the *Prose*

Tristan King Marc murders his nephew. Apart from the representation of the barons' demand that Marc marry and produce an heir, the *Tristan* romances do not explicitly acknowledge dynastic concerns.

The disregard for succession would seem to correspond to Duby's suggestion that illegitimacy is not a literary matter, that its serious consequences in medieval society precluded its representation in a literature read for pleasure. There is, however, at least one romance narrative that recounts the story of a queen's illegitimate child who inherits the throne even though he is not the king's son. *Le livre de Caradoc* demonstrates that illegitimacy is not always suppressed in romance narratives. *Caradoc* suggests that the representation of the adulterous queen as a barren queen is not only a response to a "fear" of illegitimacy that extends even into literary representations, but that it is also part of a negotiation of the queen's place in the political structure of the romance court. The importance of reproduction in defining that place is the subject of this chapter.

Adultery and Dynasty

I begin with the curious representation of adultery in *Eracle*, a twelfth-century romance by Gautier d'Arras that recounts a fictionalized version of the life of Heraclius, a seventh-century Byzantine emperor.[3] This romance tells the story of a senator's son, Eracle, whose widowed mother renounces her wealth and position out of religious piety, gives away all her worldly goods and, with her son's consent, sells him into slavery. Eracle is acquired by the senechal of the Roman emperor and when he proves his extraordinary talents to the emperor, he becomes his trusted advisor. One of the responsibilities entrusted to Eracle is to choose the emperor's wife from among all the women of Rome, and after scrutinizing the assembled candidates, Eracle names a poor orphan, Athanaïs, as the virgin most worthy of marriage to the emperor.

The story of the empress's adultery begins when her husband leaves Rome to lead a military campaign.[4] Against the advice of his wise counselor, Eracle, and despite the irreproachable behavior of the empress during seven years of marriage, the emperor does not trust

his wife to remain chaste while he is away and he locks her in a tower
to be closely guarded by twenty-four knights and their wives during
his absence. After her husband's departure the empress Athanaïs, accompanied by her chaperons, attends a celebration in the city, where
she sees a handsome senator's son playing a harp and falls in love
with him. The empress and the harpist, Parides, secretly exchange
messages of love, and Athanaïs arranges to escape her prison to meet
her lover. She goes out riding with her entourage, deliberately falls
off her horse into a muddy spot in the road, and then goes to warm
herself in a nearby house where, by a prearranged plan, Parides waits
for her, and the couple spend several hours making love.[5]

The emperor learns of the empress's adultery and returns to
Rome to punish his wife. However, Eracle refutes the emperor's assumption of his wife's guilt and puts the blame for the empress's
transgression on her husband. Athanaïs is not guilty of the transgression because she acted in response to a wrongful imprisonment.

"[N]'alés mais, sire, demenant
la dame si vilainnement;
car je vos dis bien plainnement:
n'i doit avoir honte ne lait,
que c'est par vos canqu'ele a fait.
Ele ert et chaste et fine et monde,
ele ert li miudre riens del monde;
quant le mesistes en prison,
si fesistes grant mesproison . . . .
Sont vos les colpes, ce saciés;
ce est grans dels et grans peciés
que vos le dame laidengiés." (*Eracle*, vv. 4968–5001)

("Do not blame the lady so vilely, sire, for I say to you plainly that she should
not have any shame or injury, for it is because of you that she did it. She was
chaste and fine and simple, and she was the best thing in the world when you
imprisoned her; that was a wrongful act. . . . You should know that all this is
your fault, and it is a sad and sinful thing that you slander her.")

The emperor accepts responsibility for provoking the adultery, he
pardons his wife's transgression, and following Eracle's advice, he re-
leases the empress from their marriage so that she can wed her lover.[6]

Lorenzo Renzi has suggested the possibility that *Eracle* is a sort of literary exercise based on the story of Tristan and Iseut, similar (though inferior, in his judgment) to Chrétien's rewriting of *Tristan* in *Cligés*. Renzi asks what might have been the fate of Tristan and Iseut if Marc had had a counselor like Eracle instead of the three barons, and he suggests that *Eracle* provides an answer.[7] I find Renzi's question a provocative one, particularly as it relates to queenship. The subject of the adultery story in *Eracle* is an empress, like Fenice, and not a queen, like Iseut, and her fate is more like Fenice's than Iseut's: both empresses escape their marriages, Fenice through the use of a magic potion, Athanaïs through her husband's clemency. However, the differences between the two empresses' stories are as striking as the similarities. Athanaïs is released from her marriage when her adultery is discovered. Emperor Alis does not consent to Fenice's union with his nephew, Cligés, but rather dies in the attempt to find the two lovers and bring them to justice. After Fenice's death all of the empresses who follow her on the throne of Constantinople are kept locked up in seclusion to guarantee their fidelity to their husbands—a situation that echoes the imprisonment of Athanaïs that Eracle identifies as the *reason* for her adultery. However, in *Cligés* the enclosure of the empress seems to be intended to guarantee legitimacy as much as fidelity, particularly if the fate of the empresses who follow Fenice is read in the context of Fenice's desire to disrupt succession. In *Eracle* the emperor is concerned about whether his wife will remain faithful to him while he is out of his country, but he does not mention succession concerns in his explanation of his desire to imprison her. *Eracle* seems to ignore the dynastic concerns of the twelfth-century French noblemen and women who were probably its audience and that are represented more explicitly in *Cligés*. Friedrich Wolfzettel has characterized Gautier's narrative as an anti-aristocratic romance that emphasizes the fundamental equality of human beings and rejects social elevation through noble blood or inheritance. Unlike romances like *Cligés* and *Tristan*, in which kings are urged to marry in order to produce an heir, in Gautier's romance genealogical dynasty is absent. The emperor is elected, and as Wolfzettel suggests, this may to some extent explain the emperor's pardon of his wife's adultery.[8]

If, as Renzi proposes, *Eracle* recounts what would have happened in the *Tristan* stories if King Marc's counselors had been wiser, the story requires that the king's advisors not be his vassals, or at least that they not compete with his nephew for influence over the king, and it requires that the queen's lover not be an important knight in the king's court. *Eracle* takes place in a court that is structured differently from the feudal courts of *Tristan* or *Cligés*; as Wolfzettel notes, the emperor is elected, he is not part of a royal dynasty, and his children will not inherit his throne. The continuation of a royal lineage is not an issue in *Eracle*, not even a hidden issue, and although the empress's adultery is still a betrayal, it does not threaten succession. Nor does the empress's sexual transgression mediate contests for power in her husband's court; adultery is not the subject of the rumors, accusations, proofs, and exculpations that define the royal wife's secret adultery as a symbol of the sovereign's authority, nor is it the focus for challenges to the empress's lover in Gautier's romance.

Even though the empress's children—legitimate or illegitimate—would not inherit the imperial throne, she is still barren after seven years of marriage and exemplary fidelity. *Eracle* conforms to Duby's observation that children are always absent in stories of adultery, yet the absence of children in the elected emperor's family suggests that the fear of illegitimacy, at least to the extent that it potentially corrupts succession, may not be the primary reason for the representation of the adulterous queen as barren. In Gautier's romance, the story of the queen's adultery is transformed by the absence of a royal dynasty. In its representation of the empress's adultery as a marital infidelity that does not have implications for the king's standing in his court, *Eracle* nuances the relationship between what Duby suggests are the incompatible subjects of adultery and reproduction and suggests that it is the hidden link between dynasty and adultery that makes the queen's adultery a mediating force in her husband's court. In *Eracle*, where the succession of the imperial throne is not at stake, adultery does not seem to have the same function as in romances where the king's son would inherit his throne. I am suggesting that the absence of succession concerns in *Eracle* and the romance's unique representation of the consequences of an empress's adultery are related and that they may reveal a hidden structure in romances about Iseut and Guenevere: if the queen's adultery mediates power contests in her husband's court, that mediation is only possible in a dynastic court where the queen's chastity is implicitly linked to proper succession.

This claim implies that succession concerns are a powerful absent subtext in romances about adulterous queens. I have repeatedly stated throughout this study that the absence of reproduction in stories about romance queens marks a distinct difference between fictional and nonfictional queens, that the imperative to produce royal heirs and the power and influence of royal maternity were defining factors in the construction of medieval queenship. *Eracle*, like *Cligés*, suggests that the absence of reproduction concerns in romances about adulterous queens is only apparent, that reproduction and succession imperatives are hidden, not absent.

If *Eracle* points to succession as a subtext that structures the representation of the queen's adultery as an open secret in her husband's court, as the focus of rivalries and as the symbolic representation of her husband's sovereign authority, a further contextualization of the barren queen in the romance tradition makes that subtext all the more apparent. I turn next to a short thirteenth-century narrative, *La fille du comte de Pontieu*. This romance does not recount the story of an adulterous liaison and it is not about a queen. However, in its dramatic representation of the importance of dynastic continuation and in its oblique suggestion of the dangers of illegitimacy, *La fille* may nuance Duby's explanation of the absence of children in stories of adultery by suggesting the extent to which the aristocratic wife's status and authority depend on maternity.

Illegitimacy and Islam

A desire for heirs structures and motivates the story of *La fille du comte de Pontieu*, as several critics have noted.[9] The unnamed daughter of the count of Pontieu remains childless after five years of marriage, and her husband, Thibaut, decides to go on a pilgrimage to

Campostela to pray for children. His wife begs to go with him in order to add her prayers to his. Initially Thibaut refuses her company, citing the dangers of the journey, but finally he agrees that she may accompany him, and the couple sets out for Spain. Along the way they are attacked by brigands, who tie up Thibaut and rape his wife. When the brigands leave, the wife mysteriously tries to kill her husband with his own sword, but she does not succeed. Thibaut leaves his wife in a nearby convent and he goes on to Campostela to pray for children. He then takes his wife home, where her father, the count of Pontieu, learns of the attempted assassination, decides that this dishonorable conduct must be punished, seals his daughter in a barrel, and sets her out to sea. She is rescued by merchants, who give her to the sultan of Aumarie.[10] The sultan falls in love with her, has her converted to Islam, and marries her. The daughter of the count of Pontieu then becomes a Saracen princess and has two children with the sultan, a boy and a girl.

In Pontieu the woman's husband, father, and brother regret the cruel exile they imposed on the count's daughter and decide to join a crusade to the Holy Land in order to expiate their brutal treatment of her. After their boat is swept off course in a storm, they land on the shores of the sultan of Aumarie's kingdom, where they are held as Christian captives. The daughter of the count of Pontieu recognizes the prisoners and arranges to speak with them. They tell her their story, beginning with the wife's mysterious attempt to kill her husband. The lady responds with the explanation that the wife may have been afraid that her husband would always look at her with shame after the rape. When Thibaut protests that he would never have esteemed his wife any less because of what she had suffered, the sultan's wife reveals her identity. She then pretends to the sultan that she is ill because of a new pregnancy and needs to take sea air; she sets out in a ship with her father, husband, and brother, taking her son with her but not her daughter. They flee to Rome, where the lady of Pontieu is converted back to Christianity and her Saracen son is baptized. She then returns to France, where, after having been gang raped, sealed in a barrel and set to sea, rescued by merchants, given to a sultan, and converted to Islam; after giving birth to a Saracen son and daughter, rescuing her father, husband, and brother, and reconverting to Christianity; the daughter of the count of Pontieu finally gives birth to two French, Christian sons.[11]

While *La fille du comte de Pontieu* is not a romance about a queen, nor explicitly a story about adultery, it is dominated by a quest for children, for proper succession, and for the continuation of a dynasty. These concerns are hidden in romances about adulterous queens, but they implicitly structure the story of royal adultery, as I suggested above. And although *La fille* is not the story of a queen, the heroine does become the wife of a ruler, and she is responsible for the continuation of his dynasty as well as the dynasty of the counts of Pontieu. In this story the anxiety about succession is not limited to the local genealogy of the county of Pontieu, but is part of a larger narrative of lineage that encompasses the Islamic world. In her escape from the sultan, the lady of Pontieu takes her son, but she leaves behind her daughter, who eventually becomes the grandmother of Saladin, the Muslim leader who captured Jerusalem from the Christians in 1187.

The genealogy of Saladin invented in *La fille du comte de Pontieu* is incorporated into two longer narratives: the fourteenth-century epic, *Baudouin de Sebourc*, which recounts the story of Baldwin II of Jerusalem, and the fifteenth-century *Jean d'Avesnes* compilation, which ends with the chivalric adventures of Saladin.[12] Needless to say, this genealogy is completely fictional, and the representation of the Saracen in stories about the daughter of the count of Pontieu is an early example of what Edward Said has called Orientalist discourse, a construction of the Islamic East that dramatizes anxieties of the Christian West.[13] The medieval paradigm of cultural otherness focuses on religious difference, and military defeat is seen as the natural consequence of the dependence on false gods.[14] The need to describe how Saracens are wrong leads to absurd inventions like the notoriously inaccurate and deliberately travestied picture of medieval Islam in the representation of the polytheistic, idolatrous *loi sarrasine*.[15] Fairly accurate information about Islam was not unavailable in the Christian West. Scholarly research into Islam included a translation of the Qur'an commissioned by Peter the Venerable and completed by the English scholar Robert of Ketton in July 1143.[16]

Nonetheless, distortion prevails in the literary depiction of Islam, and the description of Saracens worshiping idols or a trinity of gods is a conventional characterization in medieval French narratives. These representations were in turn cited as evidence of the obvious deficiencies in the Saracens' theological system, which explained their consistent defeat by representatives of Christian monotheism.[17]

In medieval literature Christians and Saracens share the same standards of courtesy and nobility, and religion provides the ground for the representation of difference. But what happens when the carefully drawn lines of religious difference become blurred? What happens, for example, when the Christian God is seriously challenged by the Saracen God (or gods, as the medieval tradition erroneously insists)? As, for example, when the assumed equation of Christian religion and military victory was challenged by the loss of Jerusalem to Saladin in 1187? The territory was regained by the Christians during the third Crusade, but the initial defeat put into question the assumed "right" of the Christians over the Muslims and seems to have provoked a need to redefine the borders between Saracen and Christian in fictional stories about Saladin. That redefinition is made through stories about maternity and succession: narratives about the daughter of the count of Pontieu implicitly explain the Muslim leader's military prowess and reputed courtesy by placing him in a Christian French lineage.

In the genealogy of Saladin that is part of the account of the disruption and subsequent reinstatement of the proper succession of Pontieu, *La fille* and its analogues recount the interrupted and subsequently reinstated succession of Jerusalem to Christian hands. They offer an implicit reassurance: the military successes of Saladin do not contradict the ideologically necessary opposition between the victorious Christian and the defeated Saracen because Saladin's lineage includes a noble French family. At the same time, however, these texts offer what is characterized within the stories as a troubling spectacle: a genealogy that includes a Christian mother and a Saracen son. *La fille du comte de Pontieu* pairs maternity and the Saracen religion as twin threats to the stability of the Christian family. In the story of the non-Christian child of a Christian mother, cultural borders are breached and essential identity is questioned. How can a Christian mother be the ancestor of a Saracen son? The representation of Saladin's genealogy as a disjuncture reveals an anxiety about succession and lineage that is recounted as an anxiety about Islam. In stories about the daughter of the count of Pontieu, transgression—both religious and reproductive transgression—is located in the mother and is figured not as marital infidelity, but as religious conversion. Conversions to Islam are rarely represented in medieval French literature, and the fluctuating loyalties of the daughter of the count of Pontieu not only suggest a fragile loyalty to Christianity, but disrupt and challenge the stability of the institutionalized Christian family and of its place in the structure of medieval French society.[18]

The motivation for the daughter of the count of Pontieu's conversion to Islam receives a different representation in each of the three versions of this tale. The repeated revision of the daughter's reason for accepting Islam suggests that the conversion posed a problem that each author or compiler needed to explain; it seems to indicate an anxiety about apostasy that is linked to marriage. This link is obvious on one level: the daughter converts to Islam in preparation for her marriage to the sultan. Yet the anxiety surrounding the conversion in the varying explanations of the act focuses not on the conversion itself but on the representation of the lady's desire to convert.

In the thirteenth-century *Fille du comte de Pontieu*, the conversion is represented as the inevitable outcome of the captive woman's situation. The sultan loves her and offers to marry her if she will accept the Saracen religion. The lady believes that she has little choice in the matter; if she does not choose to convert, she will be forced to do so.

Il pensa bien a çou que il veoit en li qe ele estoit haute feme, et le fist reqere se ele estoit crestienne, et ke, se ele voloit sa loi laisier, k'il le prenderoit. Ele vit bien que mix li valoit faire par amours que par force, se li manda qu'ele le feroit. Il l'espousa quant ele fu renoïe et criut en molt grant amour envers li, et petit fu avec lui quant elle conçut et eut .j. fil. (*La fille*, 23)

(He thought about the fact that he could see that she was a high-born lady, and he sent word to ask if she were a Christian and to say that if she would leave her religion he would take her as his wife. She understood that it would be better to do it because of love than because of force, and she sent word to [the sultan] that she would do it. He married her when she had renounced Christianity and his love for her grew greatly, and she was with him only a short time when she conceived a son.)

The fourteenth-century *Baudouin de Sebourc* revises the story a great deal. Here, the daughter of the count of Pontieu is rejected by a Christian knight to whom she is betrothed because the knight loves the secretly converted sister of a Saracen prince. This version of the story does not recount the problem of a barren marriage that begins the daughter's adventures and leads to her exile and conversion in the thirteenth-century narrative. In *Baudouin de Sebourc* the succession drama focuses primarily on the lineage of Saladin. As in *La fille du comte de Pontieu*, the lady of Pontieu is captured by a sultan who falls in love with her. She accepts conversion out of a desire to renounce the world of those who have insulted and betrayed her. When the sultan offers her marriage and the honor of his thirteen kingdoms, the lady is quick to accept:

"Honnis soit," dist la dame, "qui le refusera!
Et je renoië Dieu, et le pooir qu'il a;
Et Marie, sa mère, qu'on dist qui le porta;
Mahom voel aourer, aportez-le-moi chà."
. . . Li Soudans commanda
Qu'on aportast Mahom; et celle l'aoura.
A le loy Sarrasine li Soudan l'espousa;
La nuit jut o la dame. .ii. enfans engendra:
.j. fil et une fille, à che qu'on me conta;
Salatie ot à nom ichelle fille là,
Li fiex Salehadin, qui cristiens greva.[19]

("It would be shameful to refuse," says the lady, "And I renounce God and his power, and Mary his mother who carried him. I want to worship Mohomet, bring him here to me." . . . The sultan commanded that Mohomet be brought forward and she worshipped him. The sultan married her according to the Saracen religion. That night he slept with the lady and engendered two children, a son and a daughter.)

The third version of the tale, in the fifteenth-century *Jean d'Avesnes*, is very close to the thirteenth-century text. Again, the lady has no choice in the matter, she must convert to the law of the Saracens, though in this story she does put up a little more resistance than in the earlier version:

Il la fist servir et honnourer comme la princesse de sa terre, mesmement la fist soir a sa table, et tant luy fu agreable sa belle contenance que il s'enamoura d'elle mervilleusement, et la fist interroguier par gens qui savoient parler latin comme elle faisoit s'elle vouldroit renoyer la loy crestienne et le soudan la prendroit a femme. A laquelle chose elle ne s'accorda pas du primier coup, mais a chief de conclusions, comme elle veist que faire luy convenoit par amours ou par force, elle, *par fainte*, renonça au baptesme et au service de Dieu pour aourer lex ydollez. De laquelle chose le soudan fu tant joyeux qu'on ne pourroit plus, fist sez aprestez, manda sez princez et barons, et selon la maniere sarrasine espousa icelle a grant honneur, coucha avec elle, et tant firent que la dame conchupt et au chief de .ix. mois se delivra d'un beau filz. (*La fille*, 98; my emphasis)

([The sultan] had her served with honor like a princess of his country, and even had her sit at his table. Her beautiful appearance was so pleasing to him that he loved her greatly. He asked her, through people who spoke Latin as she did, whether she would renounce the Christian religion so the sultan could take her as his wife. She did not agree to the idea at first, but after deliberation she saw that it was better to do it because of love than because of force, and she *pretended* to renounce baptism and the service of God in order to worship idols. The sultan could not have been happier at this, and he made his preparations and sent for his princes and barons, and he married her with great honor according to Saracen customs. He slept with her and the lady conceived and at the end of nine months delivered a beautiful son. [my emphasis])

According to the text's editor, the idea of the lady's deception is introduced in only one manuscript, and it is a later addition above the line of the words "par feinte." [20] The lady's pretense in her conversion is an addition to the story that both reassures and troubles.

If she only pretends to convert it is clear that she wishes to resist the choice imposed on her by her circumstances, and her reconversion to Christianity at the end of the story is more plausible. At the same time, the deception puts into question other vows the lady makes: if she will lie to one husband, perhaps she will lie to another.

The three different explanations for the lady of Pontieu's decision to convert point to a need to explain a troubling development in the text. When she escapes from the sultan and goes straight to Rome to be rebaptized as a Christian, the lady of Pontieu acts in a way that does not need explanation for the Christian audience of her tale. It is the initial decision to convert that must be explained as coercion, as a perverse vengeance, or as a pretense. For medieval French readers, the renunciation of Christianity demonstrates a dangerous breakdown of the carefully constructed distinction between Christian and Saracen, but more importantly in these stories, it demonstrates the vulnerability of Christian lineage to potential corruption from within. I am not suggesting that medieval men seriously feared the religious conversion of their wives. I am suggesting, however, that the uneasy retellings of the story of the daughter of the count of Pontieu point to an anxiety about motherhood and the corruption of lineage, about the disruption of succession from inside the family, and about adultery. In these stories maternity is the means through which difference is obscured and lineage is corrupted; the maternal body is figured as a disturbing spectacle in its ability to cross borders of state, religion, and paternity. The unfaithful, converted body of the mother threatens the establishment of legitimate religion and legitimate succession. In stories about the daughter of the count of Pontieu and her Saracen great-grandson, anxiety about lineage and succession is represented in a conflation of religious conversion and motherhood that simultaneously incorporates the Saracen other into a Christian lineage and exiles the Christian mother into a Saracen otherness.

A fourteenth-century analogue of *La fille du comte de Pontieu* emphasizes the connection between adultery and conversion. In the *Dit des annelets* the story is set in motion not by a rape, but by an attempted adultery. Like the daughter of the count of Pontieu, the adulterous woman is condemned by her father, cast to sea, rescued

by a Saracen, and asked to convert. This lady refuses to renounce
Christianity, and she establishes a béguinage along the pilgrimage
route to Campostela where she eventually meets her estranged husband, who forgives her for the transgression that began the story.
In this tale adultery stands in the place of conversion as the act that
must be effaced in order to reintegrate the repudiated woman into
the Christian family.[21]

Another fourteenth-century narrative (this one not related to
the Pontieu stories) further illustrates what is implicitly at stake in
the story of the Christian mother and the Saracen son. An author
known as the Ménestrel de Reims explicitly recounts the conflation
of conversion, maternity, and adultery in a pseudo-chronicle that
encompasses the second Crusade. This story repeats a widespread
legend about Eleanor of Aquitaine's adulterous passion for Saladin.
Displeased with her husband's neglect of military action once the
royal couple arrives in the east, Eleanor falls in love with the celebrated Saracen leader.

Et quant la roine Elienor vit la deffaute que li rois avoit menée avec li, et elle
oï parleir de la bontei et de la prouesce et dou sens et de la largesce Solehadin,
si l'en ama durement en son cuer; et li manda salut par un sien druguement;
et bien seust il, se il pouoit tant faire que il l'en peust meneir, elle le penroit
à seigneur et relanquiroit sa loi. Quant Solehadins l'entendi par la letre que li
druguemenz li ot baillie, si en fu mout liez; car il savoit bien que ce estoit la
plus gentis dame de crestientei et la plus riche. (*Ménestrel de Reims*, 4–5)

(When Queen Eleanor saw the king's weakness and when she heard of the
goodness and prowess and wisdom and generosity of Saladin, then she loved
him very much in her heart. She sent him greetings by one of her messengers,
and he understood that if he could succeed in taking her away she would
marry him and renounce her religion. When Saladin understood this through
the letter her messenger had given him, he was very happy, for he knew that
she was the most noble woman of Christendom and also the richest.)

One of Eleanor's servants warns her husband of the queen's plan
to escape with Saladin and the king prevents it. On their return to
France, the king assembles his barons, reports the queen's conduct,
and asks for advice about what to do with her.

"Par foi, dient li baron, li mieudres consaus que nous vous sachiens don-
neir, ce est que vous la laissiez aleir; car c'est uns diables, et se vous la tenez
longuement nous doutons qu'elle ne vous face mourdrir. Et ensourquetout
vous n'avez nul enfant de li." A ce conseil se tint li rois, si fist que fous: mieuz
li venist l'avoir enmurée; si li demourast sa granz terre sa vie, et ne fussent
pas avenu li mal qui en avinrent si comme vous en orrez conteir ça en avant.
(*Ménestrel de Reims*, 6–7)

("By faith," said the barons, "the best advice that we can give you is that you
let her go, for she is a devil and if you keep her for a long time we fear that
she will kill you. And above all, you don't have any children with her." The
king followed this advice and he was foolish to do so. He would have done
better to wall her up; in this way he could have kept all her great lands and
would have avoided all the misfortunes that resulted from it, as you will hear
recounted below.)

The barons' counsel ("let her go . . . you don't have any children
with her") and the narrator's commentary ("he could have kept all
her great lands") demonstrate the importance of childbirth and succession that is prominent in the stories of the daughter of the count
of Pontieu.[22]

    Childbirth and succession may also have been part of the event
that is the source of this episode, Eleanor's rumored infidelity with
her uncle, Raymond of Antioch. Saladin replaces Raymond in the
Ménestrel de Reims's account and in later chronicles that use his
Récits as a source.[23] All these accounts repeat the assertion by the
king's vassals that he has no children with the queen. Eleanor did
have children with Louis—the Ménestrel of Reims ignores her two
daughters—but she had no sons, and it is perhaps the importance of
a son and a royal heir that leads the Ménestrel to claim that there
were no children in the royal family. In any case, after her divorce
Eleanor married Henry II of England and produced five sons; her
delayed fertility finds an odd echo in the story of the lady of Pontieu,
who has no children after five years of marriage to her French husband, but conceives on her wedding night with her Saracen husband.

    Adultery may produce children who illegitimately claim the
benefits of aristocratic French Christian succession. This is the threat
represented by the military successes of Saladin, the Saracen leader

who usurps the Christian position of military victory. The power to corrupt lineage is located in the maternal body, a body that occupies a position of dangerous ambiguity in the story of the daughter of the count of Pontieu. The mother is doubly marked by illegitimacy because of her own conversion and because of the birth of children out of Christian wedlock, and her reintegration into the Christian family is assured by legitimate, Christian motherhood—the two sons born after her reconversion and return to Pontieu. The reassuring reinstatement of "proper" motherhood in *La fille du comte de Pontieu* effaces the threatening spectacle of conversion and adultery by eliminating the woman as the subject of her own maternity and by inscribing that absence in a Christian teleology: "According to the will of God, Thibaut had two sons by his wife."[24] The Christian God guarantees Christian succession; adultery and otherness are left behind in Saracen lands:

[F]urent li fil monseigneur Tiebaut hoir de ces .ij. contés u il parvinrent en la fin. La boine dame vescui en grant penitance et mout fist de bien et d'aumosnes, et mesire Tiebaus vescui comme preudom k'il fu, et mout fist de bien tant com il fu en vie. (*La fille*, 48)

(The two sons of monseigneur Thibaut were heirs to two counties, which they received in the end. The good lady lived with great penitence and did many good deeds and made many offerings to the poor; Messire Thibaut lived like the gentleman he was, and did many good deeds during his lifetime.)

In this happy ending, maternity is elided as proper succession is guaranteed: Thibaut has sons, and his wife has piety.

The reinstatement of the daughter's Christian identity and subsequent Christian motherhood cover up the dangerous instability revealed by her inital conversion, but the Saracen daughter left behind in Aumarie troubles the neat resolution of the story. The count's daughter has Christian sons, but she also has a Saracen daughter and a Saracen grandson. In the world described by the formula from *La chanson de Roland*, "Christians are right and pagans are wrong," the Christian genealogy of Saladin may explain the victory of the Saracen leader in battles against Christians, but the Saracen descendants of the count's daughter trouble the reinstatement of Christian maternity at the end of the romance. In the one version of the story that presents the lady's renunciation of Christianity as a willful act of vengence and greed, the heroine is not allowed to reconvert at the end of her story. Abandoned by her French relatives, who refuse to respond to her appeals for their help, the lady never leaves her Saracen kingdom and in a development that pointedly underscores the anxious link between maternity and conversion, she dies an unredeemed Saracen while giving birth to another Saracen child.

Illegitimacy and Legitimate Succession

Le livre de Caradoc begins with a marriage and an adultery that is consummated on the wedding night.[25] King Arthur marries his wise and beautiful niece Ysave to one of his knights, King Caradoc of Vannes. Eliavrés, another knight in Arthur's court who is also a magician, loves Arthur's niece, and on Caradoc's wedding night, Eliavrés keeps Ysave from her husband's bed and in her place substitutes a dog transformed into the likeness of the bride. King Caradoc sleeps with the disguised hound, and Eliavrés sleeps with the king's new wife. On the second night Eliavrés puts an enchanted sow in Caradoc's bed and on the third night a mare magically transformed into the likeness of a beautiful young woman. On the third night the queen conceives a son with the magician, and Eliavrés ceases his deception of the king. Queen Ysave and King Caradoc return to Vannes, where the queen gives birth to a son whom the king believes is his own child, and he names the boy Caradoc. When the son is older he goes to King Arthur's court to be knighted, and while he is there Eliavrés arrives with the challenge of an exchange of mortal blows. Only Caradoc will accept the challenge, he strikes first and cuts off Eliavrés's head.[26] The decapitated knight survives and returns to court after one year to deliver his blow. Caradoc submits to the exchange, but Eliavrés finds himself unable to kill his own son. He strikes Caradoc with the flat of his sword, then draws him aside to reveal his identity. Caradoc goes to his putative father, King Caradoc, and tells him about the queen's adultery. The king imprisons his wife in a tower where Ysave entertains her magician-lover every night with great festivities. There follows a series of adventures in which Eliavrés attempts to avenge his son's betrayal and in which Caradoc escapes death with the help of his lady, Guinier, who becomes a wife of exemplary fidelity. Finally, King Caradoc dies, and his wife's son, Caradoc, inherits the throne of Vannes. The illegitimate son of the mother is not excluded from the succession to the throne, and he is the only character in the story who even raises the possibility of exclusion. In one version of the romance, when King Caradoc designates his wife's son as his heir, Caradoc initially refuses the throne because he is not the king's own son.[27]

The illegitimacy of the queen's son is neither covered up nor forgotten after the initial drama of revelation; it is explicitly acknowledged when the succession of the throne is decided. In a study of literary texts that identify Charlemagne and King Arthur as illegitimate sons, Dominique Boutet claims that it is only in the thirteenth century that bastardy begins to be seen as a disqualification for the succession of a throne.[28] But both Charles and Arthur are illegitimate sons of kings, not of queens, and the king's bastard would have had a different status in succession than the queen's illegitimate son, since royal dynasties were patrilinear in medieval France and in most medieval fictions about royal courts.

Caradoc's coronation might be explained by the fact that King Caradoc does not have any other children who might have disputed the succession of his throne to his illegitimate son, and the story does not recount that the king had any brothers who might have tried to claim the kingdom after his death, as Alis does in Chrétien's *Cligés*. Yet the lack of contenders for the king's throne does not entirely explain the seamless succession to his wife's illegitimate son. The fact that neither King Marc nor King Arthur has any other children does not open the narrative possibility of Iseut or Guenevere producing a child with their lovers. The simple absence of another direct heir does not seem to negate the problem of illegitimacy in medieval romances about adulterous queens.

Caradoc's inheritance of the throne is also enabled by his proven

prowess, and in the king's designation of his wife's son as his heir
King Caradoc seems to accept the maxim used to describe Enéas in
the thirteenth-century *Partonopeu de Blois*: "Miex vaut bons fix en
pechié nes / Que mauvais d'espouse engenrés." ("A good son born
in sin is better than a bad son engendered in a spouse." vv. 313–
14.) *Le livre de Caradoc* gestures toward an idea of kingship based on
worth rather than on lineage, although hereditary kingship is never
seriously questioned in the romance. For the illegitimate son of the
queen and her magician lover, worth is demonstrated by a renunciation of lineage: Caradoc helps the king to punish his father and
imprison his mother.

The queen is removed from her husband's court and locked in
a tower—not to guarantee the integrity of her body, as in *Cligés* or
Eracle, but to punish her for having opened her body to a lover. In
Caradoc the imprisonment of the adulterous queen seems necessary
to establish her guilt in the story. It is only after she is locked up
that Ysave is shown to have any desire for her lover. In fact, it is only
after she is shut in the tower that Ysave shows any desire whatso-
ever: up to this point in the narrative she does not speak. Caradoc's
mother is a character entirely without subjectivity in the beginning
of her story. She is objectified in the story of the seduction by Eliavrés, who "kept his lover with him" ("retint s'amie o soi," *Caradoc*, v.
2070). Ysave's reaction to the magician's appropriation of her body
is never described, nor does the narrator indicate that she complies
with the deception of her husband. Ysave does not speak to indicate
her thoughts, and before the adultery is discovered and she is imprisoned the narrator describes only the emotions and desires that she
shares with her husband: the news of Caradoc's exchange of blows
with Eliavrés reaches "the king his father and the queen his mother,
who were in great despair because of it" (". . . au roi sen pere, / Et
a la roïne sa mere / Qui'n ot molt grant duel et grant ire," *Caradoc*,
vv. 2337–39). And when the day arrives for Caradoc to receive the
blow from Eliavrés in Arthur's court, "his father did not wish to go,
for he did not wish to see him die, nor did the queen who carried
him." ("Ses peres ne vaut pas venir, / Car nel peüst veoir morir, / Ne
la roïne qel porta." *Caradoc*, vv. 2349–51.) Only when Eliavrés reveals

his paternity to Caradoc do we have any indication of Ysave's complicity in the adultery, and it is an ambiguous one.

". . . Dirai te coment
Il fu. Ele le set molt bien;
Ja ne t'en mentirai de rien.
La nuit qu'ele fu esposee,
Quant la cambre fu delivree
Et ses sires se volt coucier
Si com il dut o sa mollier,
Par sanblant fis une pucele
D'une levriere autresi bele,
Si la cocai delés le roi
Et ta mere jut delés moi." (*Caradoc*, vv. 2450–60)

("I will tell you how it happened. [The queen] knows it very well. I will not lie to you about any of it. The night she was married, when the room was prepared and her husband wanted to go to bed as he should with his wife, I made a hound into the image of a young girl just as beautiful [as the queen] and I put her in bed beside the king and your mother lay beside me.")

The queen's knowledge of the seduction is revealed in her lover's assertion that she was fully aware of what happened: "Ele le set molt bien." In the magician's retelling of the deception the queen's active participation contrasts with the narrator's original attribution of agency only to Eliavrés. Whereas the magician claims that "your mother lay down beside me" ("ta mere just delés moi"), the narrator had previously recounted that Eliavrés "kept her with him" ("retint s'amie o soi").

This may seem like a minor syntatical difference that reflects the change from the third-person to the first-person narration, but the shift in agency is important in the story. In the narrator's account of the enchantment that Eliavrés enacts on the king's third wedding night, the queen is completely passive, and the narrator seems to acknowledge that the absent representation of queen's desire will be replaced later in the story with the narration of her willing complicity in the deception of her husband.

La tierce nuit d'une jument
Refist cil par encantement
Sambler une ausi bele dame.
O le roi en liu de sa fame
La recouca, et il si jut
Avec s'amie qu'il conut.
D'un fil remest la nuit ençainte;
Puis en fu provee et atainte,
Si con li contes le retrait. (*Caradoc*, vv. 2079–87)

(On the third night he made a mare into the image of a very beautiful lady. He put her in bed with the king in place of his wife, and he lay with his *amie* whom he knew. That night she became pregnant with a son; she was later proven guilty of it as the tale recounts.)

The later proof of the queen's guilt ("Puis en fu provee et atainte") corresponds to the definition of her complicity in the adultery only late in the story.

Even though the narrator announces the eventual judgment of the queen, the narrative development of the queen's character is open-ended at the beginning of the *Livre de Caradoc*. It is the queen's son who takes responsibility for transforming his mother into an active adulteress by accepting the story of his conception recounted by Eliavrés. When the magician identifies himself to Caradoc as his true father, Caradoc states his refusal to believe the slander of his mother ("Devant tos ces bons cevaliers / Envers vos ma mere en desfent," *Caradoc*, vv. 2448–49), but the knight then returns to Vannes and tells King Caradoc the "truth" about his mother ("ains di verité," *Caradoc*, v. 2505).

Narratives about Guenevere and Iseut demonstrate that a proof of adultery is not always as definitive as it might seem, and in *Caradoc* the "truth" of the queen's adultery is based solely on Eliavrés's claim of paternity. The absence of demonstrable complicity on the part of the queen in the deception of her husband would seem to leave open several different narrative possibilities for the resolution of her story: she might have been able to hide the liaison or otherwise explain it away, or the king's love for his wife might have prompted him to dismiss her lover's accusation. What seems to preclude these narrative developments in *Le livre de Caradoc* is the queen's maternity. The king accepts the son's "truth" without demanding any other proof of the mother's guilt and asks the son how he should punish the mother. On Caradoc's advice she is locked in a tower, where, marginalized from the court, she becomes an active character in the story, holding raucous festivities with her lover, plotting with him to avenge their son's betrayal, and, finally, helping her son to escape the mortal vengeance conceived by his father.[29]

The transformation of the queen from a silent, passive object of desire to a malevolent participant in the destruction of her own son is motivated only by the discovery of her adultery, and in *Caradoc* the revelation of the queen's adultery is definitive: it cannot be covered up because it has produced a child. Maternity disrupts the structure of romances in which the repeated discoveries and concealments of the queen's adultery create an unresolved tension that contributes to the political stability of the feudal court. The maternal body, particularly the adulterous maternal body, cannot mediate political contests in the feudal court.[30] The discovery of Queen Ysave's adultery has no effect on King Caradoc's government of his court. The queen's adultery is not the pretext for contests between factions in her husband's court, nor does the adulterous liaison fit into the power structure identified by Christiane Marchello-Nizia in which the knight seeks proximity to the king and to his power through a liaison with the king's wife.[31] Capable of extraordinary feats because of his knowledge of magic, Eliavrés would not seem to need the queen or the king to ameliorate his standing in court if that is what he desired.

There is, nonetheless, a sharp rivalry between the queen's husband and her lover that takes the form of displaced confrontations. Eliavrés acts out a rivalry with King Caradoc in the seduction of Ysave and in the revelation of the true paternity of the king's son. When he learns how the magician deceived him on his wedding knight, King Caradoc forces Eliavrés to sleep with the same animals he put into the king's bed and to engender monstrous sons with them. The gradual elimination of the queen in the series of confrontations between Caradoc and Eliavrés reveals the extent to which the story is structured as a contest between the king and the magician. The revelation of Caradoc's paternity takes place in a literal contest between men, the wager between Caradoc, the son, and Eliavres, and the engendering of sons in animals underscores the woman's marginal status in the exchanges that structure the rivalry between the magician and the king.[32]

In *Le livre de Caradoc*, as in stories about Guenevere and Iseut, the queen is exchanged between men in a negotiation of power and sovereign authority. But the queen's body loses its symbolic status when she becomes a mother. The maternal body can no longer be split between men, nor can it be exchanged in rumors of adultery because it is no longer vulnerable in the same way that the queen's barren body is vulnerable to accusation. I cited earlier John W. Baldwin's description of that vulnerability as experienced by Philip Augustus's estranged barren wife, Ingeborg of Denmark, "[s]equestered in a royal monastery, unable to understand French, and deprived of all contact with her countrymen."[33] It is primarily the queen's lack of children, along with her isolation from her land of birth and kinship ties, that marks her vulnerability. The queen's relationship with the king is her only source of protection, security, and well-being while she lives in his court. In romances the queen's lover may intervene as her champion to prove the queen's innocence when she is accused of betraying the king, but the knight's intervention always depends on the king's consent. King Marc does not permit a judicial battle when the adultery of Iseut and Tristan is "proved" by the blood from Tristan's wound that stains the queen's sheets; denied recourse to her lover's chivalric skills and deprived of her husband's protection, Iseut flees into hiding with her lover. Even when the knight is allowed to prove the queen's innocence in battle, she can still lose the protection and security of her status as queen. When Guenevere is accused of being an imposter in the *Lancelot*, her lover successfully saves her from death, but the king still repudiates her as an impostor and exiles her from court.

The royal mother is not vulnerable to accusation in the same way as a childless queen; she is not isolated from her family and dependent only on her husband for protection because she has a son.

Le livre de Caradoc underscores the protection that a queen mother might expect from her son. Although Caradoc reports his mother's infidelity to King Caradoc, he also protects his mother from death, claiming that because she is his mother, he "cannot counsel death or physical harm." ("La roïne si est ma mere; / Si ne vos doi pas consellier / De l'ocirre ne mehagnier." *Caradoc*, vv. 2528–30.)

Le livre de Caradoc recounts the absent narrative that haunts more celebrated romances about the queen's adultery, and that is the story of maternity. If *La fille du comte de Pontieu* demonstrates the anxiety that illegitimacy could produce, *Caradoc* suggests that illegitimacy need not represent a threat to succession and political stability. In this story the crown passes to the illegitimate son of the queen and her lover "just as it should":

En tant avint a aventure
Que li rois Caradués morut.
Li roialmes, si com il dut,
A Caradué son fil revint;
En bone pais l'ot puis et tint. (*Caradoc*, 2860–64)

(Eventually it happened that King Caradoc died. The kingdom passed to his son Caradoc, just as it should. Thereafter he held it in good peace.)

In its representation of illegitimate succession *Le livre de Caradoc* invites a reinterrogation of the representation of adulterous queens as barren. It demonstrates that the central position of the adulterous queen in the feudal court, as the site upon which power is negotiated between her husband, her lover, and factions in the court, is possible only as long as the queen remains vulnerable to accusations of sexual transgression. The queen's vulnerability to exchange and accusation changes when she has a child. Maternity rewrites the structure of the romance court, replacing the royal couple with a royal family, and shifting the balance of power in the court. While the king's vassals might still compete with the queen's lover for influence in the court, the focus of their competition would no longer be the queen, but her son. And a queen who has a son has a status that is at least to some extent independent of her relationship with her husband.

The vulnerability of the aristocratic woman who has no children is emphasized in *La fille du comte de Pontieu*. I have claimed that this narrative also reveals a profound anxiety about illegitimacy and proper succession. Yet the unproblematic inheritance of the throne of Vannes by the queen's illegitimate son in *Le livre de Caradoc* suggests that the anxiety about illegitimacy may cover some other fear. In Chapter 5 I propose that the representation of troubled succession in *La fille*, like the untroubled succession in *Caradoc* and the absence of succession concerns in stories about Guenevere and Iseut, betrays an anxiety about women's power—both the power to corrupt lineage and the power to corrupt government.

5

Seduction, Maternity, and Royal Authority

LE ROMAN DES SEPT SAGES DE ROME recounts that when the emperor of Rome's first wife dies, leaving him with a son, his counselors advise the emperor to take another wife. The emperor follows their advice, with unfortunate results:

Molt s'esmerveillent par le regne
k'il ne prennoit une autre femme.
Concile en tinrent li baron
a .I. geudi de Rouvison.
"Sire, font il, merchi, pour Dé,
le glorïeus de maïsté!
Ne poriiés longhes garir
ne chaasté ensi tenir,
car vous estes de biel eage.
Prendés femme de haut parage.
Se vous en aviiés enfans,
vos fils aisnés seroit manans
ki lor poroit donner adiés
riches hounors et grans palais."
Tant li dirent que il le fist,
et a .i. dyable se mist
c'on deüst pendre par la geule!
D'enghien et d'art savoit plus seule
que la femme au roi Constentin,
la Salemon ne la Fortin,
ne la femme Artu de Bretaigne,
ki tant sot de male bargaigne

que par son enghien porcacha
comment Murdrés envenima.
Li rois n'a pas la dame prise,
mais ceste lui, par tel devise
qu'ele devint dame et signor;
ele a souspris l'empereor.
L'en devroit l'omme lapider
ki sa femme lait trop monter. (*Roman des sept sages*, K: 407–36)

(There was much surprise throughout the kingdom that he did not take another wife. The barons held a council on the Thursday of Rogation. "Sire," they say, "have pity, for the sake of God and the glory of his majesty! You cannot remain healthy, nor keep chaste like this for long, for you are young. Take a noble wife, and if you have children your eldest son will be powerful enough to give them rich honors and great palaces." They counseled him until he did it, and he joined himself with a devil who should have been hung! She alone knew more about trickery and magic arts than the wife of King Constantine, the wife of Solomon or of Samson the Strong, or than the wife of Arthur of Britain who knew so much about evil bargaining that she sought to poison Mordred by ruse. The king did not take the lady, she took him, and in such a way that she became lady and lord; she overcame the emperor. Any man who lets his wife rise too high should be stoned to death.)

Fenice is notably absent from this list of adulterous wives who used magic to deceive their husbands. Guenevere is present, accused of an attempt to poison Mordred that does not appear in any other story.[1]

The narrator's list of famous "women on top"[2] illustrates the dangerous consequences of women's power and suggests that the danger is averted through a collective enforcement of men's control of their wives: "Any man who lets his wife rise too high should be stoned to death." The narrator specifically points to the inappropriate rise of royal wives: the new empress became both lady and lord ("ele devint dame et signor"). Moreover, the wife's power is implicitly linked to an inappropriate sexual dominance: "the king did not take the lady, she took him." The king was meant to take her as his wife and consort, but he also should have taken her sexually in a consummation of the marriage. The narrator suggests that the king got taken—by his wife.

The association of women, political power, and sexual predation is one that is fully exploited in the *Roman des sept sages* and in several other medieval French narratives like *Le roman de Silence* and *La châtelaine de Vergi*. In these stories, a woman attempts to seduce one of her husband's vassals, he rejects her, and the woman then claims that the vassal tried to seduce her. Commonly known as the Potiphar's wife topos after the Biblical account of the attempted seduction of Joseph, when the literary motif features a queen it permits an exploration of the implicit link between transgressive sexuality and women's political authority.[3]

Jezebels

Although the story of the seductress queen is usually described as an example of the Potiphar's wife topos, early medieval historians associated a perceived misuse of political power not with Potiphar's wife, but with Queen Jezebel, whose story is told in the book of Kings. Janet L. Nelson has described how two powerful Merovingian queens were characterized as Jezebels by their contemporaries,[4] and Geneviève Bührer-Thierry has discussed this characterization of the Carolingian empress Judith, accused of adultery and of usurping the king's power.[5] By the thirteenth century the powerful position that earned Empress Judith the comparison with Jezebel was no longer available to the king's wife. The usurpation of royal power through alliances with powerful vassals and the use of kinship networks was no longer a possibility for the queen consort, whose access to the direct participation in royal government enjoyed by her predecessors was increasingly limited. Yet romances about seductress queens, queens who use their political power to pursue sexual pleasure, suggest that despite the relative loss of power by twelfth- and thirteenth-century Capetian queens consort, the idea of women's access to power still provoked anxiety. In romance narratives that anxiety is represented in a conflation of women's sexual desire and political influence that threatens royal sovereignty.

The romance figure of the seductress queen is not caught in the conflict between dynastic marriage and romantic love that characterizes the courtly adultery of Guenevere, Iseut, and Fenice. Sexual transgression is clearly motivated by shared love in stories of courtly queens like Guenevere and Iseut; even though Tristan and Iseut's unrestrainable passion may have its origins in the love philtre they drink together, their desire for each other is always described as love. In stories like *Le roman de Silence* or *Le roman des sept sages* the queen's adultery or attempted adultery is not represented as the inevitable outcome of a passion she shares with a knight, it is a sign of the queen's sexual voracity. The desire of the seductress queen is one-sided, nonreciprocal, and purely sexual. The queen is not attracted to a knight who has awakened or won her love; rather she is shown to identify the knight as a suitable object for an already existing sexual desire. In *Le roman de Silence*, Queen Eufeme twice tries to seduce the cross-dressed knight, Silence, and after both rejections she seeks revenge by accusing the knight of attempted rape. Yet Silence is not the only object of the queen's desire. At the end of the romance the queen is found to keep another lover disguised as a nun in her household. In this narrative the discovery of the queen's multiple seductions is interpreted as a confirmation of her evil nature. It suggests that the queen needs many lovers and that any attractive man will do (or even the semblance of a man, since Silence is a woman dressed as a man).

A similar scene occurs in *Le roman des sept sages*. This romance exists in several versions, but the basic story does not change: an empress tries to seduce her stepson, he rejects her, and she accuses him of having tried to seduce her. In a prose version of the romance, the falsely accused son advises his father to have the empress's favorite attendant undressed. The lady in waiting turns out to be a man, and the emperor identifies his wife's insatiable sexual desire as the origin of her treachery.

"O faulce femme et miserable creature, tu n'avoyes pas souffisance pour accomplir ta charnalité et luxure de moy ne de ton rybaul, mais vouloyes encores mon filz pour pis faire!"[6]

("O false woman and miserable creature, you didn't have enough to satisfy your carnality and luxuriousness in me and your lover, but in addition you wanted my son for your evil!")

The queen's sexual desire demonstrates her evil nature, in the king's view, and in *Le roman des sept sages* and *Le roman de Silence* queens are shown to be ruled by an indiscriminate concupiscence that disrupts the king's government of his court because the queen takes revenge by trying to turn her husband against the vassal who rejected her. In their representation of the queen's adultery as a political danger the narrators of the twelfth-century *Roman des sept sages* and thirteenth-century *Roman de Silence* echo the accusations recorded against the ninth-century empress Judith: "The palace became a place of prostitution where concubinage dominates and adultery reigns."[7] However, whereas in the case of Judith, the charge of adultery was false—Bührer-Thierry has suggested that it was part of an attempt to weaken the queen's powerful position in the court[8]—in the case of queens like Eufeme in *Le roman de Silence* or the empress in *Le roman des sept sages* the charge of adultery is true. The discovery and punishment of the queen's transgression are part of a restoration of royal sovereignty that requires the constraint and condemnation of the queen's unruly desire. *Le roman de Silence* ends with the execution of the adulterous Queen Eufeme, the redressing of the knight, Silence, as a woman, and the marriage of this newly reconstructed woman to the king. Within the context of *Le roman de Silence* and in contrast to the deposed Queen Eufeme, Silence is an excellent choice as queen. Throughout the romance she never expresses any kind of sexual desire and she explains that she dressed as a knight in order to save her patrimony, which, by the king's order, could only be inherited by a man.[9] In the representation of Silence, a figure who seems to subordinate erotic desire to a desire for property and proper succession, the romance reassuringly rewrites Queen Eufeme's desire for sexual pleasure and political authority as Queen Silence's desire for dynastic continuation.

In Béroul's *Roman de Tristan* the discovery of the queen's sexual transgression directly implicates the king's power and authority: his vassals threaten to abandon him if he does not separate the queen and her lover. The king's ambivalence toward knowledge about the adultery and the lovers' success at dissimulation prevent or distort proofs of the queen's guilt, and the political stability of the court is preserved by the repeated series of accusations that threaten to destroy it, followed by exculpations that renew its unity and the king's sovereign authority. In stories of seductress queens, the threat to royal sovereignty posed by the queen's infidelity is located not in a contest between the king and his vassals, but in an internal drama played out between the king and his wife, and in which the king's relationship with a vassal is at stake. There is no secret adultery to be discovered, but a failed attempt at adultery that must be hidden. Rejected when she speaks desire, the queen seeks acceptance for her story of treason. Reversing the roles in the attempted seduction, she claims that the king's vassal tried to seduce her. The object of desire, the vassal knight, becomes its subject in the accusation that redefines a threat from within the couple (the wife's adulterous desire) as a threat from the outside (the knight's desire).

In *Le roman de Silence*, *Le roman des sept sages*, *La châtelaine de Vergi*, and similar tales, the attempted seduction and its cover-up are recounted in explicitly political terms. The queen (or duchess in *La châtelaine*) accuses a knight of a crime against his lord and she demands a political response to her charge: in *Le roman de Silence* that the king execute his vassal, in *Le roman des sept sages* that the emperor execute his son, and in *La châtelaine de Vergi* that the duke break his feudal ties with his knight.

The queen's ability to influence her husband's government of his court—at least temporarily—is a manifestation of political influence. Since the queen consort does not govern directly (she owes her position to her marriage), and since in these romance examples she has no children through whom she might claim the authority accorded to the mother of the king's heirs, the queen's power depends on her personal relationship with her husband. In *La châtelaine de Vergi* that personal influence is located entirely in a sexual relationship: the duchess succeeds in dictating her husband's conduct toward his vassal by withholding sex. *La châtelaine* recounts the story of a duchess, not a queen, but the ducal court in this romance has the same structure as a feudal royal court. The noble wife's participation in political decisions in her husband's court, the counsel she offers him, and his desire for her advice also characterize the position of the medieval queen consort. As in romances about queens who use their influence to pursue vengeance for a sexual rejection, the duchess's power and authority take the form of a sexual manipulation that threatens the structure of the feudal court.

The queen's sexual relationship with the king as a source of power and influence is not an invention of medieval romances. Historians of medieval queenship have shown that the queen's ability to intercede effectively with the king on the behalf of petitioners is linked to her intimacy with the sovereign.[10] The fact that the queen slept with the king gave her an access to the king that was recognized as influential and important. Even more significant was the authority the queen gained through her status as mother of the king's heirs. In preceding chapters I have discussed the suppression of childbirth in narratives about adulterous queens, and I have suggested that the absence of children isolates the queen at the center of the royal court and permits the exchange of her body and rumors about her body in negotiations of power and sovereignty in her husband's court. If concerns about royal succession are hidden in romances about courtly queens like Guenevere and Iseut, in stories about seductress queens succession and dynasty are prominently featured, even though the queen herself is not a mother. This structure is particularly evident in the narrative tradition of *Le roman des sept sages de Rome*, where succession is directly implicated in adultery: the young man that the empress tries to seduce is the son of her husband. When the empress accuses him of attempted rape and demands justice, she requires not simply the emperor's rupture of a feudal relationship with one of his vassals, but the execution of his own son and heir.

The link between succession and seduction is elaborated in some versions of *Le roman des sept sages* where the young empress, married to a man who has a son near her own age, presses the young son to accept her advances by presenting herself as a mate more suitable for the son than the father. One prose version of the story recounts her claim to have saved her virginity through sorcery and science ("par sorcerie et par science") in order that she might kill the old man who is her husband and marry his son.[11] In a verse version of the romance, the empress claims not to have had sex with her husband for three months.[12] The prolonged abstinence, like the claim to virginity, is surely linked to procreation. It demonstrates that the empress is not pregnant with her husband's child, and it gives an explanation for her lack of children. The empress offers herself to her stepson as a potential mother of his heirs.

In yet another version of *Le roman des sept sages* the empress does not wish to establish a ruling dynasty with her stepson but rather to clear the way for her own children (yet to be born) to inherit her husband's throne. The seduction is the result of a desire for power, and the sexual desire of the queen is indistinguishable from her voracious desire for the power she would gain as mother of the king's heir if she could destroy the king's son from his previous marriage.

Et finablement trouvérent une tresbelle dame fille du roy de Castille laquelle luy espousérent. Et aussy tost que l'empereur la vist il en fust tresamoureux, et tellement que toute l'amour et douleur de sa premiere femme fut perdue et obliée. Lesqueux demorérent longuement sans avoir enfant, de quoy l'emperiére et royne estoit dolente et malcontente. Mais après qu'elle sceut que l'empereur avoit ung filz qui estoit commis a sept sages maistres pour le nourrir et aprendre pour estre empereur après son pére, elle disoit ainsi en soy meismes: "Pleust a Dieu qu'i n'est mort et que j'eusse ung filz, affin qu'i fut heritier de l'empire." Et sus cestui desplaisir ne faisoit que cogiter comment elle porroit trouver maniére de le faire morir.[13]

(And finally they found a very beautiful woman, the daughter of the king of Castile, and they married her to [the emperor]. And as soon as the emperor saw her he fell in love and loved her so much that he forgot all the love and pain he felt for his first wife. They remained without child for a long time and the emperor and the queen were sad and unhappy about it. But after she learned that the emperor had a son who had been sent to seven wise masters to be educated and to learn to be emperor after his father, she said to herself, "Please God that he would die and that I would have a son, so that he could inherit the empire." And she was unhappy and spent all her time thinking about how she could find a way to make him die.)

The representation of succession concerns acknowledges the important reproductive role of the queen in a monarchy and the power she might exercise as mother to the future ruler of an empire.

The queen is never already a mother in the various versions of *Le roman des sept sages*, she only aspires to the power of a royal mother. And her desire for the power that maternity might give her is constructed as an evil desire because it is enacted through an adulterous seduction. Romances about seductress queens represent the queen's power to intervene in her husband's government and they offer a view of the queen's political power that is suppressed in stories about Guenevere and Iseut. These courtly adulterous queens enjoy the privileges of queenship, but the ways in which they use their influence in the royal court are marginal to direct government. Guenevere and Iseut are shown to arrange marriages and, on occasion, to counsel their husbands, but they rarely intervene in the king's government of his court except when they try to reconcile their husbands with their lovers. Seductress queens participate directly in the king's decisions about the court. They do not govern, but they affect the king's relationship with his vassals. As in the case of the Carolingian empress Judith, the queen's power is seen as a dangerous complement to royal sovereignty, and in *Le roman des sept sages* its transgressive nature is demonstrated in the queen's "unnatural" sexuality that leads her to seek multiple lovers and to dominate her royal spouse: "the king didn't take the queen, she took him."

Rejection and Revenge

In the long history of fictional and nonfictional representations of queens who usurp their husbands' royal authority, women's misuse of power is conflated with transgressive sexuality. Stories about seductress queens accept this model—but not always in a seamless, uncontested appropriation. Romance narratives may leave gaps through which it is possible to read beyond the narrative conflation of royal marriage, political power, and transgressive sexual desire to see how fictional representations of seductress queens may participate in an ongoing negotiation of the disputed relationship between royal wives and political authority in medieval France.

   One seemingly essential element of the seductress queen's story is the queen's violent reaction to rejection. The desire for revenge seems to be related to the queen's power to enact revenge. Other female characters in romance narratives do not react with violence when they offer their love or their bodies to a knight who rejects them. In romances that give a prominent place to the narration of knights' adventures in the forest, demoiselles are often rejected by knights errant who refuse to accept their love. In the *Prose Lancelot* one young woman reveals her love to Lancelot, who claims that he will never love her. This *pucelle* vows to retain her virginity as a sign of her devotion to the knight even though she knows he will never return her love.[14]

Queens and noblewomen with power, like the duchess in *La châtelaine de Vergi*, do not accept rejection with resignation; they seek vengeance. But the logic that structures the association of queenship, seduction, and vengeance is not always linked to rejected queens in medieval romance, as the example of *Le romans de la dame a la lycorne et du biau chevalier au lyon* demonstrates. In this story the Queen of Hungary falls in love with the Fair Knight and declares her love to him. When the knight claims that he will never love her, the queen goes away sad and angry, but does not seek to take revenge. The queen's lack of coercive threats and vengeful accusations may be a courtly response to the the nature of the knight's rejection. That is, the queen's reaction may be dictated by the kind of story that the romance recounts. But this is exactly the point I wish to make with respect to seductress queens. The seeming inevitability of the queen's violent desire for revenge in stories about seductress queens is a narrative convention. *La dame a la lycorne* suggests that an examination of the individual elements of that convention may reveal the assumptions about women, power, and sovereignty that define it as a compelling narrative structure for many twelfth- and thirteenth-century poets.

In *La dame a la lycorne* the knight's refusal of the queen's seduction is uniquely emotional: he says that he will never love the queen, but in an implicit recognition of her power, he offers her his body.

"Ma dame," dist-il, "vraiement
De tout mon cors vus fai present;

Mes je vous di que a nul fuer
Vous ne pöes avoir mon coer;
Car en tel lieu l'ai assené,
Dont ja nul jour ne l'osteré." . . .
La roynne u coer tant de doel a
Que maintenant el le laissa;
En sa chambre s'en est entree
Conme dolente et couroucee.[15]

("My lady," he said, "truly, I give you my body. But I tell you that you can
never have my heart. For I have consigned it to a place from which it can
never be taken." . . . The queen had so much pain in her heart that she left
him. Sad and angry, she went to her chamber.)

In the knight's resigned submission to the queen's declaration of
love, he seems to adopt what is usually constructed as a female
position in medieval narratives. Kathryn Gravdal has suggested that
courtly romances "[conflate] the themes of love and force so that
male domination and female submission are coded as emotionally
satisfying and aesthetically pleasing."[16] *La dame a la lycorne* suggests
that the gendered positions of this structure cannot be reversed:
although the knight is willing to take (or resigned to taking) the
submissive role, the queen does not take the dominant position.
She does not use her power to claim the knight because, unlike the
queens in *Le roman des sept sages* and *Le roman de Silence*, she seeks the
pleasures of mutual love. And in these romances, where the queen is
willing to act the role of masculine domination, the knight is unwilling to submit.[17] What then are the specific narrative motivations for
the queen's misuse of power when she is rejected?

It is not always possible to discern why a queen has such a violent reaction to rejection that she seeks revenge. The absence of an
explicitly recounted motivation for the queen's actions may be explained by a narrator's acceptance of misogynist characterizations
like the one the romance helps to establish, or the lack of explicit motivation may simply be characteristic of a genre that focuses more on
actions than on introspection. A seductress queen may first appear
in the story with already formed evil intentions, as in *Le roman des
sept sages*, or she may inexplicably change character, as in *Le roman de*

Silence. When Queen Eufeme first appears in the romance she is described briefly, but in positive terms.[18] As Silence gains stature in the romance, Eufeme turns into a vengeful, sexually voracious woman willing to use her influence to destroy a vassal.[19] In Chapter 4 I discussed a similar transformation in *Le livre de Caradoc*, where Queen Ysave at first appears ignorant of the magic seduction enacted by Eliavrés and only later is represented as having actively participated in the deception of her husband. In *Caradoc* the queen's metamorphosis into an evil character willing to destroy her own son takes place only after her adultery is discovered and she is locked up in a tower. The transformation and imprisonment permit the alliance of Caradoc and his putative father, King Caradoc, and the successful transition of the throne to the illegitimate son of the queen. While the transformation of Ysave into a willing accomplice of her magician-lover in *Le roman de Caradoc* and the motivation for the voracious and vengeful actions of queens in romances like *Le roman des sept sages* and *Le roman de Silence* remain unexplained, other stories about seductress queens may offer at least a partial deconstruction of the narrative process through which vengeance and transgressive sexuality are linked to women's power.

Power, Proof, and Procreation

In *Lanval* Marie de France recounts the attempted seduction of one of King Arthur's vassals by the king's unnamed wife. The story follows a familiar pattern: the knight rejects the queen's advances because he already has a secret lover, and the queen accuses the knight of her own crime. She claims that he tried to seduce her and that when she rejected him, the knight insulted her by claiming that the lowest servant of his lover was more desirable than the queen. The queen makes a formal accusation against the knight to the king and demands justice. In Marie's tale the queen's complaint is not a private exchange that takes place in the royal bedroom, but a public accusation to be followed by the formal judgment offered by the king's barons. Although there is also a public judgment in some ver-

sions of *Le roman des sept sages*, in that romance the empress attempts
to influence her husband's decision privately or she encourages him
to overrule his barons and execute his son without relying on their
decision. Likewise, in *Le roman de Silence* Queen Eufeme urges her
husband to "Take vengeance on this [knight] without waiting for
a trial!" ("Prendés de cestui vengement / C'onques n'atendés jugement!" *Roman de Silence*, 4147–48), and in *La châtelaine de Vergi*, the
duchess gains a hearing for her accusation against the duke's knight
by feigning illness and by withholding sex. In *Lanval* the queen does
not use sexual threats to bring attention to her charge. She seems to
appeal to a well-established judicial procedure when she makes her
accusation that the king will submit to a formal trial:

> Li reis fu del bois repeiriez;
> Mut out le jur esté haitiez.
> Es chambres la reïne entra.
> Quant el le vit, si se clamma;
> As piez li chiet, merci li crie,
> E dit que Lanval l'ad hunie:
> De druërie la requist;
> Pur ceo qu'ele l'en escundist,
> Mut la laidi e avila;
> De tel amie se vanta
> Ki tant iert cuinte e noble e fiere
> Que mieuz valeit sa chamberiere,
> La plus povre ki la serveit,
> Que la reïne ne feseit.
> Li reis s'en curuçat forment;
> Juré en ad sun serement,
> S'il ne s'en peot en curt defendre,
> Il le ferat ardeir u pendre. (*Lanval*, vv. 311–28)

(The king had returned from the woods after an extremely happy day. He
entered the queen's apartments and when she saw him, she complained
aloud, fell at his feet, cried for mercy and said that Lanval had shamed her.
He had requested her love and because she had refused him, had insulted
and deeply humiliated her. He had boasted of a beloved who was so well
bred, noble and proud that her chambermaid, the poorest servant she had,
was worthier than the queen. The king grew very angry and swore on oath

that, if Lanval could not defend himself in court, he would have him burned or hanged. [*Lais*, 77])

As in the stories of courtly adultery where accusations of the queen's sexual transgression mediate relationships between the king and his vassals, in *Lanval* a story about the queen becomes the basis of a negotiation between the king and his knight. Here the accusation comes from the queen herself, but her words are immediately appropriated by the king. Once she states her accusation, the queen loses her place as its subject. She is present only as an observer at the trial and she does not speak again in the story.

Li reis li dit par maltalant:
"Vassal, vus m'avez mut mesfait;
Trop començastes vilein plait
De mei hunir e avillier
E la reïne ledengier!
Vantez vus estes de folie:
Trop par est noble vostre amie,
Quant plus est bele sa meschine
E plus vaillanz que la reïne!" (*Lanval*, vv. 362–70)

(The king said to him angrily: "Vassal, you have wronged me greatly! You were extremely ill-advised to shame and vilify me, and to slander the queen. You boasted out of folly, for your beloved must be very noble for her hand-maiden to be more beautiful and more worthy than the queen." [*Lais*, 77])

In the king's accusation the queen's claim to shame ("[la reïne] dit que Lanval l'ad hunie," v. 315) becomes the knight's act of sham-ing the king ("de mei hunir," v. 366); the insult to the queen's body is an insult to the king's corporate body. The link between the state of the queen's body and the integrity of the king's rule is one that I have discussed throughout this study. Here, however, the consequences for the symbolic representation of the king's sovereignty are different since it is not the guilty queen who is on trial, but the falsely accused knight. Lanval's innocence can be proved—his lady is indeed more beautiful than the queen—without damage to the king's status, particularly since the knight disappears with his extraordinarily beautiful lady as soon as he proves his innocence of slander and of seduction.[20]

In *Lanval* the queen's attempted seduction is a secondary development in a tale about the importance of secrecy in loyal love service: it provides the pretext for the knight's betrayal of his lady's command to silence and her forgiveness of his transgression.[21] The portrait of the queen is not well developed in this story; she does not even have a name. Despite the ancillary function of the queen's seduction in the *lai*, in its representation of the negotiation of status and privilege through the relative beauty of women *Lanval* may question the extent to which the queen's personal relationship with the king could influence the practice of government. Marie shows that any influence the queen could bring to bear on the king would be contained or at least limited by the king's relationship of mutual obligation with his vassals, a relationship represented as already troubled at the beginning of the story. The *lai* opens with an account of the king's unjust treatment of his vassal, Lanval, whom he has neglected to reward with lands and wealth in return for his faithful service. A fairy maiden comes to the impoverished Lanval's aid, providing love and riches on demand and requiring that the knight keep their relationship secret.

In Marie's story a political system structured by feudal obligations and by feudal systems of justice negates any fantasy of significant power on the part of a queen. A queen may influence her husband, but her advice and even her requests for justice are subsumed in the king's negotiation of relationships with his vassals, which are regulated by established judicial procedure.[22] Marie suggests that although a queen can claim some influence over her husband, she does not have enough power to destroy her husband's relationship with his vassals through her sexual transgressions.

In *Lanval* it is the king who pursues the accusation against the knight, not the queen, and it is the king's desire for vengeance that must be contained. The barons are divided between those who wish to pardon Lanval because he has been falsely accused and those who wish to do the king's will and condemn the knight. The judges' dilemma seems to focus on how to prove the knight's innocence; the queen's accusation is widely disbelieved, and in the counsel given to the barons by the count of Cornwall, the king takes the place of the accusor:

Ceo dist li quoens de Cornẅaille:
"Ja endreit nus n'i avra faille,
Kar ki qu'en plurt ne ki qu'en chant,
Le dreit estuet aler avant.
Li reis parla vers sun vassal
Que jeo vus oi numer Lanval;
De felunie le retta
E d'un mesfait l'acheisuna,
D'une amur dunt il se vanta,
E ma dame s'en curuça.
Nuls ne l'apele fors le rei.
Par cele fei ke jeo vus dei,
Ki bien en veut dire le veir,
Ja n'i deüst respuns aveir
Si pur ceo nun qu'a sun seignur
Deit hum partut fairë honur.
Uns seremenz l'en gagera
E li reis le nus pardura.
E s'il peot aveir sun guarant
E s'amie venist avant,
E ceo fust veir k'il en deïst,
Dunt la reïne se marist,
De ceo ara il bien merci,
Quant pur vilté nel dist de li." (*Lanval*, vv. 433–56)

(Thus spoke the Count of Cornwall: "There shall be no default on our part. Like it or not, right must prevail. The king accused his vassal, whom I heard you call Lanval, of a felony and charged him with a crime, about a love he boasted of which angered my lady. Only the king is accusing him, so by the faith I own you, there ought, to tell the truth, to be no case to answer, were it not that one should honour one's lord in all things. An oath will bind Lanval and the king will put the matter in our hands. If he can provide proof and his beloved comes forward, and if what he said to incur the queen's displeasure is true, then he will be pardoned, since he did not say it to spite her." [*Lais*, 78–79])

I noted above that romance characterizations of the queen as a Jezebel whose sexual voracity corrupts government repeat accusations made against early medieval queens. By the late twelfth century Capetian queens consort had lost the sometimes powerful position enjoyed by their predecessors as the king's advisor and partner in government. In its representation of the nameless queen marginalized in her husband's demand for justice, Marie's tale may more accurately recount the limited sphere of influence of twelfth-century queens than stories like *Le roman de Silence* and *Le roman des sept sages* that present the queen's at least initially successful manipulation of her husband's relationship with a vassal. These women do not exercise direct political power, but their great influence over their husbands is an effective persuasion that leads to a disregard of feudal loyalties. Marie de France questions the extent of the king's wife's influence in the royal court: the queen disappears after she makes her accusation against Lanval, and the king takes her place as the wronged party in the judgment of the knight. In the words of the count of Cornwall, "Only the king is accusing him" ("Nuls ne l'apele fors le rei," v. 443).

In stories of seductress queens, as in most romances about adulterous queens, the king and the queen do not have any children together. Arthur does not have any children with his unnamed queen in *Lanval*, and the vulnerability of the childless queen is evident in her position in the *lai*. The difference that children might make in the formulation of a queen's accusation against her husband's vassal is suggested by a sixteenth-century version of the story of attempted seduction and revenge. Four centuries after Marie de France wrote *Lanval*, another woman writer turned to the story of the seductress queen and incorporated into it the story of maternity. In the seventieth tale of the *Heptaméron*, Marguerite de Navarre recounts a story that, like *Lanval*, suggests the limits of the power available to noble wives in feudal courts. Marguerite suggests that power is limited even when those wives are mothers.

Marguerite's source is the medieval story known in the thirteenth-century romance *La châtelaine de Vergi*. There is a fifteenth-century prose version of the romance called *L'istoire de la chastelaine du Vergier et de Tristan le chevalier*, and a 1540 printed version in dialogue called *La chastelaine du Vergier*.[23] It is not known which texts Marguerite may have consulted; the first complete version of the

Heptaméron was published in 1559. In *Heptaméron* 70, as in *La châtelaine de Vergi*, a duchess tries to seduce her husband's vassal and he rejects her. In Marguerite's version of the story, the duchess then creates the fiction of a pregnancy in an effort to gain her husband's sympathy and support for her accusation against the knight. Among the changes Marguerite makes to the earlier versions of the story, the most striking is the addition of the duchess's false pregnancy. Marguerite speaks what remains hidden in most medieval narratives about adultery: the power that maternity offered to women in a society structured by aristocratic dynasty.[24] Yet the pregnancy in *Heptaméron* 70 is a false claim to the influence of motherhood by an evil character in the story.

The complex and disputed relationship between power and sexual desire is at stake in all the versions of this story; Marguerite adds reproduction and succession to the representation of power in the tale. She further revises the structure of the earlier versions of the story by shifting its focus from the relationship between the knight and his secret lover, the châtelaine, to the relationship between the duke, the knight's feudal lord, and the duchess. The earliest version of the story, the thirteenth-century *La châtelaine de Vergi*, begins with an explanation of the lovers' pact of secrecy, then describes the knight and the duchess's attempt to seduce him. The anonymous fifteenth- and sixteenth-century rewritings of the story add a long scene describing the courtship of the châtelaine and the knight to the beginning of the story. Marguerite opens her tale with a description of the *duchess*.

Another important change in Marguerite's version of the story is found in the description of the knight's secret lover, the châtelaine de Vergier. In the thirteenth-century story, the châtelaine is married; in *Heptaméron* 70 she is a widow,[25] and Marguerite characterizes her secret liaison with her lover, the knight, as a "chaste, noble and most virtuous love" (Chilton, 527). The knight regularly visits the châtelaine to spend the night in talk. It has been suggested that this chaste "parler" is a euphemism for love-making; the lovers clearly spend the night in bed in the medieval version of the story. However, it does not seem likely that Marguerite would be reticent to name a sexual relationship if that is what she meant to suggest; elsewhere in the *Heptaméron* she does not hesitate to describe nights spent in sexual activity. In tale 18 Marguerite distinctly marks the difference between discourse and sex: a lady tests the sincerity of her suitor's love by inviting him to her bed to spend the night in talk, but forbids him to remove his nightshirt and to demand anything more than her words and chaste kisses. Marguerite also makes it clear when lovers spend nights together without talking in the *Heptaméron*. In several stories men secretly take the place of a husband or a lover in a lady's dark bedchamber, and their silence disguises their identity and permits the sex act. In *Heptaméron* 70 the nights that the châtelaine and her knight spend talking together are part of a narrative strategy that rewrites the châtelaine's adultery as a "chaste love."[26] Patricia Cholokian has suggested that female characters in the *Heptaméron* claim autonomy in the form of an exaggerated insistence on female chastity and honor.[27] I wish to focus not on the châtelaine and her concern for secrecy, chastity, and honor, but on the duchess and the way in which Marguerite's portrayal of what Cholakian defines as the demands of male honor—motherhood and succession—dictate her role in the story.[28]

In *Heptaméron* 70 Marguerite eliminates the actual adultery of the medieval story and focuses on the desired adultery between the duchess and the knight. Marguerite's interest in the figure of the duchess is evident in the prominent place she gives her in the story and in the detailed descriptions of the character.[29] In a significant departure from the other versions of the tale, the duchess is a mother and she uses her motherhood to influence her husband. In her first complaint about the knight's supposed seduction attempt, she pushes the duke to action by appealing to the honor of his lineage. She encourages her husband to shun the knight who "has now committed so mean and cruel an act as to seek to sully the honour of your wife upon which the honour of your family and your children rests" (". . . a osé entreprendre chose si cruelle et misérable que de pourchasser à faire perdre l'honneur de votre femme où gît celui de votre maison et de vos enfants," *Heptaméron*, 470–71; Chilton 517). The duchess exploits her position as mother of the duke's children to strengthen her demand that her husband punish the knight.

The subsequent invention of a false pregnancy has the same function. The duchess tries to claim the duke's solicitous attention by pretending to be pregnant: "pour mieux venir à la fin qu'elle préten-dait, lui dit qu'elle pensait être grosse, et que sa grossesse lui avait fait tomber un rhume dessus les yeux, dont elle était en fort grand peine" (*Heptaméron*, 470). The duke listens to his wife's accusation against the knight, he confronts him with the duchess's charge, and he ac-cepts the knight's denial. When the duke tells the duchess that the knight cannot have attempted to seduce her because he loves another woman, the duchess insists that the knight prove his innocence by revealing the name of his secret love. After the knight breaks his pact of secrecy with the châtelaine and speaks her name to the duke, the duchess again uses her pretended pregnancy to persuade her husband to reveal the name to her.

La Duchesse . . . feignit sentir bouger son enfant, dont le Duc fut si joyeux qu'il s'en alla coucher auprès d'elle. Mais à l'heure qu'elle le vit le plus amour-eux d'elle, se tournait de l'autre côté lui disant: "Je vous supplie, monsieur, puisque vous n'avez amour ni à femme ni à enfant, laissez-nous mourir tous deux." Et avec ces paroles jeta tant de larmes et de cris que le Duc eut grand peur qu'elle perdît son fruit. . . . [L]e bon prince, craignant de perdre sa femme et son enfant ensemble, se délibéra de lui dire vrai du tout. (*Hepta-méron*, 477–78)

([The duchess] pretended that she could feel her unborn child stirring within her, and the poor Duke was so overjoyed at this that he came to her bed. But as his passion was mounting, she turned on her side, and said: "I im-plore you, my husband, since you feel no love, either for your wife or for your child, let us go to our death together!" These words were accompanied by such cries and floods of tears that the Duke was afraid that she would lose the fruit of her womb. . . . [T]he good Duke, terrified lest he lose both wife and child, decided to tell her the whole truth. [Chilton, 524–25])

The pregnancy in *Heptaméron* 70 gives the duchess a way of influenc-ing her husband's policy in his court: she tries to disrupt feudal ties by manipulating the duke's paternal love and his desire for dynastic continuity.

The duchess's effort to influence her husband is not new in Mar-guerite's version of the tale. In the thirteenth-century *Châtelaine de*

Vergi the duchess also seeks to manipulate the duke: she feigns an illness (but not a pregnancy) before she accuses the knight and then, to persuade the duke to reveal the châtelaine's identity, she refuses to have sex with him. Marguerite makes an important shift in the focus of this story. The pregnancy gives the duchess added leverage over the duke, of course, and this is implicit in the suggestion by some critics that Marguerite introduces the pregnancy to explain the duke's shifting loyalties.[30] But the pregnancy also suggests the importance of succession in *Heptaméron* 70. The emphasis on lineage is new in Marguerite's version of the story, and it is further demonstrated in the ending that she adds to the story. After the deaths of the châtelaine and the knight, and after the execution of the duchess, the duke joins a crusade against the Turks. Upon his return he retires to a monastery and relinquishes his duchy to his son. The explicitly recounted succession is not found in the other versions of the story, where there is no concern for the fate of the duchy and no indication of who will inherit it.

In *Heptaméron* 70 a medieval story about the conflict between the constraints of secret love and the obligations of feudal service becomes a drama motivated at least in part by succession concerns. As I suggested earlier, although *La châtelaine de Vergi* does not recount the story of a royal court, the duke's court closely resembles the royal court in similar stories, like *Le roman des sept sages*, *Le roman de Silence*, and *Lanval*. Marguerite's version of the story clearly shows that the duchy is hereditary, and her addition of the duchess's false pregnancy expresses an awareness of succession concerns that is absent in the thirteeth-century version of the story.

This shift may have some links to changes in the French monarchy over the course of the centuries between the composition of *La châtelaine de Vergi* and the *Heptaméron*. In the thirteenth century the Capetians could boast of a relatively long possession of the French crown. Whether due to good luck or to good marriage politics, the Capetians kings had always had sons to inherit the throne. The anxiety about dynasty that overtly structures *La fille du comte de Pontieu* had, in the thirteenth century, always been successfully resolved through the birth of a royal heir. By the time that Marguerite de Navarre wrote the *Heptaméron* the transition of the French crown from Capetian king to Capetian king had long been interrupted. Because none of Philip the Fair's sons produced a surviving male heir, the throne passed to the Valois branch of the royal family in 1328, and then in 1515 to Marguerite's own brother, François I.

Succession anxieties must have been familiar to Marguerite de Navarre. The precarious status first of her father and then of her brother as heir to the king of France dominated her life until the accession of François I in 1515. Marguerite's mother, Louise de Savoie, writes in her journal of the tense period of waiting that she experienced each time the queen of France became pregnant, and she frankly describes her joy at each of the queen's failures to produce a son—which secured her own son's position as future king. Marguerite herself remained childless throughout her fifteen-year marriage to Charles d'Alençon, and her letters to her confidant Briçonnet demonstrate the sorrow and frustration she experienced as a result of her inability to conceive. It is easy to imagine Marguerite's happiness and, perhaps, her relief when she gave birth to her daughter Jeanne d'Albret in 1528, ten months after her marriage to Henri de Navarre. Marguerite also had a son two years after the birth of her daughter, but he died at the age of five and a half months. She had no other surviving children.

At the end of 1531, the year after her son's death, Marguerite de Navarre had a false pregnancy. For several months she believed she was pregnant and refused to travel because of her condition. Jean du Bellay, who was at her court during this period, noted that even Marguerite's doctor believed her to be pregnant. His letters and those of Marguerite herself make it clear that the queen had a hysterical pregnancy, not a miscarriage.[31] Marguerite appears to have had at least two other pregnancies, the last when she was fifty years old.[32] It ended in miscarriage after six months. Marguerite received condolences from her brother, François I, after the loss of this child, and in her reply she tells him that his letter comforted her and "will give her the strength to have yet one more child" ("lui donnera la force d'en avoir encore un").[33]

In the dramatization of succession in *Heptaméron* 70, Marguerite explicitly recounts the importance of maternity that is suppressed in medieval stories of adultery, yet fully played out in medieval and Renaissance aristocratic society. Mothers are powerful and respected figures in Marguerite's tales, yet in *Heptaméron* 70 she assigns the power associated with maternity to the malevolent duchess, who makes an false claim to motherhood and seeks empowerment by appealing to the duke's desire for heirs. However, a consideration of the importance of maternity and succession in the *Heptaméron* and in Marguerite's own life suggests a two-sided representation of the duchess in *Heptaméron* 70.[34] As the direct cause of the tale's tragic ending, the duchess is an evil character. Yet just as Marie de France's tale of the seductress queen represents the queen's manipulation of justice but at the same time shows the fundamental powerlessness of the childless queen in the feudal court, Marguerite's rewriting of the story of the duchess may represent the vulnerability of women to dynastic demands, to the need for heirs that Marguerite herself had certainly experienced.

In *Heptaméron* 70 Marguerite shows that while maternity may empower women, it also figures the limits of women's power, that motherhood may represent a position of influence but that it is the only position of authority available to noblewomen. The duchess's use of motherhood to deceive is not excused in Marguerite's tale—it is shown to be a treacherous act—but Marguerite suggests that the duchess needs the pregnancy to influence her husband to take action against the knight. After hearing the duchess's accusation, the duke confronts the knight but accepts his protests of innocence without proof, or rather the duke accepts as proof the knight's claim of the duchess's undesirability:

"Vous suppliant, Monseigneur, croire deux choses de moi: l'une, que je vous suis si loyal que, quand Madame votre femme serait la plus belle créature du monde, si n'aurait Amour la puissance de mettre tache à mon honneur et fidélité; l'autre est que quand elle ne serait point votre femme, c'est celle que je vis onques dont je serais aussi peu amoureux; et y en a assez d'autres où je mettrais plutôt ma fantaisie." (*Heptaméron*, 472)

("I would ask of you, my lord, to accept my word concerning two things. The first is that my loyalty to you is so true that even were Madame your wife the most beautiful creature in the world, still love would never have the power to stain my honor and my faith; and the second is that even were she not your wife, she of all the women in the world is the one whose love I least would seek; there are many others to whom [my fancy] would be sooner drawn." [Chilton, 519])

Far from insulted at the knight's appraisal of his wife, the duke accepts the knight's defense even though at this point it is simply a question of the duchess's word against the knight's: "Hearing these truthful words, the Duke began to soften, and said: 'I assure you that I have not believed her'" ("je ne l'ai pas crue").[35] The bond between the duke and the knight seems to outweigh the duke's bond to his wife. It is only her claim of pregnancy that gives the duchess's accusation enough credibility to provoke the duke to seek proof of the knight's innocence. The duchess uses her position as a mother to gain authority.

In adding the pregnancy to the story of the seductress queen, Marguerite de Navarre restores maternity to the representation of women's power. She acknowledges a source of influence and authority for royal women that is obscured in medieval stories of adulterous aristocratic women. Yet as a position of power, motherhood has definite limits in *Heptaméron* 70. In her rewriting of the story of the seductress queen, Marguerite may be seen to extend the exploration of the link between sexual desire and power in *Le roman des sept sages*, *Le roman de Silence*, and *Lanval*. Marguerite's duchess is ultimately ineffectual; her power, like that of other seductress queens, is thwarted. However, where medieval narratives focus on the potential or actual disruption in feudal bonds caused by the queen's attempt to manipulate her husband, Marguerite concentrates on the form of agency available to the noble wife in a way that implicitly critiques its limitations. Marguerite's own involvement throughout her life in a series of anxieties about succession surely influenced the introduction of dynastic concerns in *Heptaméron* 70: she writes from experience of both the influence and power available to women because of family ties and of the limits of a power that must be grounded in and legitimized by maternity.

Maternity and Power

While both Marguerite de Navarre and Marie de France acknowledge the political power that a woman might gain as wife of a powerful lord or as mother of his heirs, they also demonstrate the limited
scope of that power. In *Lanval* a wife's demand for justice cannot
supersede the king's obligations to consider the advice of his advisors, and in *Heptaméron* 70 the duchess succeeds in manipulating her
husband by speaking as the mother of his children, but her maternity
cannot save her from the duke's punishment when he learns of her
attempted adultery and vengeance. *Lanval* and *Heptameron* 70 might
be seen to offer a reassuring response to romances like *Le roman des
sept sages* and *Le roman de Silence*. The structure of the feudal court,
defined by mutual obligations between men, between the sovereign
and his vassals, contains and destroys the malevolent influence of
the woman who would use political power in the service of sexual
pleasure.

Royal maternity defines not only a relationship between a king
and a queen, but also, and perhaps more importantly, between a
queen and her son. A queen's influence over her son may represent
a less precarious avenue to political agency than the uncertain reception her words may receive from her husband. Many romances
recount the story of a powerful mother who intervenes in her son's
court. Like the seductress queen, the romance queen mother who
exercises political authority is usually an evil character, but whereas
seductress queens use political power to pursue sexual desire, queens
who are evil mothers act out of a desire to preserve political power.
In the thirteenth-century *Roman de la Manekine* and its analogues, a
queen views her son's wife as a younger, more beautiful rival for her
son's affection and for power in his court. When her daughter-in-law
gives birth in the king's absence, the queen mother sends word to
her son of a monstrous birth. She uses a story of corrupted lineage to
eliminate the king's wife and son from court and to preempt the influence her daughter-in-law might gain as mother of the king's heir.

While the story of the duchess in *Heptaméron* 70 exposes the
limits of the influence aristocratic women might gain through ma-

ternity, romances about evil mothers suggest that the position of the mother of a powerful man was itself a powerful position. Both kinds of stories ultimately condemn women who intervene in political decisions, but they also suggest that a woman's access to power through maternity represented an unsettling possibility in medieval society.

The representation of evil mothers who profit from their sons' absence to increase their own political power in thirteenth-century romances may represent one voice in a larger contemporary debate about mothers and political power in the French monarchy, a debate possibly intensified by the regency of Blanche of Castile after the death of Louis VIII in 1226. The idea of a regency was not well defined in thirteenth-century France and the term "régente" does not appear until close to a century later.[36] According to feudal custom, a widow could retain the custody of her children and govern a fief after her husband's death, but she acted according to the advice and direction of vassals. Robert Fawtier claims that

To all intents and purposes [Blanche] may be counted among the kings of France. For from 1226 until her death in 1252 she governed the kingdom. Twice she was regent: from 1226 to 1234, while Louis IX was a minor, and from 1248 to 1252 during his first absence on crusade. Between 1234 and 1248 Blanche bore no official title, but her power was no less effective.[37]

As regent, Blanche became the focus for attacks against the increasing centralization of royal power. She was accused of using her power as regent to serve her own interests, and in particular, of sending funds from the royal treasury to Spain.[38] Attacks against royal power focused not on the monarchy but on the fitness of women to rule. The poet Hugues de la Ferté claims that the legitimate paternity of the *patria* is corrupted by a woman's rule ("Bien est France abatardie . . . Quant feme l'a en baillie"; "France is made a bastard . . . when a woman rules" [39]), and this maxim is applied to Blanche's regency, according to the author of the *Chroniques de Saint-Denis*: "The barons objected to the king that Queen Blanche, his mother, should not govern such a great thing as the kingdom of France and that it was not appropriate that a woman do such a thing."[40]

This anxiety about women and government also takes a predictable form for readers of Old French romances: Blanche of Castile was also accused of sexual transgression. The queen was accused first of being the lover of the cardinal's envoy Romain Frangipani and subsequently of being pregnant with his child. The Ménestrel de Reims records that when the royal councillors did not immediately reject the accusations, the queen appeared before them in her chemise, climbed up on a table, "turned around before them so that each one could see her, and it was clear that she had no children in her belly."[41] Although Queen's Blanche's fidelity during her marriage was never questioned by her enemies, the queen's sexual misconduct was nonetheless linked to illegitimacy: the "bastardization" of the kingdom cited by Hugues de la Ferté. In other words, if maternity represents a potential source of power for medieval royal women, it also dictates the form of attacks against that power: accusations of adultery and illegitimacy. These are also the accusations that motivate the official exclusion of women from royal succession in France.

Conclusion: Gendering Sovereignty in Medieval France

IN 1314 KING PHILIP IV THE FAIR had the wives of his three sons arrested on charges of adultery. Marguerite of Burgundy, wife of Prince Louis, king of Navarre and the future Louis X, and Blanche of Burgundy, wife of Charles, count of La Marche and the future Charles IV, were accused of having carried on a three-year liaison with two brothers, Philip and Gautier d'Aunay. Jeanne of Burgundy, wife of Philip, count of Poitiers and the future Philip V, was charged with having a complicitious knowledge of the affairs. The charges against Jeanne were dropped soon after they were made. Marguerite died in prison. Blanche continued to defend her innocence during seven years of imprisonment. She was repudiated by her husband Charles in 1322, the year of his accession to the throne, and she died in a convent in 1326. The two knights accused of being the lovers of the king's daughters-in-law were executed immediately after their arrest.[1]

The adultery scandal during the last year of the reign of Philip the Fair also marks the chronological end-point of the representation of the courtly adulterous queen in medieval romances. This is not a causal relationship, but it is not an arbitrary one either. I began this study by citing the rumors that accused Eleanor of Aquitaine of adultery with her uncle, Raymond of Antioch. Whatever Eleanor's relationship to the poetry of courtly love might have been, it is implausible to assert that she attempted to live according to the ethic of *fine amors*. Nor did she invent the figure of the adulterous queen. Eleanor's relationship to twelfth-century literary representations of queenship and adultery is less direct and more subtle, as I have tried to suggest. Both fictional and nonfictional queens are defined by cultural ideas about sovereignty and its symbolic networks, about succession and royal dynasty, about women and power. As these ideas evolve over time they are negotiated in institutional changes like the gradual marginalization of queens from government in the Capetian monarchy, and they are debated in literary representations like romances. Narratives about adulterous queens recount in fictional form some of the most important negotiations in the evolution of queenship in the twelfth and thirteenth centuries: the importance of royal succession and the relative influence of the queen in her husband's court. Romances about adulterous queens from this period also participate in an increasingly explicit definition of royal sovereignty as masculine. I return to the adultery scandal in Philip the Fair's court to explore this idea.

Adulterous queens were well-known literary characters in the Middle Ages, but they did not appear in Capetian courts. The rumors about Eleanor of Aquitaine's liaison with her uncle were as close as any Capetian queen came to being accused of adultery. Until the fourteenth century, Capetian kings had enjoyed not only a long series of faithful wives, but also a long period of uninterrupted succession; they always had sons to inherit the throne. When Philip the Fair died, each of his three sons reigned in turn. None produced a surviving male heir, and in 1328 the Capetian throne passed to Philip VI of Valois. The discovery of the adultery of Philip the Fair's daughters-in-law thus directly precedes the end of the Capetian dynasty and it realizes the anxieties that underlie romance representations of adulterous queens: the discovery of the queen's adultery and the suspicion of a corrupted lineage. An examination of the end of the Capetian succession in the early fourteenth century may suggest why romance representations of courtly adulterous queens end with the Capetian dynasty.

If romance queens can combine transgressive sexual pleasure and the privileges of queenship it is of course because they are fictional queens. Despite the rumors that followed Eleanor of Aquitaine's visit to Antioch, nonfictional queens were in general models of chastity, and if romance adulterous queens were part of a cultural debate on the nature of queenship, their place in this process depended on their fictional status. Once the uniquely fictional status of the adulterous queen is challenged, as in the accusations of adultery against two royal daughters-in-law, the representation of challenges to royal sovereignty in the form of fictions about the queen's sexual transgression is no longer possible. Romances composed after the adultery scandal in the last year of Philip IV's reign ignore the courtly adulterous queens of twelfth- and thirteenth-century romance. *Ysaÿe le Triste*, a fifteenth-century prose romance, may illustrate the new form of the adulterous queen's story. This romance recounts the adventures of the son of Tristan and Iseut, a son whose story is silenced in earlier romances about the lovers, according to its narrator.[2] Iseut gives birth to this illegitimate son and abandons him in a forest. After introducing his origins, the narrator goes on to recount Ysaÿe's adventures, but even as a frame narrative, Iseut's story is striking in its emphasis on the queen's maternity and on the problem of illegitimacy.

It would be rash to suggest that the disappearance of the courtly adulterous queen as a subject of romance is entirely due to an adultery scandal in the court of Philip the Fair. It is also influenced by the introduction of the grail quest into the stories of Iseut and Guenevere in the thirteenth-century prose romances that recount their stories, and by evolutions in the form of romance, particularly the growing prominence of allegorical narratives. Nonetheless, it is not implausible to suggest that after the adultery scandal in Philip's court, and particularly after the failure of the Capetian succession, the representation of the courtly adulterous queen whose transgressive sexuality contributes to the political stability of her husband's court is no longer a viable way to imagine a relationship between women and power.

Throughout this study I have emphasized the importance of succession concerns as an unacknowledged but important aspect of the representation of the barren adulterous queen. Succession is not directly disrupted as a result of the adultery scandal of 1314, but it is implicated in the deliberations that replaced the king with his brother rather than his daughter. Louis X, who succeeded his father, Philip the Fair, in 1314, had a daughter from his marriage to Marguerite of Burgundy, and when he died in 1316 his second wife, Clemence of Hungary, was pregnant. The queen gave birth to a son, John I, who lived only a few days. Philip of Poitiers, the king's brother, then claimed the throne, displacing Louis's daughter, Jeanne. The role of gender in the succession is disputed. Charles T. Wood cautions that, although there was already considerable sentiment against the succession rights of women, it would be dangerous to assert that gender played a decisive role in excluding Jeanne from the throne. Wood suggests that it is the possible illegitimacy of Jeanne—her mother's alleged adulterous affair dated from the year before her birth—that excluded her from the inheritance and that "succession devolved on Philip V largely because, given Jeanne's possible illegitimacy he was Louis X's closest blood heir."[3]

Andrew W. Lewis also valorizes the importance of blood relationships in Philip's succession and acknowledges the role played by Jeanne's possible illegitimacy, but he emphasizes not illegitimacy but a newly formed idea of the royal family that includes the exclusion of women's inheritance as a defining characteristic:

The accession of Philip V was based on, and produced, a rejection of the laws of patrimonial inheritance in favor of a special law applied to the kingdom. The new ordering of the royal succession made the royal family different from any other. Several factors contributed to this turn of events, but the essential and perhaps determinate one seems to have been that the preeminence of the French crown excluded women from the royal succession.[4]

Like Wood, Lewis notes that the sentiment in favor of the exclusion of women from succession predates Philip V's accession, and as probable evidence of Philip the Fair's opposition to women's rule he cites a marriage negotiation that was begun for Jeanne during the final years of Philip the Fair's reign. In the document prepared by the king's chief minister, Enguerrand de Marigny, it was stipulated that Jeanne could not inherit the throne of France or of Navarre except by special grace of the king.[5] Wood cites the reversion clause in Philip IV's award of Poitiers to his son Philip as further evidence of the preparation for the exclusion of Jeanne.[6] Wood also notes the uncertainty surrounding the succession: "While the fact that no woman had ever held the throne might have suggested that no woman could, . . . thanks to the regencies of queen mothers, both real and contingent, the principle of male succession was far from being established."[7] After Philip V was crowned in 1317, effectively excluding Jeanne, an assembly held in Paris ruled that a woman could not succeed to the French throne.[8] The exclusion was repeated when Philip V and then his brother Charles IV died without male heirs, and it prepared the way for the elaboration of the Salic law later in the century.

In a rhetorical sense, royal sovereignty has always been conceptualized as male in medieval Europe; even when a reigning queen occupied the throne she was named with masculine pronouns in treatises that described her functions in the royal court. Ernst Kantorowicz has suggested that the corporate body of the ruler is sexless, and he cites the example of the late eighth-century Athenian empress Irene who was spoken of as "emperor" in official documents while she was regent for her son.[9] But Janet Nelson notes that a view of gendered "imperium" was also possible during this period. She cites an explanation of why Charlemagne became emperor on Christmas day in 800:

Because the title of emperor was at this time lacking among the Greeks and they had among them the rulership of a woman [femineum imperium], it seemed to the pope, the holy fathers and the rest of the Christian people that they ought to give Charles himself the title of emperor.[10]

Nelson notes that "femineum imperium" is used in this document as "a contradiction in terms."[11] Kantorowicz also admits that, when women are excluded from succession, "the king's 'Body corporate' could probably not claim sexlessness."[12]

The developments in the last years of the Capetian monarchy seem to realize the worst anxieties represented in medieval romance narratives about adulterous queens. Adultery is discovered and cannot be covered up; two potential queens are condemned, one dies in prison, one is repudiated; and an heir to the royal throne is excluded because of suspicions of illegitimacy. The similarities are not entirely coincidental. Romances do not predict or inspire historical events, but they are part of the intellectual and imaginative preparation for those events. If the early fourteenth century sees the exclusion of women from the succession of the royal throne, it is not because of a sudden distaste for women's rule but because of a questioning of the appropriateness of women's succession that is evidenced in oblique form in the debates surrounding the twelfth-century queens Urraca of Castile and León, Melisende of Jerusalem, and Matilda of England,[13] and in fictional narratives about adulterous queens. Fictional adulterous queens are queens consort, but their access to royal power is always at issue, whether in the form of the symbolic representation of the king's sovereignty in the state of the queen's body, in the queen's ability to deceive her husband and enjoy both royal privilege and sexual pleasure, or in the queen's manipulation of her husband to protext her own (sexual) interests.

In an examination of the portrayal of royal women by medieval clerics, Pauline Stafford has shown how the vocabulary available for descriptions of women and their access to power evolved through changes in narrative conventions. She notes that, in the mid- to late tenth century, that vocabulary "was heavily influenced by hagiographical conventions casting women in limited and predictable roles. It already utilized images adapted from women's family roles."[14] Stafford traces an evolution in the representation of royal power to the twelfth century, a period that "had begun to produce a language of politics, a way of talking about the problems of power."[15] It has been the goal of this study to situate romance narratives within the evolution described by Stafford as one of the discourses about women and power available to writers in the twelfth and thirteenth centuries. Romances about adulterous queens seem to lose their utility as discourses about government at the beginning of the fourteenth century. At the same time that discovery of adultery among Philip the Fair's daughters-in-law enacts some of the consequences for royal sovereignty imagined in romance narratives, it also resolves some of the tensions that motivate the representation of the fictional adulterous queen. If the subject becomes a dangerous one after the adultery scandal of 1314, in the wake of the exclusion of women from royal succession it also loses urgency as a subject of narrative that negotiates anxieties about women's access to political power.

Notes

Introduction

1. The *"Historia Pontificalis" of John of Salisbury*, ed. and trans. Marjorie Chibnall (Oxford: Oxford University Press, 1986), 52–62.

2. William of Tyre, "Historia rerum in partibus transmarinis gestarum," *Recueil des historiens des croisades. Historiens occidentaux* (Paris: Imprimerie Nationale, 1845), 1: 752; translation from William, Archbishop of Tyre, *A History of Deeds Done Beyond the Sea*, trans. Emily Atwater Babcock and A.C. Krey, 2 vols. (New York: Columbia University Press, 1943), II: 180.

3. Georges Duby, *The Knight, the Lady and the Priest: The Making of Marriage in Medieval France*, trans. Barbara Bray (New York: Pantheon, 1983), 189–96. I discuss this incident in the context of succession politics below, 12–13.

4. Rita Lejeune, "Le rôle littéraire d'Aliénor d'Aquitaine et de sa famille," *Cultura Neolatina* 14 (1954): 5–57; and "Le rôle littéraire de la famille d'Aliénor d'Aquitaine," *Cahiers de Civilisation Médiévale* 1 (1958): 303–20; Moshé Lazar, "Cupid, the Lady, and the Poet: Modes of Love at Eleanor of Aquitaine's Court," *Eleanor of Aquitaine: Patron and Politician*, ed. William W. Kibler, Symposia in the Arts and the Humanities 3 (Austin: University of Texas Press, 1976), 35–59; D. D. R. Owen, *Eleanor of Aquitaine: Queen and Legend* (Oxford: Blackwell, 1993), 162–212; Edmond-René Labande, "Pour une image véridique d'Aliénor d'Aquitaine," *Bulletin de la Société des Antiquaires de l'Ouest* 4th ser. 2 (1952): 175–234; Ruth E. Harvey, *The Troubadour Marcabru and Love* (London: Westfield College, University of London Committee for Medieval Studies, 1989), 131–39.

5. For various approaches to courtly love, see Roger Boase, *The Origin and Meaning of Courtly Love* (Manchester: Manchester University Press, 1977); C. S. Lewis, *The Allegory of Love* (Oxford: Oxford University Press, 1958); Christiane Marchello-Nizia, "Amour courtois, société masculine, et figures du pouvoir," *Annales: Economies, Sociétés, Civilisations* 36, 6 (1981): 969–82; F. X. Newman, ed., *The Meaning of Courtly Love* (Albany, N.Y.: SUNY Press, 1968); and Francis L. Utley, "Must We Abandon the Concept of Courtly Love?" *Medievalia et Humanistica* n.s. 3 (1972): 299–324.

6. Janet L. Nelson, "Queens as Jezebels: The Careers of Brunhild and Balthild in Merovingian History," *Medieval Women*, ed. Derek Baker (Oxford: Blackwell, 1978), 39.

7. Nelson, "Queens as Jezebels," 36–39.

8. Geneviève Bührer-Thierry, "La reine adultère," *Cahiers de Civilisation Médiévale* 35 (1992): 300.

9. Bührer-Thierry, "La reine adultère," 300–301. For other sources that recognize the importance of the queen's role within the palace and the kingdom and for further discussion of the model of Esther, see Lois L. Huneycutt, "Intercession and the High-Medieval Queen: The Esther Topos," *The Power of the Weak: Studies on Medieval Women*, ed. Jennifer Carpenter and Sally-Beth MacLean (Urbana and Chicago: University of Illinois Press, 1995), 126–46.

10. Bührer-Thierry, "La reine adultère," 299.

11. Marion F. Facinger, "A Study of Medieval Queenship: Capetian France, 987–1237," *Studies in Medieval and Renaissance History* 5 (1968): 27–29; see also Robert Fawtier, *The Capetian Kings of France: Monarchy and Nation, 987–1328*, trans. Lionel Butler and R. J. Adam (London: Macmillan, 1960), 27–28. Roger Collins notes that in the royal charters of the tenth-century kingdom of Pamplona, kings and queens are represented as ruling jointly. "Queens-Dowager and Queens-Regent in Tenth-Century León and Navarre," *Medieval Queenship*, ed. John Carmi Parsons (New York: St. Martin's Press, 1993), 90.

12. Facinger, "A Study of Medieval Queenship," 28–29. See also Andrew W. Lewis, *Royal Succession in Capetian France: Studies on Familial Order and the State* (Cambridge, Mass.: Harvard University Press, 1981), 55.

13. Facinger, "A Study of Medieval Queenship," 32–40.

14. Facinger, "A Study of Medieval Queenship," 38–39; John W. Baldwin, *The Government of Philip Augustus: Foundations of French Royal Power in the Middle Ages* (Berkeley and Los Angeles: University of California Press, 1986), 83–84, 357; Inge Skovgaard-Petersen with Nanna Damsholt, "Queenship in Medieval Denmark," *Medieval Queenship*, ed. John Carmi Parsons (New York: St. Martin's Press, 1993), 29.

15. Gabrielle M. Spiegel, "The *Reditus Regni ad Stirpem Karoli Magni*: A New Look," *French Historical Studies* 7 (1971): 156–57.

16. Lewis, *Royal Succession in Capetian France*, 47–50.

17. John Carmi Parsons, "The Queen's Intercession in Thirteenth-Century England," *The Power of the Weak: Studies on Medieval Women*, ed. Jennifer Carpenter and Sally-Beth MacLean (Urbana and Chicago: University of Illinois Press, 1995), 149.

18. Parsons, "The Queen's Intercession," 149–50.

19. Claire Richter Sherman, "The Queen in Charles V's 'Coronation Book': Jeanne de Bourbon and the 'Ordo ad reginam benedicendam,'" *Viator* 8 (1977): 293.

20. Joan A. Holladay, "The Education of Jeanne d'Evreux: Personal Piety and Dynastic Salvation in Her Book of Hours at the Cloisters," *Art History* 17, 4 (1994): 603–4.

21. Madeline H. Caviness, "Patron or Matron? A Capetian Bride and a Vade Mecum for Her Marriage Bed," *Speculum* 68 (1993): 343.

22. Huneycutt, "Intercession and the High-Medieval Queen," 131.

23. Huneycutt, "Intercession and the High-Medieval Queen," 131–38; Pauline Stafford, *Queens, Concubines, and Dowagers: The King's Wife in the Early Middle Ages* (Athens: University of Georgia Press, 1983), 195.

24. Huneycutt, "Intercession and the High-Medieval Queen," 126–46.

25. Parsons, "The Queen's Intercession," 162.

26. Parsons, "The Queen's Intercession," 153–54. Parsons cites Victor Turner's definition of Mary as "the Church in nonlegalistic form." For a perceptive and provocative discussion of liminality and sovereignty, see Louise Olga Fradenburg, *City, Marriage, Tournament; Arts of Rule in Late Medieval Scotland* (Madison: University of Wisconson Press, 1991), 73–83, esp. 73–75.

27. Paul Strohm, *Hochon's Arrow: The Social Imagination of Fourteenth-Century Texts* (Princeton, N.J.: Princeton University Press, 1992), 101.

28. Strohm, *Hochon's Arrow*, 99–102; quote p. 101.

29. John Carmi Parsons, "Ritual and Symbol in the English Medieval Queenship to 1500," *Women and Sovereignty*, ed. Louise Olga Fradenburg, Cosmos 7 (Edinburgh: Edinburgh University Press, 1992), 67.

30. Sharon Farmer, "Persuasive Voices: Clerical Images of Medieval Wives," *Speculum* 61 (1986): 517–43.

31. Stafford, *Queens, Concubines, and Dowagers*, 152.

32. André Poulet, "Capetian Women and the Regency: The Genesis of a Vocation," *Medieval Queenship*, ed. John Carmi Parsons (New York: St. Martin's Press, 1993), 110. Elizabeth McCartney has shown how comparisons of Louise de Savoie to Blanche of Castile were used to justify the regency of a king's mother who had never been a queen. "The King's Mother and Royal Prerogative in Early-Sixteenth-Century France," *Medieval Queenship*, ed. John Carmi Parsons (New York: St. Martin's Press, 1993), 117–41.

33. John Carmi Parsons, "Mothers, Daughters, Marriage, Power: Some Plantagenet Evidence, 1150–1500," *Medieval Queenship*, ed. Parsons (New York: St. Martin's Press, 1993), 63–78.

34. Caviness, "Patron or Matron?" 346, 355.

35. *Speculum dominarum*, Bibliothèque Nationale ms. latin 6784. The text was rewritten for Marguerite de Navarre by Ysambert de Saint-Leger in the sixteenth century. For a discussion of the various forms of the text, see Ysambert de Saint-Leger, *Le miroir des dames*, ed. Camillo Marazza (Lece: Micella, 1978).

36. Pauline Stafford, "The Portrayal of Royal Women in England,

Mid-Tenth to Mid-Twelfth Centuries," *Medieval Queenship*, ed. John Carmi Parsons (New York: St. Martin's Press, 1993), 145.

37. Huneycutt, "Intercession and the High-Medieval Queen," 138.

38. Bührer-Thierry, "La reine adultère," 300.

39. Stafford, *Queens, Concubines, and Dowagers*, 82.

40. John Carmi Parsons, "Introduction. Family, Sex, and Power: The Rhythms of Medieval Queenship," *Medieval Queenship*, ed. Parsons (New York: St. Martin's Press, 1993), 5; Duby, *The Knight, the Lady and the Priest*, 204–5; Baldwin, *The Government of Philip Augustus*, 206–7.

41. Duby, *The Knight, the Lady and the Priest*, 57–58; Robert Bartlett, *Trial by Fire and Water : The Medieval Judicial Ordeal* (Oxford: Oxford University Press, 1986), 16–17; Dyan Elliott, *Spiritual Marriage: Sexual Abstinence in Medieval Wedlock* (Princeton, N.J.: Princeton University Press, 1993), 129–131.

42. Bartlett, *Trial by Fire and Water*, 17; Parsons, "Introduction," 5.

43. Elliott, *Spiritual Marriage*, 129.

44. John of Salisbury, *Historia Pontificalis*, 53; William of Tyre, *A History of Deeds*, 2: 196.

45. "licet reginam affectu fere immoderto diligeret," *Historia Pontificalis*, 53.

46. Jane Martindale, "Eleanor of Aquitaine," *Richard Coeur de Lion in History and Myth*, ed. Janet L. Nelson, King's College London Medieval Studies 7 (London: King's College London Centre for Late Antique and Medieval Studies, 1992), 41. On doubts about the queen's fertility, see p. 39, and Poulet, "Capetian Women and the Regency," 103.

47. "[L]i mieudres consaus que nous vous sachiens donner, ce est que vous la laissiez aleir; car c'est uns diables, et se vous la tenez longuement nous doutons qu'elle ne vous face mourdrir. Et ensourquetout vous n'avez nul enfant de li." *Récits d'un ménestrel de Reims au treizième siècle*, ed. Natalis de Wailly (Paris: Renouard, 1876), 6. See below pp. 132–33 for a discussion of this text.

48. Strohm, *Hochon's Arrow*, 96.

49. Parsons, "Ritual and Symbol," 69.

50. Bernard F. Reilly, *The Kingdom of León-Castilla Under Queen Urraca, 1109–1126* (Princeton, N.J.: Princeton University Press, 1982), 45–86.

51. Hans Eberhard Mayer, "Studies in the History of Queen Melisende of Jerusalem," *Dumbarton Oaks Papers* 26 (1972): 93–182; Bernard Hamilton, "Women in the Crusader States: The Queens of Jerusalem (1100–1190)," *Medieval Women*, ed. Derek Baker (Oxford: Blackwell, 1978), 149–57.

52. Marjorie Chibnall, *The Empress Matilda: Queen Consort, Queen Mother and Lady of the English* (Oxford: Blackwell, 1991), 64–87.

53. Cary J. Nederman and N. Elaine Lawson, "The Frivolities of Courtiers Follow the Footprints of Women: Public Women and the Crisis of

Virility in John of Salisbury," *Ambiguous Realities: Women in the Middle Ages and Renaissance*, ed. Carole Levin and Jeanie Watson (Detroit: Wayne State University Press, 1987), 85–86. Nederman and Lawson claim that John recognized and accepted the inevitability of women's involvement in public affairs (93).

54. Lois L. Huneycutt, "Female Succession and the Language of Power in the Writings of Twelfth-Century Churchmen," *Medieval Queenship*, ed. John Carmi Parsons (New York: St. Martin's Press, 1993), 195.

55. Huneycut, "Female Succession," 198.

56. Reilly, *The Kingdom of León-Castilla*, 46; Mayer "Studies in the History of Queen Melisende," 102–6, 110.

57. For coronations, see Parsons, "Ritual and Symbol," Sherman, "The Queen in Charles V's *Coronation Book*"; on books of hours, see Caviness, "Patron or Matron?" and Holladay, "The Education of Jeanne d'Evreux"; on financial records, Margaret Howell, "The Resources of Eleanor of Provence as Queen Consort," *English Historical Review* 102 (1987): 372–93.

58. Sarah Kay, "The Tristan Story as Chivalric Romance, Feudal Epic and Fabliau," *The Spirit of the Court: Selected Proceedings of the Fourth Congress of the International Courtly Literature Society*, ed. Glyn S. Burgess and Robert A. Taylor (Cambridge: D. S. Brewer, 1985), 187; Matilda Tomaryn Bruckner, *Shaping Romance: Interpretation, Truth, and Closure in Twelfth-Century French Fictions* (Philadelphia: University of Pennsylvania Press, 1993), 94.

59. Joan Tasker Grimbert provides a thorough discussion of the different developments of the Tristan story and their different emphases in her introduction to *Tristan and Isolde: A Casebook*, ed. Grimbert (New York: Garland, 1995), xiii–ci. On the relationship of the *Prose Tristan* to the French verse versions of the romance, see also Emmanuèle Baumgartner, *Le Tristan en prose: Essai d'interprétation d'un roman médiéval* (Geneva: Droz, 1975), 110–17.

60. W. J. McCann, "Tristan: The Celtic and Oriental Material Reexamined," *Tristan and Isolde: A Casebook*, ed. Joan Tasker Grimbert (New York: Garland, 1995), 3–35.

61. For a discussion of the history of the *commune/courtoise* distinction and a discussion of its usefulness, see Grimbert, "Introduction," xxvii–xxviii.

62. Tony Hunt, "The Significance of Thomas's *Tristan*," *Reading Medieval Studies* 7 (1981): 41–61; Joan Tasker Grimbert, "*Voleir* v. *Poeir*: Frustrated Desire in Thomas's *Roman de Tristan*," *Philological Quarterly* 69 (1990): 153–65.

63. Douglas Kelly, "*Fine Amor* in Thomas's *Tristan*," *Studies in Honor of Hans-Erich Keller*, ed. Rupert T. Pickens (Kalamazoo, Mich.: Medieval Institute Publications, 1993), 175.

64. Jean-Charles Payen, "Lancelot contre Tristan: la conjuration d'un

mythe subversif (réflexions sur l'idéologie romanesque au moyen âge)," *Mélanges de langue et de littérature médiévales offerts à Pierre Le Gentil* (Paris: SEDES et CDU, 1973), 617–32.

65. F. Douglas Kelly, *Sens and Conjointure in the* Chevalier de la charrete (The Hague: Mouton, 1966), 6. For an overview of the sources and traditions of the Lancelot and Guenevere story, see Lori J. Walters, "Introduction," *Lancelot and Guinevere: A Casebook*, ed. Walters (New York: Garland, 1996), xiii–lxix.

66. On the "relative severity" of the prose authors toward adultery in the *Prose Lancelot*, see Jean-Charles Payen, "Figures féminines dans le roman médiéval français," *Entretiens sur la renaissance du douzième siècle*, ed. Maurice de Gandillac and Edouard Jeauneau (Paris: Mouton, 1968), 416.

67. On the different qualities of the potion in the various versions of the *Tristan* story, see Jean Frappier, "Structure et sens du Tristan: version commune, version courtoise," *Cahiers de Civilisation Médiévale* 6 (1963): 273–74, and Renée L. Curtis, "The Character of Iseut in the Prose Tristan (Parts I and II)," *Mélanges de littérature du moyen âge au XXe siècle offerts à Mlle Jeanne Lods*, 2 vols. (Paris: Ecole Normale Supérieure de Jeunes Filles, 1978), 1: 174–75.

68. *Erec et Enide*, v. 424.

69. Erich Köhler, *L'aventure chevaleresque: Idéal et réalité dans le roman courtois*, trans. Eliane Kaufholz (Paris: Gallimard, 1974); Georges Duby, "Les 'jeunes' dans la société aristocratique dans la France du Nord-Ouest au XIIIe siècle," in his *Hommes et structures au moyen âge* (Paris: Mouton, 1973), 213–25; R. Howard Bloch, *Medieval French Literature and Law* (Berkeley and Los Angeles: University of California Press, 1977) and *Etymologies and Genealogies: A Literary Anthropology of the French Middle Ages* (Chicago: University of Chicago Press, 1983); Sandra Hindman, *Sealed in Parchment: Rereadings of Knighthood in the Illuminated Manuscripts of Chrétien de Troyes* (Chicago: University of Chicago Press, 1994).

70. Georges Duby, "Women and Power," *Cultures of Power: Lordship, Status, and Process in Twelfth-Century Europe*, ed. Thomas N. Bisson (Philadelphia: University of Pennsylvania Press, 1995), 71.

71. Simon Gaunt, *Gender and Genre in Medieval French Literature* (Cambridge: Cambridge University Press, 1995), 109.

72. On the displacement of a moral structure in twelfth-century *Tristan* romances, see Jean-Claude Payen, *Le motif du repentir dans la littérature médiévale française* (Geneva: Droz, 1967), 331–64; on the *Prose Lancelot*, see Elspeth Kennedy, *Lancelot and the Grail: A Study of the Prose Lancelot* (Oxford: Oxford University Press, 1986), 77–78.

Chapter One

1. My translation. "Mult fu de grant afaitement / Et de noble cun-tienement; / Mult fu large et buene parliere, / Artur l'ama mult et tint chiere; / Mais entr'els dous n'orent nul eir / Ne ne porent emfant aveir" (Wace, *Le roman de Brut*, ed. Ivor Arnold, 2 vols. [Paris: SATF, 1938–40], vv. 9653–58).

2. Layamon, *Brut*, ed. G. L. Brook and R. F. Leslie, 2 vols., EETS o.s. 250, 277 (Oxford: Oxford University Press, 1963), vv. 2025. It has been suggested that Wace's description of Arthur's coronation was modeled on Henry II's. See Rebecca A. Baltzer, "Music in the Life and Times of Eleanor of Aquitaine," *Eleanor of Aquitaine: Patron and Politician*, ed. William W. Kibler (Austin: University of Texas Press, 1976), 66. Baltzer cites Yvonne Rokseth, *Polyphonies du XIIIe siècle: Le manuscrit H 196 de la Faculté de Méde-cine de Montpellier*, 4 vols. (Paris: Editions de l'Oiseau-Lyre, 1935–39), 4: 40.

3. Owen, *Eleanor of Aquitaine*, 182–83.

4. Owen, *Eleanor of Aquitaine*, 183.

5. However, M. Victoria Guerin argues that Geoffrey of Monmouth, Wace's source, was aware of the tradition that makes Mordred the son of Arthur's incestuous relationship with his sister. *The Fall of Kings and Princes: Structure and Destruction in Arthurian Tragedy* (Stanford, Calif.: Stanford University Press, 1995), 10–15.

6. For medieval medical views on conception and fertility, see Joan Cadden, *Meanings of Sex Difference in the Middle Ages: Medicine, Science, and Culture* (Cambridge: Cambridge University Press, 1993), 54–104; Danielle Jacquart and Claude Thomasset, *Sexuality and Medicine in the Middle Ages*, trans. Matthew Adamson (Princeton, N.J.: Princeton University Press, 1988), 66–69, 130–38.

7. *Le haut livre du graal, Perlesvaus*, ed. William A. Nitze and T. Atkin-son Jenkins, 2 vols. (Chicago: University of Chicago Press, 1932), 1: 272–73. This is one of only two texts that explicitly name Loholt as the son of Guene-vere, though Arthur is commonly named as his father. For a comparative discussion of Loholt in medieval literature, see Keith Busby, "The Enigma of Loholt," *An Arthurian Tapestry: Essays in Memory of Lewis Thorpe*, ed. Kenneth Varty (Glasgow: French Department of the University of Glasgow, 1981), 28–36.

8. Although the chaos of disputed paternity for the queen's son is consistently refused in medieval romance, it is fully exploited in the stories of the king's illegitimate children, the most famous example being Arthur's son Mordred, who enacts the destruction of his father's kingdom. See *La mort le roi Artu*, 211.

9. Marchello-Nizia, "Amour courtois," 980. I will return to Marchello-Nizia's analysis of how the queen's adultery functions in a political dynamic later in this chapter and thoroughout this study.

10. Duby, *The Knight, the Lady and the Priest*, 222.

11. Even Arthur and Charlemagne are illegitimate sons in some narratives. For a discussion of these figures and of illegitimate sons of kings (but not of queens), see Dominique Boutet, "Bâtardise et sexualité dans l'image littéraire de la royauté (XIIe–XIIIe siècles)," *Femmes: Mariages-lignages, XIIe–XIVe siècles: Mélanges offerts à Georges Duby*, Bibliothèque du Moyen Age 1 (Brussels: De Boeck-Wesmael, 1992), 55–68.

12. As in Gottfried's *Tristan*: "Thereafter Mark's councillors adopted a policy of importuning him morning and evening with urgent advice to take a wife from whom he could get an heir, either a son or a daughter" (Gottfried, 151). James A. Schultz has shown how Mark's decision to marry functions as both a cause and an efect in the structure of narrative motivation in Gottfried's romance. "Why Does Mark Marry Isolde? And Why Do We Care? An Essay on Narrative Motivation," *Deutsche vierteljahrs Schrift für Literaturwissenschaft und Geistesgeschichte* 61, 2 (1987): 206–22, esp. 219.

13. "Cil qui fist d'Erec et d'Enide, / Et les comandemenz d'Ovide / Et l'art d'amors an romans mist, / Et le mors de l'espaule fist, / Del roi Marc et d'Ysalt la blond" (*Cligés*, vv. 1–5).

14. Foerster first posited the "anti-*Tristan*" reading of *Cligés* in the introduction to his edition of the romance (Halle: Niemeyer, 1901). In his review of Foerster's edition, Gaston Paris suggested a view of *Cligés* as a "nouveau *Tristan*" and suggested its origins in the protests of twelfth-century women who objected precisely to the "partage de la femme entre l'amant et le mari" in the Tristan story and demanded a story in which the woman would belong only to her lover. "*Cligés*," *Journal des Savants* ser. 3, 67 (1902): 443–44.

15. David Shirt has discussed Chrétien's representation of Fenice's marriage within the context of the evolving formation of matrimonial legislative practices in Europe during the second half of the twelfth century, and he shows how Alis's subversion of legal procedure in the marriage arrangements casts the emperor as an aggressor. "Cligés—A Twelfth-Century Matrimonial Case-Book?" *Forum for Modern Language Studies* 18 (1982): 81–82.

16. Paris faults Fenice for her refusal to accomplish her marital duties and cites her deception as support for his reading of *Cligés* as a "nouveau *Tristan*," a more refined version of the Tristan story, but not one that promotes an ideal of love in marriage ("*Cligés*," 444–45). Marie-Noëlle Lefay-Tourry faults Fenice not for preserving herself from her husband's embraces but for making him think that he possessed her. She situates this "amoralisme" in a progressive degradation of female characters in Chrétien's romances, and

does not interrogate the premises (largely established by the tenets of courtly love) on which she evaluates the behavior of the women. "Roman breton et mythes courtois: L'évolution du personnage féminin dans les romans de Chrétien de Troyes," *Cahiers de Civilisation Médiévale* 15 (1972): 202. Rita Lejeune characterizes Fenice as "faussement vertueuse" ("La femme dans les littératures française et occitaine du XIe au XIIIe siècle," *Cahiers de Civilisation Médiévale* 20 [1977]: 213), and Myrrha Lot-Borodine sees her rejection of Iseut's example as motivated by "a virgin's instinct" (*La femme et l'amour au XIIe siècle d'après les poèmes de Chrétien de Troyes* [Paris: Picard, 1909], 106–8).

17. Claire Richter Sherman, "The Queen in Charles V's 'Coronation Book,' " 293; John Carmi Parsons, "Ritual and Symbol," 67, and "The Pregnant Queen as Counsellor and the Medieval Construction of Motherhood," *Medieval Mothering*, ed. John Carmi Parsons and Bonnie Wheeler (New York: Garland, 1996), 39–61; Paul Strohm, *Hochon's Arrow*, 101.

18. Recent studies of the place of the female body in society permit us to recast the kinds of questions we ask about the body and the symbolic order that constructs it in medieval romance. See, for example, the essays in *The Female Body in Western Culture: Contemporary Perspectives*, ed. Susan Rubin Suleiman (Cambridge, Mass.: Harvard University Press, 1985), and *Fragments for a History of the Human Body*, ed. Michel Feher, with Ramona Naddaff and Nadia Tazi, 3 vols. (New York: Urzone, 1989). Volume 3 is particularly concerned with political metaphors using the body. For studies by medievalists, see the essays in *Feminist Approaches to the Body in Medieval Literature*, ed. Linda Lomperis and Sarah Stanbury (Philadelphia: University of Pennsylvania Press, 1993), and *Framing Medieval Bodies*, ed. Sarah Kay and Miri Rubin (Manchester: Manchester University Press, 1994).

19. Mary Douglas, *Purity and Danger: An Analysis of the Concepts of Pollution and Taboo* (New York and London: Routledge and Kegan Paul, 1966), 115.

20. Douglas, *Purity and Danger*, 122. Douglas notes that in caste societies, where a place in the hierarchy of privilege and purity is transmitted biologically, pollution rituals focus on sexuality: "Both male and female physiology lend themselves to the analogy with the vessel which must not pour away or dilute its vital fluids. Females are correctly seen as, literally, the entry by which the pure content may be adulterated. Males are treated as pores though which the precious stuff may ooze out and be lost, the whole system being thereby enfeebled. . . . Through the adultery of a wife impure blood is introduced to the lineage. So the symbolism of the imperfect vessel appropriately weighs more heavily on the women than on the men." *Purity and Danger*, 126.

21. Alice M. Colby-Hall, *The Portrait in Twelfth-Century Literature* (Geneva: Droz, 1965).

22. The liaison of Tristan and Iseut differs from that of Lancelot and Guenevere in that the queen's lover is also the king's heir; the liaison of Marc's wife and his nephew constitutes the double transgression of adultery and incest. Cligés is also the nephew and heir of his lover's husband, who is his paternal uncle. According to Donald Maddox, the paternal line in *Cligés* and the maternal one in *Tristan* provoke different moral problems. "Kinship Alliances in the *Cligés* of Chrétien de Troyes," *L'Esprit Créateur* 12 (1972): 5. Maddox concentrates on the nephew-uncle relationship. My focus on the queen's role in the adulterous triangle rather than on the motivations of her lover or the implications of his betrayal of his paternal/maternal uncle will bring a different perspective to the political implications of adultery.

Adultery of a vassal with his lord's wife is also a crime of treason, and John F. Benton sees the treasonous potential of courtly love as evidence that it was a purely literary phenomenon. "Clio and Venus: An Historical View of Medieval Love," *The Meaning of Courtly Love*, ed. F. X. Newman (Albany, N.Y.: SUNY Press, 1968), 24–28. I will suggest that the representation of treasonous adultery against the king, as a conflation of sexual, dynastic, and political anxieties, may be read as an exploration of notions of women's power and the place of women in government.

23. Julia Kristeva, *Powers of Horror: An Essay on Abjection*, trans. Leon S. Roudiez (New York: Columbia University Press, 1982), 67.

24. Kristeva, *Powers of Horror*, 67.

25. Renée L. Curtis claims that Fenice's criticism of Iseut is not supported by extant forms of the Tristan story and that it reflects neither the audience's nor Chrétien's attitude toward the legend. "The Validity of Fenice's Criticism of Tristan and Iseut in Chrétien's *Cligés*," *Bibliographical Bulletin of the International Arthurian Society* 41 (1989): 293–300.

26. Michelle A. Freeman, *The Poetics of* Translatio studii *and* Conjointure*: Chrétien de Troyes's* Cligés (Lexington, Ky.: French Forum, 1979), 174.

27. Queen Iseut is also doubled in the character of Iseut aux Blanches Mains, but these are two different characters and the doubling is located in Tristan's wish to duplicate the object of his love, not in the woman's desire to avoid adultery. Susan Dannenbaum [Crane] suggests that the doubling in *Tristan* is a narrative reflection of the internal contradictions in the story, while Terrence Scully sees the doubling of Iseut as a way to "split the personality of the heroine," the first Iseut representing carnal love and the second, sentimental, chaste love. Dannenbaum, "Doubling and Fine Amor in Thomas' *Tristan*," *Tristania* 5 (1979): 1–14; Scully, "The Two Yseults," *Medievalia* 3 (1977): 34.

28. On paired narrative structures in the romance, see Patricia Harris Stablein, "Transformation and Stasis in *Cligés*," *An Arthurian Tapestry: Essays in Memory of Lewis Thorpe*, ed. Kenneth Varty (Glasgow: French Department

of the University of Glasgow, 1981), 155–56. Stablein suggests that change in the romance is only illusory, that its structure is one of reflective stasis. I will return below to the question of how effectively Fenice "changes" her body through its illusory doubling.

29. Shirt suggests that the irregularities of Alis's marriage with respect to twelfth-century matrimonial law enabled Chrétien to justify Fenice's liaison with and eventual marriage to Cligés in the eyes of his audience. "Cligés —A Twelfth-Century Matrimonial Case-Book?" 84–85.

30. The question of Fenice's motivation in *Cligés* has long occupied critics. A. G. Van Hamel suggested that Fenice is concerned more with her literary reputation than for her reputation as empress of Constantinople. "*Cligés* and *Tristan*," *Romania* 33 (1904): 467. Gaston Paris claimed that the idea of belonging to two men "horrified" Fenice more than the fear that someone might suspect her adultery. "Cligés," 443–44.

31. For a brief discussion and overview of the political use of body metaphors from antiquity through the Middle Ages, see Jacques Le Goff, "Head or Heart? The Political Use of Body Metaphors in the Middle Ages," *Fragments for a History of the Human Body*, 3: 12–27. For a more detailed study, see Ernst H. Kantorowicz, *The King's Two Bodies: A Study in Medieval Political Theology* (Princeton, N.J.: Princeton University Press, 1957).

32. Parsons, "The Pregnant Queen," 52–53.

33. Chrétien, 151–52; *Cligés*, vv. 5251–53.

34. "Encor i a de tex reduiz / Que nus hom ne porroit trover . . . Ne ja l'uis trover n'i porrez / Ne antree de nule part" (vv. 5508–23).

35. Thibaut, *Le roman de la poire par Tibaut*, ed. Christiane Marchello-Nizia, SATF (Paris: Picard, 1984), vv. 73–76.

36. For a description of the manuscripts, see Marchello-Nizia's introduction, *Le roman de la poire*, lxvi–lxxii; on the illumination program, see xlxix–lvi.

37. Sylvia Huot, *From Song to Book: The Poetics of Writing in Old French Lyric and Lyrical Narrative Poetry* (Ithaca, N.Y.: Cornell University Press, 1987), 177, 179.

38. Bloch, *Etymologies and Genealogies*, 189.

Chapter 2

1. Bührer-Thierry, "La reine adultère," 301–2.

2. "Concitati itaque sunt spiritus filiorum imperatoris racionabili zelo, videntes maculatum stratum paternum, sordidatum platium, confusum regnum et obscurantum nomen Francorum, quod actenus clarum fuerat in

toto orbe." Agobard, *Liber pro filii et contra Judith*, book 1, ch. 2, cited by Bührer-Thierry, "La reine adultère," 302; my translation.

3. Bührer-Thierry, "La reine adultère," 299.

4. Stafford, *Queens, Concubines, and Dowagers*, 93–94.

5. Bührer-Thierry, "La reine adultère," 310.

6. Bührer-Thierry, "La reine adultère," 310.

7. Even in the grail quest where chivalric prowess is joined to sexual purity, the grail knights are publicly put to the test in bodily combat, not in proofs of their chastity. The knight's virginity may be tested by demons, but not in a combat publicized in reports to the court.

8. Dominique Boutet, *Charlemagne et Arthur, ou le roi imaginaire* (Paris: Champion, 1992), 40–41.

9. Kantorowicz, *The King's Two Bodies*, 193–272; Le Goff, "Head or Heart?" 12–27.

10. Emmanuèle Baumgartner traces its filiation in "A propos du mantel mautaillié," *Romania* 96 (1975): 315–32. Tom Peete Cross discusses the origins of the story in "Notes on the Chastity-Testing Horn and Mantle," *Modern Philology* 10 (1913): 289–99.

11. R. Howard Bloch, *The Scandal of the Fabliaux* (Chicago: University of Chicago Press, 1986), 23–24.

12. "Vostre cort en sera blasmée; / S'en ira en mainte contrée / La novele qui par tout cort, / Et sachiez que en vostre cort / En vendront aventures mains." *Mantel*, 26.

13. Emmanuèle Baumgartner, "Caradoc ou de la séduction," *Mélanges de langue et de littérature offerts à Alice Planche* (Nice: Les Belles Lettres, 1984), 66.

14. "Guignie[r] sa fame [r]envoia / En sa terre, car bien savoit / Que la roïne le haoit." *Caradoc*, vv. 3262–64.

15. Baumgartner considers the couple's departure from court in the context of *lais* like *Graelent* and *Lanval*, and suggests that, in each case, the knight's departure suggests that the Arthurian court and/or chivalric society cannot admit the knight who is capable of grounding his power on the love he inspires ("Caradoc ou de la séduction," 68). I would modify Baumgartner's formulation slightly to claim that the court cannot tolerate the presence of the woman who offers such a love.

16. Fradenburg, *City, Marriage, Tournament*, 69.

17. Bloch has suggested chastity tests in narratives like *Du mantel mautaillié* and *Le lai du corn* participate in the narrative tradition of the "trials of marriage" (*molestiae nuptiarum*) that extends from the Church fathers through the late Middle Ages, and he reads the trial of chastity as an example of "a paradigm of exorbitance inherent to medieval articulations of the question of woman." "The Arthurian Fabliau and the Poetics of Virginity,"

Continuations: Essays on Medieval French Literature and Language in Honor of John L. Grigsby, ed. Norris J. Lacy and Gloria Torrini-Roblin (Birmingham, Ala.: Summa Publications, 1989), 233–34. In what follows I explore how the test of chastity is also about a historically situated idea of queenship.

18. For a discussion of the discovery of adultery within medieval judicial procedures and an examination of its representation in *La mort le roi Artu*, see Bloch, *Medieval French Literature and Law*, 53–62.

19. Gregory of Tours cites one example of an adulterous woman condemned to burn; Godfrey of Viterbo recounts that María of Aragon, wife of Otto III, was burned for an attempted adultery; St. Florent of Saumur alleges that Fulk of Nerra burned his wife Elizabeth because of a suspicion of adultery. For a discussion of these cases and for an overview of legal procedures involving burning, see J. R. Reinhard, "Burning at the Stake in Medieval Law and Literature," *Speculum* 16 (1941): 186–209. For a further discussion of judicial procedure and for its relevance to Béroul's *Tristan*, see A. H. Diverres, "Tristan and Iseut's Condemnation to the Stake in Béroul," *Rewards and Punishments in the Arthurian Romances and Lyric Poetry of Medieval France: Essays Presented to Keith Varty on the Occasion of His Sixtieth Birthday*, ed. Peter V. Davies and Angus J. Kennedy (Cambridge: D. S. Brewer, 1987), 21–29.

20. "Sire, sire, dit la roïne, or m'est avis se a morir vient par l'espreve de cest cor, je n'i morrai mie sole, car ceste dame en est corpable, se corpe i avient, aussi com je sui." Curtis, 2: 133.

21. "[I]l est faiz par enchantement por correcier les hautes dames qui n'ont mie fait a la volenté de toz les enchanteors ne de totes les enchanteresses de la Grant Bretaigne. Et certes, je sai bien que ceste chose vint de la Grant Breteigne, ou sont tuit li enchantement, et qu'il vos est envoiez por metre descorde entre moi et vos, ou entre autre bone gent de Cornouaille." Curtis, 2: 132.

22. See also *La mort le roi Artu*, 192–93, and the discussion in Bloch, *Medieval French Literature and Law*, 13–62.

23. Paul Rousset, "La croyance en la justice immanente à l'époque féodale," *Le Moyen Age* 54, 4th ser. 3 (1948): 225–48.

24. For example, Paul R. Hyams, "Trial by Ordeal: The Key to Proof in the Early Common Law," *On the Laws and Customs of England: Essays in Honor of Samuel E. Thorne*, ed. Morris S. Arnold et al., Series in Legal History (Chapel Hill: University of North Carolina Press, 1981), 90–126.

25. John W. Baldwin, "The Intellectual Preparation for the Canon of 1215 Against Ordeals," *Speculum* 36 (1961), 613–36, esp. 626; Bartlett, *Trial by Fire and Water*, 72–75.

26. Rebecca V. Colman, "Reason and Unreason in Early Medieval Law," *Journal of Interdisciplinary History* 4 (1974): 571–91.

27. Bartlett, *Trial by Fire and Water*, 83.

28. Bartlett, *Trial by Fire and Water*, 94. See Colman for a discussion of the possible ritual use of the ordeal as a "communal purging" ("Reason and Unreason," 589–90).

29. For a discussion of the possible origins of the episode, see Helaine Newstead, "The Equivocal Oath in the Tristan Legend," *Mélanges offerts à Rita Lejeune*, 2 vols. (Gembloux: Duculot, 1969), 2: 1077–85. Ernest C. York situates Iseut's trial in the context of medieval judicial practice and emphasizes how the elimination of the ordeal heightens the focus on the duplicity of the oath in Béroul and in *La folie d'Oxford*: "Isolt's Trial in Béroul and *La Folie Tristan d'Oxford,*" *Medievalia et Humanistica* n.s. 6 (1975): 157–61.

30. Bartlett, *Trial by Fire and Water*, 30.

31. In the drinking horn episode of the *Prose Tristan* the king's distrust of judicial battle is stated *after* the proof of adultery is demonstrated on the queen's body by the magic drinking horn. See above, p. 68.

32. Duby, *The Knight, the Lady and the Priest*, 220.

33. Bloch describes Béroul's narrative of the discovery of the lovers in the forest and of the queen's trial as inaugurating a new "theocratic notion of active kingship in which power descends from above through the monarch to the community and in which the king is at once above positive but below natural law." "Tristan, the Myth of the State and the Language of the Self," *Yale French Studies* 51 (1974): 79. I see the trial scene as representing a newly explicit appropriation of the queen's body as a symbol of the king's sovereignty, but not one that changes the king's relationship to his vassals.

34. E. Jane Burns, "How the Lovers Lie Together: Infidelity and Fictive Discourse in the *Roman de Tristan,*" *Tristania* 8, 2 (1983): 15–30, esp. 15–17.

35. E. Jane Burns, *Bodytalk: When Women Speak in Old French Literature* (Philadelphia: University of Pennsylvania Press, 1993), 210–13; and "How the Lovers Lie Together," 23–26. See also François Rigolot, "Valeur figurative du vêtement dans le *Tristan* de Béroul," *Cahiers de Civilisation Médiévale* 10 (1967): 447–53.

36. See also vv. 2880–88: "Du col li a osté la chape, / Qui ert d'escarlate molt riche. / Ele out vestu une tunique / Desus un grant bliaut de soie. / De son mantel que vos diroie? / Ainz l'ermite, qui l'achata, / Le riche fuer ne regreta. / Riche ert la robe et gent le cors: / Les eulz out vers, les cheveus sors."

37. "Pensez de moi . . . / Aidiez a noveler mes dras." Béroul, vv. 3688–90. For a discussion of clothing as a figure of representation in medieval narratives, see Bloch, *The Scandal of the Fabliaux*, 22–58.

38. Burns notes how the gifts of clothing repeat the shifts in visible truth in the ordeal scene: "[As] each character uncovers himself, by divesting himself of soiled or superfluous garments, he contributes indirectly to

Tristan's cover. . . . While others expose their naked truth and vulnerability, Tristan shelters himself in the protective cloak of borrowed appearances." "How the Lovers Lie Together," 23.

39. Burns, *Bodytalk*, 229; emphases in text.

40. Burns, *Bodytalk*, 208, 230; emphases in text.

41. Burns, *Bodytalk*, 7.

42. Fradenburg, *City, Marriage, Tournament*, 75.

43. Michel Foucault, *Discipline and Punish: The Birth of the Prison*, trans. Alan Sheridan (New York: Vintage, 1979), 48.

44. Burns, *Bodytalk*, 233.

45. For a discussion of Mark's investment in a successful ordeal in Gottfried's romance, see Kelley Kucaba, "Höfisch inszenierte Wahrheiten: Zu Isolds Gottesurteil bei Gottfried von Strassburg," *fremdes Wahrnehmen— Fremdes wahrnehmen*, ed. Wolfgang Harms and C. Stephen Jaeger, with Alexandra Stein (Stuttgart: S. Hirzel, 1997), 73–93.

46. Lacy, 151. "J'ai trois felons, d'ancesorie, / Qui heent mon amendement; / Mais se encor nes en desment, / Que nes enchaz for de ma terre, / Li fel ne criement mais ma gerre." Béroul, vv. 3186–90.

47. Hyams, "Trial by Ordeal," esp. 96–99; Peter Brown, "Society and the Supernatural: A Medieval Change," *Society and the Holy in Late Antiquity* (Berkeley: University of California Press, 1982), 302–32; and Colman, "Reason and Unreason," 589–90.

48. "Cumque nullus inventus esset, qui quodlibet illi malum inferret, purificavit se secundum iudicium Francorum de omnibus quibus accusata fuerat." *Annales de Saint-Bertin*, cited by Bührer-Thierry, "La reine adultère," 310; my translation.

49. Foucault, *Discipline and Punish*, 25–26.

Chapter 3

1. See, for example, Bloch, *Etymologies and Genealogies*, 182–83; and J. M. Stary, "Adultery as a Symptom of Political Crisis in Two Arthurian Romances," *Parergon* n.s. 9,1 (1991): 65.

2. Marchello-Nizia, "Amour courtois," 979.

3. Marchello-Nizia, "Amour courtois," 981.

4. Karma Lochrie, "Women's 'Pryvetees' and Fabliau Politics in the Miller's Tale," *Exemplaria* 6, 2 (1994): 289.

5. See Bloch, *Medieval French Literature and Law*, 53–62.

6. See above, p. 63–65.

7. Philippe de Beaumanoir, *Coutumes de Beauvaisis*, ed. A. Salmon, 2 vols. (Paris: Picard, 1899), art. 934, 1: 472–73; *The* Coutumes de Beauvaisis

of Philippe de Beaumanoir, trans. F. R. P. Akehurst (Philadelphia: University of Pennsylvania Press, 1992), 330–31. In Beaumanoir's text, a huband who discovers his wife and her lover in bed or alone in a private place together may kill them both with impunity.

8. Bloch, "Tristan, the Myth of the State and the Language of the Self," 70. Bloch notes the function of adultery in structuring the changing balance of power between the barons and Tristan (69), but he does not insist on the queen's role in this negotiation, and he does not discuss it as a stabilizing force in the court. His essay focuses on a changing notion of sovereignty in the form of kingship, not of queenship.

9. Bloch, "Tristan, the Myth of the State and the Language of the Self," 78.

10. Bloch, "Tristan, the Myth of the State and the Language of the Self," 79.

11. I compare the function of the secret in the story of the queen's adultery to its use in *La châtelaine de Vergi*, a narrative about a failed attempt at adultery, in "The Queen's Secret: Adultery in the Feudal Court," *Romanic Review* 86 (1995): 289–306.

12. "qui enquierent autrui amours," v. 958. The prologue begins: "Une maniere de gent sont / qui d'estre loial samblant font / et de si bien conseil celer / qu'il / se covient en aus fier; / et quant vient qu'aucuns s'i descuevre / tant qu'il sevent l'amor et l'uevre, / si l'espandent le païs, / puis en font lor gas et lor ris" (vv. 1–8).

13. Payen, "Lancelot contre Tristan," 619, n. 11.

14. In the *Prose Tristan* King Marc's nephew Audret takes the place of the barons.

15. Lacy 31; "Savoir le puet qui c'onques veut." Béroul, v. 608.

16. Pierre Jonin, *Les personnages féminins dans les romans français de Tristan au XIIe siècle: Étude d'influences contemporaines* (Aix-en-Provence: Ophrys, 1958), 186–90; Payen, "Lancelot contre Tristan," 618–19.

17. Jonin, *Les personnages féminins*, 577–78.

18. Thomas recounts that Brangien reproaches Marc for his complicity in the queen's conduct, but she does not accuse Iseut of adultery, only of the desire for adultery, and she identifies Iseut's potential lover as Cariado. Thomas, Douce, vv. 392–94.

19. Curtis, 2: 143–44. For Béroul and Thomas, see Alexandre Micha, "Le mari jaloux dans la littérature romanesque," *Studi Medievali* 17 (1951): 307–8; and Jonin, *Les personnages féminins*, 279–81. For the *Prose Tristan*, see Emmanuèle Baumgartner, *Le Tristan en Prose*, 224–30.

20. Bruckner, *Shaping Romance*, 17.

21. Bloch, "Tristan, the Myth of the State and the Language of the Self," 69, and *Etymologies and Genealogies*, 182–83.

22. Stary, "Adultery as a Symptom of Political Crisis," 63–73. John H. Fisher explains the adultery with reference to the political context of the earliest versions of the legend, which in his reading provides a better explanation of the acceptance of adultery than do twelfth-century "social influences." "*Tristan* and Courtly Adultery," *Comparative Literature* 9 (1957): 152. I claim that twelfth- and thirteenth-century romances about adultery are part of what forms twelfth- and thirteenth-century cultural attitudes about political institutions.

23. Marchello-Nizia, "Amour courtois," 980–81.

24. Marchello-Nizia, "Amour courtois," 980.

25. Huneycutt, "Intercession and the High-Medieval Queen," and Parsons, "The Queen's Intercession."

26. See *Lancelot*, 1:354 for another version of this episode where the king "tient tot a mensoinge quanque la damoisele dist et respont a ce que la roine a dit que si li aït Diex, il voldroit que Lancelos l'eust esposee par covenant que il seroit tote sa vie ses compains et vesquit son droit eage."

27. I am grateful to Carol Dover for bringing this illumination to my attention.

28. ". . . car autrement ne doit reïne morir qui desloiauté fet, puis que ele est sacree," *La mort le roi Artu*, 121–22; see above, pp. 89–90.

29. Eve Kosofsky Sedgwick has given this structure a theoretic development in *Between Men: English Literature and Male Homosocial Desire* (New York: Columbia University Press, 1985).

30. Guenevere's advice to Arthur to postpone the end of the white stag hunt at the beginning of Chrétien's *Erec et Enide* is a good example of the queen's counsel to her husband (vv. 335–39). In Chapter 5 I discuss the queen's use of marital intimacy to manipulate her husband in romances that represent the queen as a woman governed by a voracious sexuality.

31. Roberta L. Krueger, *Women Readers and the Ideology of Gender in Old French Verse Romance* (Cambridge: Cambridge University Press, 1993), 39–51.

32. Krueger, *Women Readers*, 61. Krueger cites Reto R. Bezzola, *Le sens de l'aventure et de l'amour* (Paris: La Jeune Parque, 1947), 44; Eugène Vinaver, *A la recherche d'une poétique médiévale* (Paris: Nizet, 1970), 114; Douglas Kelly, *Sens and Conjointure in the Chevalier de la charrete*, 58; and Jean Frappier, *Chrétien de Troyes; l'homme et l'oeuvre* (Paris: Hatier-Boivin, 1957), 130–32, 142–43.

33. Krueger, *Women Readers*, 60.

34. Krueger, *Women Readers*, 61.

35. Krueger, *Women Readers*, 66.

36. The queen's role in arranging marriages is also represented in the *Chevalier de la charrete*. In Guenevere's absence the maidens of Arthur's court

lose hope of being married and arrange a tournament in order to choose their own husbands.

37. For differences in the effectiveness of the philtre in Béroul and Thomas, see Jean Frappier, "Structure et sens du Tristan," 273–74. Renée L. Curtis claims that in the *Prose Tristan* Tristan and Iseut love each other for their qualities, not simply because of the magic philtre. "The Character of Iseut," 174–75.

38. Baldwin, *The Government of Philip Augustus*, 83–84.

39. Baldwin, *The Government of Philip Augustus*, 86.

40. Baldwin, *The Government of Philip Augustus*, 206–7.

41. Baldwin, *The Government of Philip Augustus*, 210.

42. Baldwin, *The Government of Philip Augustus*, 357.

43. Pierre Jonin, "Le songe d'Iseut dans la forêt du Morrois," *Le Moyen Age* 64 (1958): 110–13.

44. Burns, *Bodytalk*, 214. See discussion above, pp. 78–79.

45. Emmanuèle Baumgartner has suggested that the refusal to leave the court may be part of a narrative strategy to preserve the stature of the hero: he decides where he will go; he does not simply flee. "Du Tristan de Béroul au Roman en Prose de Tristan, étude comparée de l'idéologie et de l'écriture romanesques à partir de l'épisode de la forêt du Morois," *Der altfranzösische Prosaroman*, ed. Ernstpeter Puhe and Richard Schwaderer (Munich: Wilhelm Fink, 1979), 13–14.

46. Krueger, *Women Readers*, 61.

47. Krueger, *Women Readers*, 66.

Chapter 4

1. Duby, *The Knight, the Lady and the Priest*, 222.

2. Gottfried, *Tristan*, 151.

3. The composition of *Eracle* is located between 1176 and 1184 by Anthime Fourrier, *Le courant réaliste dans la roman courtois en France au moyen âge* (Paris: Nizet, 1960), 179–207.

4. Norris J. Lacy has noted that the section of the romance containing the story of the emperor's marriage is a "complete, self-contained narrative" integrated into the long romance. "The Form of Gautier d'Arras's *Eracle*," *Modern Philology* 83 (1986): 230.

5. The story of the woman who arranges a meeting with her lover by pretending to fall off her horse and to dirty her clothes is found in a number of texts. In all except *Eracle* it is used as an exemplum to illustrate the perfidy of women. Medieval examples of the story are found in Jacques de Vitry, *The Exempla or Illustrative Stories from the Sermones Vulgares of Jacques de Vitry*,

ed. Thomas Frederick Crane (London: Folklore Society, 1890), no. 230 (pp. 95–96); repeated by Etienne de Bourbon, who names Jacques de Vitry as his source, *Anecdotes historiques, légendes et apologues tirés du recueil inédit d'Etienne de Bourbon*, ed. A. Lecoy de la Marche (Paris: Renouard, 1877), no. 457 (pp. 394–95). There are also a number of post-medieval versions of the story.

Yves Lefevre suggests that Gautier d'Arras probably took the story from an oral popular tale rather than from a written source. "Du rêve idyllique au goût de la vraisemblance," *Le roman jusqu'à la fin du XIIIe siècle*, ed. Jean Frappier and Reinhold R. Grimm, Grundriss der romanischen Literaturen des Mitelalters 4.1 (Heidelburg: Carl Winter, 1978), 270. Fourrier discusses the "maladresses" of the episode in Gautier's romance in *Le courant réaliste*, 229–32.

6. William C. Calin sees this resolution as a justification of courtly love "through its synthesis with marriage and the Christian life," and he puts it in the context of the romance's concern not with abstract notions of justice, but with "the enactment of justice in the world." "Structure and meaning in the *Eracle* of Gautier d'Arras," *Symposium*, 16 (1962): 284. I am interested in the specific form of justice when it relates to the adultery of a royal wife.

7. Lorenzo Renzi, *Tradizione cortese et realismo in Gautier d'Arras* (Padova: CEDAM, 1964), 194, n. 48.

8. Friedrich Wolfzettel, "La recherche de l'universel: Pour une nouvelle lecture des romans de Gautier d'Arras," *Cahiers de Civilisation Médiévale* 33 (1990), 118. Karen Pratt suggests that the adulterous relationship is represented as an honorable love "because the couple love *finement* and are ennobled by their love." *Meister Otte's Eraclius as an Adaptation of Eracle by Gautier d'Arras*, Göppingen Arbeiten zur Germanistik 392 (Göppingen: Kümmerle Verlag, 1987), 292.

9. For two perceptive analyses of the genealogical structure of this romance see Evelyn Birge Vitz, "Story, Chronicle, History: *La fille du comte de Pontieu*," in her *Medieval Narrative and Modern Narratology: Subjects and Objects of Desire* (New York: New York University Press, 1989), 96–125; and Donald Maddox, "Domesticating Diversity: Female Founders in Medieval Genealogical Literature and *La fille du comte de Pontieu*," *The Court and Cultural Diversity*, ed. Evelyn Mullally and John Thompson (Bury St. Edmunds: D. S. Brewer, 1997), pp. 97–107. I see the daughter's place in genealogy as a more troubled position than do these two studies.

10. "Aumarie" is the French name of the Spanish city Almeria, but here it most certainly used without any geographic specificity. Gaston Paris, "La légende de Saladin," *Journal des Savants* (1893): 358.

11. Danielle Régnier-Bohler notes that the problem of the daughter's sterility is resolved only after exile from the feudal world and its values.

"Figures féminines et imaginaire généalogique: étude comparée de quelques récits bref," *Le récit bref au moyen âge*, ed. Danielle Buschinger (Paris: Champion, 1980), 90.

12. *Baudouin de Sebourc* and the *Saladin* section of *Jean d'Avesnes* are part of the second cycle of crusade epics. See Robert F. Cook and Larry S. Crist, *Le deuxième cycle de la croisade: Deux études sur son développement* (Geneva: Droz, 1972); Edmond-René Labande, *Etude sur Baudouin de Sebourc* (Paris: Droz, 1940); and Larry S. Crist's thoroughly annotated edition of the prose Saladin, *Saladin: Suite et fin du deuxième cycle de la croisade* (Geneva: Droz, 1972).

13. Edward W. Said, *Orientalism* (New York: Pantheon, 1978).

14. In *Heroes and Saracens: An Interpretation of the Chansons de Geste*, Norman Daniel provides a detailed analysis of how Saracens and Christians are alike, except in religion and defeat (Edinburgh: Edinburgh University Press, 1984); see also C. Meredith Jones, "The Conventional Saracen of the Songs of Geste," *Speculum* 17 (1942): 201–225, esp. 223.

15. The term "Saracen" appears in both Latin and Greek in late Antiquity, and means simply "Arab." In fictional texts it names not only Muslims but any non-Christian, including Saxons, Irishmen, Danes, even Vandals. See Daniel, *Heroes and Saracens*, 8–9; R. W. Southern, *Western Views of Islam in the Middle Ages* (Cambridge, Mass: Harvard University Press, 1962), 16–17 ; William Wister Comfort, "The Literary Rôle of the Saracens in the French Epic," *PMLA* 55 (1940): 629–30.

16. For descriptions of the extent to which Islam was studied and known in the West, see Norman Daniel, *Islam and the West; The Making of an Image* (Edinburgh: Edinburgh University Press, 1960), esp. 17–45; Southern, *Western Views of Islam*, 34–66.

17. Daniel, *Islam and the West*, 118–20.

18. Macaire, in *Aiol*, is perhaps the best-known convert in medieval French literature; for other examples, see Comfort, "The Literary Rôle of the Saracens," 646–47; for converts in medieval society, see Daniel, *Islam and the West*, 132.

19. *Li romans de Baudouin de Sebourc, IIIe roy de Jhérusalem*, ed. L. N. Boca (Valenciennes: B. Henry, 1841), vv. 320–33.

20. *La fille*, 98. Régine Colliot calls this addition a "pieuse retouche." "Un exemple de révolte et de libération féminines au XIII siècle: La fille du comte de Pontieu," *Mélanges de langue et de littérature offerts à Alice Planche* (Nice: Les Belles Lettres, 1984), 110. Whatever its effect, the change demonstrates a need to make sense of the conversion.

21. *Nouveau recueil de contes, dits, fabliaux et autres pièces inédites des XIIIe, XIVe, et XVe siècles*, ed. A. Jubinal (Paris: Edouard Pannier, 1839), 1: 1–32.

22. For a discussion of the evolution of the story, see Paris, "La légende de Saladin," 435–38.

23. These include Pierre Cochon, *Chronique normande*, ed. Charles de

Robillard de Beaurepaire (Rouen: A. Le Brument, 1870), 2–3; *La chronique de Flandres*, in *Istoire et chroniques de Flandres d'après les textes de divers manuscrits*, ed. Kervyn de Lettenhove (Brussels: F. Hayez, 1879), 44–45; and *La chronique abrégée*, Bibliothèque Nationale manuscrit français 9222, fol. 16v–17v.

24. "... messires T. eut par le volenté de Dieu .ij. fiex de sa fame." *La fille*, 47.

25. Roger Sherman Loomis discusses the origins of the story in "The Strange History of Caradoc de Vannes," *Studies in Medieval Literature, A Memorial Collection of Essays* (New York: Burt Franklin, 1970), 91–98.

26. On the different versions of this episode in the *Livre de Caradoc*, see Michelle Szkilnik, "Les deux pères de Caradoc," *Bibliographical Bulletin of the International Arthurian Society* 40 (1988): 276, n. 9.

27. *The Continuations of the Old French Perceval*, I: 222, mss. TVD.

28. Boutet, "Bâtardise et sexualité," 59.

29. Marguerite Rossi stresses that the mother's infidelity has almost tragic consequences for her son and that responsibility for the destructive effects of Eliavrés's spells is displaced entirely onto the mother. "Sur l'épisode de Caradoc dans la *Continuation Gauvain*," *Marche Romane* 30 (1980): 248. Despite her role in the vengeance against her son, Ysave is also ultimately the source of his delivrance from the devouring serpent. This change of attitude, although explained in the story, is another example of the ambiguous characterization of Ysave's complicity with Eliavrés's desires.

30. Rossi assimilates the representation of adultery in *Le livre de Caradoc* to Jean-Charles Payen's notion of the destruction of courtly myths in Arthurian romances. I claim that this representation reveals the cultural and literary presuppositions about women, power, and sexual transgression upon which courtly representations of adultery are grounded. Rossi, "L'épisode de Caradoc," 251; Payen, "La destruction des myths courtois dans le roman arthurien: la femme dans le roman en vers après Chrétien de Troyes," *Revue des Langues Romanes* 78 (1969): 213–28.

31. Marchello-Nizia, "Amour courtois," 969–82.

32. Szkilnik emphasizes the weakness of King Caradoc and identifies Eliavrés as the source of movement and narrative development in the romance. I see the king's passivity as dictated by the structure of royal adultery in medieval romances. "Les deux pères de Caradoc," 276.

33. Baldwin, *Government of Philip Augustus*, 83–84. See above, p. 113–14.

Chapter 5

1. On the tradition of evil wives in this passage, see *Le roman des sept sages de Rome*, 301–2.

2. I quote Natalie Zemon Davis's use of the phrase in her study of the uses of the unruly woman topos in popular festivities and ordinary life in Renaissance Europe. "Women on Top," in *Society and Culture in Early Modern France* (Stanford, Calif.: Stanford University Press, 1965), 124–51.

3. On the historical stereotyping of the "wicked queen" to illustrate the "pernicious influence of women wielding independent authority," see Susan Mosher Stuard, "Fashion's Captives: Medieval Women in French Historiography," *Women in Medieval History and Historiography*, ed. Stuard (Philadelphia: University of Pennsylvania Press, 1987), 64–65.

4. Nelson stresses the necessity of examining the careers of Brunhild and Balthild in the context not only of women's power, but of the evolution of Merovingian kingship. These queens were not accused of sexual transgression. "Queens as Jezebels," 31–79.

5. Bührer-Thierry, "La reine adultère," 304.

6. *L'ystoire des sept sages* in *Deux rédactions du roman des sept sages de Rome*, ed. Gaston Paris, SATF (Paris: Firmin Didot, 1876), 160.

7. "Fit palatium prostibulum, ubi moechia dominatur et adulter regnat," *Radberti Epitaphium Arsenii*, cited by Bührer-Thierry, "La reine adultère," 304.

8. Bührer-Thierry, "La reine adultère," 300.

9. I discuss cross-dressing, gender identification, and inheritance in this romance in "'The Boy Who Was a Girl': Reading Gender in the *Roman de Silence*," *Romanic Review* 85 (1994): 517–36.

10. Parsons, "The Queen's Intercession," and Huneycutt, "Intercession and the High-Medieval Queen."

11. *Les sept sages de Romme*, in *Deux rédactions du roman des sept sages de Rome*, ed. Gaston Paris (Paris: Firmin Didot, 1876), 3. See also *L'ystoire des sept sages*, in *Deux rédactions*: "je te fais sçavoir que pour l'amour de toy j'ai gardé ma verginité, affin que tu l'eussez. Parle a moy hardiement, et puis dormirons ensemble" (67).

12. *Le roman des sept sages*, K: 795–802.

13. *L'ystoire des sept sages*, 62–63.

14. *Lancelot*, 4: 157.

15. *Le romans de la dame a la lycorne et du biau chevalier au lyon*, ed. Friedrich Gennrich (Halle: Niemeyer, 1908), vv. 5076–97; my translation.

16. Kathryn Gravdal, *Ravishing Maidens: Writing Rape in Medieval French Literature and Law* (Philadelphia: University of Pennsylvania Press, 1991), 43.

17. The Potiphar's wife topos does have a form that reverses gender positions. On stories in which the false accusation of sexual transgression is made against a woman, see Krueger's analysis in *Women Readers*, 128–55.

18. ". . . moult est franche la mescine" (*Silence*, v. 188); "Quant il le vit,

gent le salue. / Cele li rent moult biel salu; / Cho a le roi moult bien valu." (*Silence*, vv. 240–42).

19. Tami Scheibach has suggested to me that if Silence's story continued past her marriage, she, too, might become a seductress queen. This is a provocative idea that Eufeme's transformation would seem to support.

20. Sharon Kinoshita identifies this departure as a rejection of feudal and chivalric values and suggests that it is in "this dissent from the fundamental premises of courtly society that the 'feminism' of the *Lais* of Marie de France might ultimately reside." "Cherchez la Femme: Feminist Criticism and Marie de France's *Lai de Lanval*," *Romance Notes* 34 (1994): 272.

21. On the poetics of secrecy in the *lai* as a discourse about the dilemma of the poet, see R. Howard Bloch, *Medieval Misogyny and the Invention of Western Romantic Love* (Chicago: University of Chicago Press, 1991), 113–42.

22. E. A. Francis stresses Lanval's status as an "alien" in Arthur's court as a complication in the trial. "The Trial in *Lanval*," *Studies in French Language and Mediaeval Literature Presented to Professor Mildred K. Pope* (Manchester: Manchester University Press, 1939), 124. I see Marie's representation of the trial as focusing more closely on the king/vassal relationship than on particular differences between the king's vassals.

23. On the different versions of the story, see Gaston Raynaud, "La châtelaine de Vergi," *Romania* 82 (1992): 145–93; and Jean Frappier, "*La chastelaine de Vergi*, Marguerite de Navarre et Bandello," *Du moyen âge à la renaissance: Etudes d'histoire et de critique littéraire* (Paris: Champion, 1976), 393–473.

24. Frappier calls the duchess's invention of a pregnancy to gain a hearing for her accusation an "idée assez bizarre sans doute" ("*La chastelaine de Vergi*," 432), but pregnancy was linked to supplication in a number of medieval fictional and nonfictional accounts of queens' intercessions. Parsons has studied many of these in "The Pregnant Queen."

Patricia Francis Cholakian sees the use of motherhood in the story rather differently: "[the duchess] knows that [female chastity] ensures masculine honor and the father's name. Consequently she veils her own evil desire for revenge in the only acceptable form of female sexuality—motherhood." *Rape and Writing in the "Heptaméron" of Marguerite de Navarre* (Carbondale: Southern Illinois University Press, 1991), 189. I will claim that Marguerite problematizes the characterization of the duchess as evil precisely through the use of maternity.

25. The status as a widow gives her "more choices that either single or married women," according to Cholakian, *Rape and Writing*, 192.

In the fifteenth-century *L'istoire de la chastelaine du Vergier et de Tristan le chevalier*, the châtelaine is married; in the sixteenth-century *Chastelaine du Vergier* her marital status is not indicated. The châtelaine's status in the medieval text has been debated; see Joselyn Reed, "*La Chastelaine de Vergi*: Was the Heroine Married?" *Romance Notes* 16 (1974): 197–204; and Renée L. Curtis, "The Chastelaine de Vergi's Husband," *French Studies Bulletin* 24 (1987): 1–5, and "The Chastelaine de Vergi's Marital Status: A Further Reflection," *French Studies Bulletin* 27 (1988): 11–12.

26. Jules Gelernt, *World of Many Loves: The Heptameron of Marguerite de Navarre* (Chapel Hill: University of North Carolina Press, 1966), 84–85.

27. Cholakian, *Rape and Writing*, 205.

28. Cholakian, *Rape and Writing*, 189.

29. Leigh A. Arrathoon, "Le 'Compte en viel langaige': Behind *Heptaméron LXX*," *Romance Philology* 30 (1976): 194.

30. For example, Frappier, "*La Chastelaine de Vergi*," 433.

31. DuBellay's letter is cited by Pierre Jourda, *Marguerite d'Angoulême, duchesse d'Alençon, reine de Navarre (1492–1549): Etude biographique et littéraire*, 2 vols. (Paris: Champion, 1930), 1: 162; Marguerite's letters are reprinted in Jourda, ed., *Répertoire analytique et chronologique de la correspondance de Marguerite d'Angoulême, duchesse d'Alençon, reine de Navarre (1492–1549)* (1930; rpt. Geneva: Slatkine, 1973), nos. 503, 505, and 506.

32. She writes of these pregnancies in *Répertoire* nos. 899, 901, 903, 906, 912, 928, 930, 934, and 939.

33. Jourda, ed., *Répertoire*, no. 941.

34. Cholakian has called the *Heptaméron* "a profoundly autobiographical text." *Rape and Writing*, xiii.

35. Chilton, 519. "Le Duc commença à s'adoucir, oyant ce véritable propos, et lui dit: 'Je vous assure aussi que je ne l'ai pas crue.'" *Heptaméron*, 472.

36. The term is first used in 1315, according to Elizabeth M. Hallan, *Capetian France, 987–1328* (London: Longman, 1980), 207.

37. Robert Fawtier, *The Capetian Kings of France*, 28.

38. Hugues de la Ferté, in *Le romancero français*, ed. Paulin Paris (Paris: Techner, 1833), pp. 182–85.

39. Hugues de la Ferté, in *Le romancero français*, pp. 188; my translation. See also Fawtier, *The Capetian Kings of France*, 27.

40. Cited by Gérard Sivéry, *Blanche de Castille* (Paris: Fayard, 1990), 149; my translation.

41. "[E]lle monta sour une table dormant à deus piez, et dist, oiant l'evesque de Biauvais qui estoit presenz: 'Seigneur, esgardeiz moi tuit; aucurns dit que je sui enceinte d'enfant.' Et lait cheoir son mantel sour la table, et se tourne devant et derriere tant que tuit l'orent veue; et bien paroit qu'elle n'avoit enfant en ventre." *Le ménestrel de Reims*, 98.

Conclusion

1. Charles T. Wood, *The French Apanages and the Capetian Monarchy, 1224–1328* (Cambridge, Mass.: Harvard University Press, 1966), 48–65; Fawtier, *The Capetian Kings of France*, 53; Hallan, *Capetian France, 987–1328*, 284; Lewis, *Royal Succession in Capetian France*, 150–54; and Joseph R. Strayer, *The Reign of Philip the Fair* (Princeton, N.J.: Princeton University Press, 1980), 19–20.

2. *Ysaÿe le Triste*, ed. André Giacchetti (Rouen: Publications de l'Université de Rouen, 1983), 27.

3. Charles T. Wood, "Queens, Queans, and Kingship: An Inquiry into Theories of Royal Legitimacy in Late Medieval England and France," *Order and Innovation in the Middle Ages*, ed. William C. Jordan, Bruce McNab, and Teofilo F. Ruiz (Princeton, N.J.: Princeton University Press, 1976), 387.

4. Lewis, *Royal Succession in Capetian France*, 154.

5. . . . senz ceu que elle ne puisse venir a succession dou roy de France ne dou roy de Navarre, se de grace espéciaul ne le voloient ordoner." Cited by Lewis, *Royal Succession in Capetian France*, 152, 291, n. 243.

6. Wood, *The French Apanages*, 48–49.

7. Wood, *The French Apanages*, 58.

8. Lewis, *Royal Succession in Capetian France*, 150. Lewis cites Guillaume de Nangis, *Chronique latine*, "Tunc etiam declaratum fuit quod ad coronam regni Franciae mulier non succedit," and John of St. Victor, "in regno Franciae mulieres succedere non debebant. Hoc autem probari non poterat evidenter." (288–89, n. 223).

9. Kantorowicz, *The King's Two Bodies*, 80.

10. *The Lorsch Annals*, cited by Janet L. Nelson, "Women at the Court of Charlemagne: A Case of Monstrous Regiment?" *Medieval Queenship*, ed. John Carmi Parsons (New York: St. Martin's Press, 1993), 49.

11. Nelson, "Women at the Court of Charlemagne," 49.

12. Kantorowicz, *The King's Two Bodies*, 394, n. 271.

13. See above, Introduction, pp. 14–15.

14. Stafford, "The Portrayal of Royal Women," 153.

15. Stafford, "The Portrayal of Royal Women," 161.

Bibliography

Editions and Translations

Béroul. *The Romance of Tristran*. Ed. and trans. Norris J. Lacy. Garland
    Library of Medieval Literature, Series A, 36. New York: Garland, 1989.
La châtelaine de Vergi. Ed. Gaston Raynaud, rev. Lucien Foulet. Paris: Cham-
    pion, 1921.
Chrétien de Troyes. *Le chevalier de la charrete*. Ed. Mario Roques. Paris:
    Champion, 1958.
———. *Cligés*. Ed. Wendelin Foerster. Halle: Niemeyer, 1901.
———. *Cligés ou la fausse mort*. Ed. Alexandre Micha. Paris: Champion, 1957.
———. *The Complete Romances of Chrétien de Troyes*. Trans. David Staines.
    Bloomington: Indiana University Press, 1990.
———. *Erec et Enide*. Ed. Mario Roques. Paris: Champion, 1952.
Cochon, Pierre. *Chronique normande*. Ed. Charles de Robillard de Beaure-
    paire. Rouen: A. Le Brument, 1870.
The Continuations of the Old French Perceval of Chrétien de Troyes. Ed. William
    Roach. 5 vols. Philadelphia: University of Pennsylania Press and Ameri-
    can Philosophical Society, 1949–83.
Deux rédactions du roman des sept sages de Rome. Ed. Gaston Paris. Société des
    Anciens Textes Français. Paris: Firmin Didot, 1876.
Etienne de Bourbon. *Anecdotes historiques, légendes et apologues tirés du recueil
    inédit d'Etienne de Bourbon*. Ed. A. Lecoy de la Marche. Paris: Re-
    nouard, 1877.
La fille du comte de Pontieu, conte en prose, versions du XIIIe et du XVe siècle.
    Ed. Clovis Brunel. Paris: Champion, 1923.
La folie Tristan de Berne. Ed. Ernest Hoepffner. Paris: Les Belles Lettres,
    1949.
La folie Tristan d'Oxford. Ed. Ernest Hoepffner. Paris: Les Belles Lettres,
    1963.
Gautier d'Arras. *Eracle*. Ed. Guy Raynaud de Lage. Paris: Champion, 1976.
Geoffrey of Monmouth. *Historia Regum Britanniae*. Ed. Acton Griscom.
    New York: Longmans, 1929.
Gottfried von Strassburg. *Tristan*. Trans. A. T. Hatto. New York: Penguin,
    1960.

Le haut livre du graal, Perlesvaus. Ed. William A. Nitze and T. Atkinson Jenkins. 2 vols. Chicago: University of Chicago Press, 1932.

Heldris de Cornuälle. *Le roman de Silence, a Thirteenth-Century Arthurian Verse Romance.* Ed. Lewis Thorpe. Cambridge: Heffer, 1972.

Istoire et chroniques de Flandres d'après les textes de divers manuscrits. Ed. Kervyn de Lettenhove. Brussels: F. Hayez, 1879.

Jacques de Vitry. *The Exempla or Illustrative Stories from the Sermones Vulgares of Jacques de Vitry.* Ed. Thomas Frederick Crane. London: Folklore Society, 1890.

John of Salisbury. *The "Historia Pontificalis" of John of Salisbury.* Ed. and trans. Marjorie Chibnall. Oxford: Oxford University Press, 1986.

Lancelot: roman en prose du XIIIe siècle. Ed. Alexandre Micha. 9 vols. Geneva: Droz, 1978–83.

Layamon. *Brut.* Ed. G. L. Brook and R. F. Leslie. 2 vols. Early English Text Society o.s. 250, 257. Oxford: Oxford University Press, 1963.

Mantel et cor: deux lais du XIIe siècle. Ed. Philip Bennett. Exeter: University of Exeter Press, 1975.

Marguerite de Navarre. *L'heptaméron.* Paris: Garnier-Flammarion, 1982.

———. *The Heptameron.* Trans. P. A. Chilton. New York: Penguin, 1957.

Marie de France. *Lais.* Ed. Jean Rychner. Paris: Champion, 1966.

———. *The Lais of Marie de France.* Trans. Glyn S. Burgess and Keith Busby. New York: Penguin, 1986.

La mort le roi Artu. Ed. Jean Frappier. Geneva: Droz, 1964.

Nouveau recueil de contes, dits, fabliaux et autres pièces inédites des XIIIe, XIVe, et XVe siècles. Ed. A. Jubinal. 2 vols. Paris: Edouard Pannier, 1839.

Partonopeu de Blois, a French Romance of the Twelfth Century. Ed. Joseph Gildea. Villanova, Pa.: Villanova University Press, 1967.

Philippe de Beaumanoir. *Coutumes de Beauvaisis.* Ed. A. Salmon. 2 vols. Paris: Picard, 1899.

———. *The* Coutumes de Beauvaisis *of Philippe de Beaumanoir.* Trans. F. R. P. Akehurst. Philadelphia: University of Pennsylvania Press, 1992.

Raoul de Houdenc. *Messire Gauvain ou la Vengeance de Raguidel.* Ed. Celestin Hippeau. Geneva: Slatkine Reprints, 1969.

Récits d'un ménestrel de Reims au treizième siècle. Ed. Natalis de Wailly. Paris: Renouard, 1876.

Recueil général et complet des fabliaux des XIIIe et XIVe siècles. Ed. Anatole de Montaiglon. 6 vols. Paris: Librairie des Bibliophiles, 1872.

Le roman de Tristan en prose. Ed. Renée L. Curtis. 3 vols., 1963–85; rpt. Cambridge: D. S. Brewer, 1985.

Le roman de Tristan en prose. General ed. Philippe Ménard. 9 vols. Geneva: Droz, 1987–97.

Le roman des sept sages de Rome: A Critical Edition of the Two Verse Redactions of a Twelfth-Century Romance. Ed. Mary B. Speer. Lexington, Ky.: French Forum, 1989.

Le romancero français. Ed. Paulin Paris. Paris: Techner, 1833.

Li romans de Baudouin de Sebourc, IIIe roy de Jhérusalem. Ed. L. N. Boca. Valenciennes: B. Henry, 1841.

Le romans de la dame a la lycorne et du biau chevalier au lyon. Ed. Friedrich Gennrich. Halle: Niemeyer, 1908.

Saladin: Suite et fin du deuxième cycle de la croisade. Ed. Larry S. Crist. Geneva: Droz, 1972.

Thibaut. *Le roman de la poire par Tibaut*. Ed. Christiane Marchello-Nizia. Société des Anciens Textes Français. Paris: Picard, 1984.

Thomas. *Les fragments du roman de Tristan, poème du XIIe siècle*. Ed. Bartina H. Wind. Geneva: Droz, 1960.

Wace. *Le roman de Brut*. Ed. Ivor Arnold. 2 vols. Paris: Société des Anciens Textes Français, 1938–40.

William of Tyre. "Historia rerum in partibus transmarinis gestarum." *Recueil des historiens des croisades: Historiens occidentaux*. Paris: Imprimerie Nationale, 1845.

———. *A History of Deeds Done Beyond the Sea*. Trans. Emily Atwater Babcock and A. C. Krey. 2 vols. New York: Columbia University Press, 1943.

Ysambert de Saint-Leger. *Le Miroir des Dames*. Ed. Camillo Marazza. Lece: Micella, 1978.

Ysaÿe le Triste. Ed. André Giacchetti. Rouen: Publications de l'Université de Rouen, 1983.

SECONDARY STUDIES

Arrathoon, Leigh A. "Le 'Compte en viel langaige': Behind *Heptaméron* LXX." *Romance Philology* 30 (1976): 192–99.

Baldwin, John W. "The Intellectual Preparation for the Canon of 1215 Against Ordeals." *Speculum* 36 (1961): 613–36.

———. *The Government of Philip Augustus: Foundations of French Royal Power in the Middle Ages*. Berkeley and Los Angeles: University of California Press, 1986.

Baltzer, Rebecca A. "Music in the Life and Times of Eleanor of Aquitaine." *Eleanor of Aquitaine: Patron and Politician*, ed. William W. Kibler. Symposia in the Arts and the Humanities 3. Austin: University of Texas Press, 1976. Pp. 61–80.

Bartlett, Robert. *Trial by Fire and Water: The Medieval Judicial Ordeal*. Oxford: Oxford University Press, 1986.

Baumgartner, Emmanuèle. "A propos du mantel mautaillié." *Romania* 96 (1975): 315–32.

———. *Le* Tristan en prose: *Essai d'interprétation d'un roman médiéval.* Geneva: Droz, 1975.

———. "Du Tristan de Béroul au Roman en Prose de Tristan, étude comparée de l'idéologie et de l'écriture romanesques à partir de l'épisode de la forêt du Morois." *Der altfranzösische Prosaroman,* ed. Ernstpeter Puhe and Richard Schwaderer. Munich: Wilhelm Fink, 1979. Pp. 11–25.

———. "Caradoc ou de la séduction." *Mélanges de langue et de littérature médiévales offerts à Alice Planche.* Nice: Les Belles Lettres, 1984. Pp. 61–69.

Benton, John F. "Clio and Venus: An Historical View of Medieval Love." *The Meaning of Courtly Love,* ed. F. X. Newman. Albany, N.Y.: SUNY Press, 1968. Pp. 19–42.

Bezzola, Reto R. *Le sens de l'aventure et de l'amour.* Paris: La Jeune Parque, 1947.

Bloch, R. Howard. "Tristan, the Myth of the State and the Language of the Self." *Yale French Studies* 51 (1974): 61–81.

———. *Medieval French Literature and Law.* Berkeley and Los Angeles: University of California Press, 1977.

———. *Etymologies and Genealogies: A Literary Anthropology of the French Middle Ages.* Chicago: University of Chicago Press, 1983.

———. *The Scandal of the Fabliaux.* Chicago: University of Chicago Press, 1986.

———. "The Arthurian Fabliau and the Poetics of Virginity." *Continuations: Essays on Medieval French Literature and Language in Honor of John L. Grigsby,* ed. Norris J. Lacy and Glora Torrini-Roblin. Birmingham, Ala.: Summa Publications, 1989. Pp. 231–49.

———. *Medieval Misogyny and the Invention of Western Romantic Love.* Chicago: University of Chicago Press, 1991.

Boase, Roger. *The Origin and Meaning of Courtly Love: A Critical Study of European Scholarship.* Manchester: Manchester University Press, 1977.

Boutet, Dominique. "Bâtardise et sexualité dans l'image littéraire de la royauté (XIIe–XIIIe siècles)." *Femmes: Mariages-lignages, XIIe–XIVe siècles: Mélanges offerts à Georges Duby.* Bibliothèque du Moyen Age 1. Brussels: De Boeck-Wesmael, 1992. Pp. 55–68.

———. *Charlemagne et Arthur, ou le roi imaginaire.* Paris: Champion, 1992.

Brown, Peter. *Society and the Holy in Late Antiquity.* Berkeley: University of California Press, 1982.

Bruckner, Matilda Tomaryn. *Shaping Romance: Interpretation, Truth, and Closure in Twelfth-Century French Fictions.* Philadelphia: University of Pennsylvania Press, 1993.

Bührer-Thierry, Geneviève. "La reine adultère." *Cahiers de Civilisation Médiévale* 35 (1992): 299–312.

Burns, E. Jane. "How the Lovers Lie Together: Infidelity and Fictive Discourse in the *Roman de Tristan*." *Tristania* 8, 2 (1983): 15–30.

———. *Bodytalk: When Women Speak in Old French Literature*. Philadelphia: University of Pennsylvania Press, 1993.

Busby, Keith. "The Enigma of Loholt." *An Arthurian Tapestry: Essays in Memory of Lewis Thorpe*, ed. Kenneth Varty. Glasgow: French Department of the University of Glasgow, 1981. Pp. 28–36.

Cadden, Joan. *Meanings of Sex Difference in the Middle Ages: Medicine, Science, and Culture*. Cambridge: Cambridge University Press, 1993.

Calin, William C. "Structure and Meaning in the *Eracle* of Gautier d'Arras." *Symposium* 16 (1962): 275–87.

Carpenter, Jennifer and Sally-Beth MacLean. *The Power of the Weak: Studies on Medieval Women*. Urbana and Chicago: University of Illinois Press, 1995.

Caviness, Madeline H. "Patron or Matron? A Capetian Bride and a Vade Mecum for Her Marriage Bed." *Speculum* 68 (1993): 333–62.

Chibnall, Marjorie. *The Empress Matilda: Queen Consort, Queen Mother and Lady of the English*. Oxford: Blackwell, 1991.

Cholakian, Patricia Francis. *Rape and Writing in the "Heptaméron" of Marguerite de Navarre*. Carbondale: Southern Illinois University Press, 1991.

Colby-Hall, Alice M. *The Portrait in Twelfth-Century Literature*. Geneva: Droz, 1965.

Collins, Roger. "Queens-Dowager and Queens-Regent in Tenth-Century León and Navarre." *Medieval Queenship*, ed. John Carmi Parsons. New York: St. Martin's Press, 1993. Pp. 79–92.

Colliot, Régine. "Un exemple de révolte et de libération feminines au XIIIe siècle: La fille du comte de Pontieu." *Mélanges de langue et de littérature offerts à Alice Planche*. Nice: Les Belles Lettres, 1984. Pp. 105–15.

Colman, Rebecca V. "Reason and Unreason in Early Medieval Law." *Journal of Interdisciplinary History* 4 (1974): 571–91.

Comfort, Willam Wister. "The Literary Rôle of the Saracens in the French Epic." *PMLA* 55 (1940): 628–59.

Cook, Robert F. and Larry S. Crist. *Le deuxième cycle de la croisade: Deux études sur son développement*. Geneva: Droz, 1972.

Cross, Tom Peete. "Notes on the Chastity-Testing Horn and Mantle." *Modern Philology* 10 (1913): 289–99.

Curtis, Renée L. "The Character of Iseut in the *Prose Tristan* (Parts I and II)." *Mélanges de littérature du moyen âge au XXe siècle offerts à Mlle Jeanne Lods*. 2 vols. Paris: Ecole Normale Supérieure de Jeunes Filles, 1978. 1: 173–82.

———. "The Chastelaine de Vergi's Husband." *French Studies Bulletin* 24 (1987): 1–5.

———. "The Chastelaine de Vergi's Marital Status: A Further Reflection." *French Studies Bulletin* 27 (1988): 11–12.

———. "The Validity of Fenice's Criticism of Tristan and Iseut in Chrétien's *Cligés*." *Bibliographical Bulletin of the International Arthurian Society* 41 (1989): 293–300.

Daniel, Norman. *Islam and the West; The Making of an Image*. Edinburgh: Edinburgh University Press, 1960.

———. *Heroes and Saracens: An Interpretation of the Chansons de Geste*. Edinburgh: Edinburgh University Press, 1984.

Dannenbaum [Crane], Susan. "Doubling and Fine Amor in Thomas' *Tristan*." *Tristania* 5 (1979): 1–14.

Davis, Natalie Zemon. *Society and Culture in Early Modern France*. Stanford, Calif.: Stanford University Press, 1965.

Diverres, A. H. "Tristan and Iseut's Condemnation to the Stake in Béroul." *Rewards and Punishments in the Arthurian Romances and Lyric Poetry of Medieval France: Essays Presented to Keith Varty on the Occasion of His Sixtieth Birthday*, ed. Peter V. Davies and Angus J. Kennedy. Cambridge: D. S. Brewer, 1987. Pp. 21–29.

Douglas, Mary. *Purity and Danger: An Analysis of the Concepts of Pollution and Taboo*. New York and London: Routledge and Kegan Paul, 1966.

Duby, Georges. "Les 'jeunes' dans la société aristocratique dans la France du Nord-Ouest au XIIIe siècle." *Hommes et structures au moyen âge*. Paris: Mouton, 1973. Pp. 213–25.

———. *The Knight, the Lady and the Priest: The Making of Marriage in Medieval France*. Trans. Barbara Bray. New York: Pantheon, 1983.

———. "Women and Power." *Cultures of Power: Lordship, Status, and Process in Twelfth-Century Europe*, ed. Thomas N. Bisson. Philadelphia: University of Pennsylvania Press, 1995. Pp. 69–85.

Elliott, Dyan. *Spiritual Marriage: Sexual Abstinence in Medieval Wedlock*. Princeton, N.J.: Princeton University Press, 1993.

Facinger, Marion F. "A Study of Medieval Queenship: Capetian France, 987–1237." *Studies in Medieval and Renaissance History* 5 (1968): 1–48.

Farmer, Sharon. "Persuasive Voices: Clerical Images of Medieval Wives." *Speculum* 51 (1986): 517–43.

Fawtier, Robert. *The Capetian Kings of France: Monarchy and Nation, 987–1328*. Trans. Lionel Butler and R. J. Adam. London: Macmillan, 1960.

Feher, Michel, ed., with Ramona Naddaff, and Nadia Tazi. *Fragments for a History of the Human Body*. 3 vols. New York: Urzone, 1989.

Fisher, John H. "*Tristan* and Courtly Adultery." *Comparative Literature* 9 (1957): 150–64.

Foucault, Michel. *Discipline and Punish: The Birth of the Prison*. Trans. Alan Sheridan. New York: Vintage, 1979.

Fourrier, Anthime. *Le courant réaliste dans le roman courtois en France au moyen âge*. Paris: Nizet, 1960.

Fradenburg, Louise Olga. *City, Marriage, Tournament: Arts of Rule in Late Medieval Scotland*. Madison: University of Wisconsin Press, 1991.

———, ed. *Women and Sovereignty*. Cosmos 7. Edinburgh: Edinburgh University Press, 1992.

Francis, E. A. "The Trial in *Lanval.*" *Studies in French Language and Mediaeval Literature Presented to Professor Mildred K. Pope*. Manchester: Manchester University Press, 1939. Pp. 115–24.

Frappier, Jean. *Chrétien de Troyes; l'homme et l'oeuvre*. Paris: Hatier-Boivin, 1957.

———. "Structure et sens du Tristan: version commune, version courtoise." *Cahiers de Civilisation Médiévale* 6 (1963): 255–80, 441–54.

———. "*La Chastelaine de Vergi*, Marguerite de Navarre et Bandello." *Du moyen âge à la renaissance: Etudes d'histoire et de critique littéraire*. Paris: Champion, 1976. Pp. 393–473.

Freeman, Michelle A. *The Poetics of* Translatio studii *and* Conjointure: *Chrétien de Troyes's* Cligés. Lexington, Ky.: French Forum, 1979.

Gaunt, Simon. *Gender and Genre in Medieval French Literature*. Cambridge: Cambridge University Press, 1995.

Gelernt, Jules. *World of Many Loves: The* Heptameron *of Marguerite de Navarre*. Chapel Hill: University of North Carolina Press, 1966.

Gravdal, Kathryn. *Ravishing Maidens: Writing Rape in Medieval French Literature and Law*. Philadelphia: University of Pennsylvania Press, 1991.

Grimbert, Joan Tasker. "*Voleir* v. *Poeir*: Frustrated Desire in Thomas's *Roman de Tristan.*" *Philological Quarterly* 69 (1990): 153–65.

———. "Introduction." *Tristan and Isolde: A Casebook*, ed. Grimbert. New York: Garland, 1995. Pp. xiii–ci.

———, ed. *Tristan and Isolde: A Casebook*. Arthurian Characters and Themes 2. New York: Garland, 1995.

Guerin, M. Victoria. *The Fall of Kings and Princes: Structure and Destruction in Arthurian Tragedy*. Stanford, Calif.: Stanford University Press, 1995.

Hallan, Elizabeth M. *Capetian France, 987–1328*. London: Longman, 1980.

Hamilton, Bernard. "Women in the Crusader States: The Queens of Jerusalem (1100–1190)." *Medieval Women*, ed. Derek Baker. Oxford: Blackwell, 1978. Pp. 143–174.

Harvey, Ruth E. *The Troubadour Marcabru and Love*. London: Westfield College, University of London Committee for Medieval Studies, 1989.

Hindman, Sandra. *Sealed in Parchment: Rereadings of Knighthood in the Illu-*

minated Manuscripts of Chrétien de Troyes. Chicago: University of Chicago Press, 1994.

Holladay, Joan A. "The Education of Jeanne d'Evreux: Personal Piety and Dynastic Salvation in her Book of Hours at the Cloisters." *Art History* 17, 4 (1994): 585–611.

Howell, Margaret. "The Resources of Eleanor of Provence as Queen Consort." *English Historical Review* 102 (1987): 372–93.

Huneycutt, Lois L. "Female Succession and the Language of Power in the Writings of Twelfth-Century Churchmen." *Medieval Queenship*, ed. John Carmi Parsons. New York: St. Martin's Press, 1993. Pp. 189–201.

———. "Intercession and the High-Medieval Queen: The Esther Topos." *The Power of the Weak: Studies on Medieval Women*, ed. Jennifer Carpenter and Sally-Beth MacLean. Urbana and Chicago: University of Illinois Press, 1995. Pp. 126–46.

Hunt, Tony. "The Significance of Thomas's *Tristan*." *Reading Medieval Studies* 7 (1981): 41–61.

Huot, Sylvia. *From Song to Book: The Poetics of Writing in Old French Lyric and Lyrical Narrative Poetry.* Ithaca, N.Y.: Cornell University Press, 1987.

Hyams, Paul. "Trial by Ordeal: The Key to Proof in the Early Common Law." *On the Laws and Customs of England: Essays in Honor of Samuel E. Thorne*, ed. Morris S. Arnold et al. Series in Legal History. Chapel Hill: University of North Carolina Press, 1981. Pp. 90–126.

Jacquart, Danielle and Claude Thomasset. *Sexuality and Medicine in the Middle Ages.* Trans. Matthew Adamson. Princeton, N.J.: Princeton University Press, 1988.

Jones, C. Meredith. "The Conventional Saracen of the Songs of Geste." *Speculum* 17 (1942): 201–25.

Jonin, Pierre. *Les personnages féminins dans les romans français de Tristan au XIIe siècle: Etude d'influences contemporaines.* Aix-en-Provence: Ophrys, 1958.

———. "Le songe d'Iseut dans la forêt du Morrois." *Le Moyen Âge* 64 (1958): 101–13.

Jourda, Pierre. *Marguerite d'Angoulême, duchesse d'Alençon, reine de Navarre (1492–1549): Etude biographique et littéraire.* 2 vols. Paris: Champion, 1930.

———. *Répertoire analytique et chronologique de la correspondance de Marguerite d'Angoulême, duchesse d'Alençon, reine de Navarre (1492–1549).* 1930; rpt. Geneva: Slatkine, 1973.

Kantorowicz, Ernst H. *The King's Two Bodies: A Study in Medieval Political Theology.* Princeton, N.J.: Princeton University Press, 1957.

Kay, Sarah. "The Tristan Story as Chivalric Romance, Feudal Epic and Fabliau." *The Spirit of the Court: Selected Proceedings of the Fourth Con-*

gress of the International Courtly Literature Society, ed. Glyn S. Burgess and Robert A. Taylor. Cambridge: D. S. Brewer, 1985. pp. 185–95.

Kay, Sarah and Miri Rubin, eds. *Framing Medieval Bodies*. Manchester: Manchester University Press, 1994.

Kelly, Douglas. Sens *and* Conjointure *in the* Chevalier de la charrete. The Hague: Mouton, 1966.

———. "*Fine amor* in Thomas's Tristan." *Studies in Honor of Hans-Erich Keller*, ed. Rupert T. Pickens. Kalamazoo, Mich.: Medieval Institute Publications, 1993. Pp. 167–80.

Kennedy, Elspeth. *Lancelot and the Grail: A Study of the Prose Lancelot*. Oxford: Oxford University Press, 1986.

Kibler, William W., ed. *Eleanor of Aquitaine: Patron and Politician*. Symposia in the Arts and the Humanities 3. Austin: University of Texas Press, 1976.

Kinoshita, Sharon. "Cherchez la Femme: Feminist Criticism and Marie de France's *Lai de Lanval*." *Romance Notes* 34 (1994): 263–73.

Köhler, Erich. *L'aventure chevaleresque: Idéal et réalité dans le roman courtois*. Trans. Eliane Kaufholz. Paris: Gallimard, 1974.

Kristeva, Julia. *Powers of Horror: An Essay on Abjection*. Trans. Leon S. Roudiez. New York: Columbia University Press, 1982.

Krueger, Roberta L. *Women Readers and the Ideology of Gender in Old French Verse Romance*. Cambridge: Cambridge University Press, 1993.

Kucaba, Kelley. "Höfisch inszenierte Wahrheiten: Zu Isolds Gottesurteil bei Gottfried von Strassburg." *fremdes Wahrnehmen/Fremdes wahrnehmen*. Ed. Wolfgang Harms and C. Stephen Jaeger, with Alexandra Stein. Stuttgart: S. Hirzel, 1997. Pp. 73–93.

Labande, Edmond-René. *Etude sur Baudouin de Sebourc*. Paris: Droz, 1940.

———. "Pour une image véridique d'Aliénor d'Aquitaine." *Bulletin de la Société des Antiquaires de l'Ouest* 4th ser. 2 (1952): 175–234.

Lacy, Norris J. "The Form of Gautier d'Arras's *Eracle*." *Modern Philology* 83 (1986): 227–32.

Lazar, Moshé. "Cupid, the Lady, and the Poet: Modes of Love at Eleanor of Aquitaine's Court." *Eleanor of Aquitaine: Patron and Politician*, ed. William W. Kibler. Symposia in the Arts and the Humanities 3. Austin: University of Texas Press, 1976. Pp. 35–59.

Le Goff, Jacques. "Head or Heart? The Political Use of Body Metaphors in the Middle Ages." *Fragments for a History of the Human Body*, ed. Michel Feher, with Ramona Naddaff and Nadia Tazi. 3 vols. New York: Urzone, 1989. 3: 12–27.

Lefay-Tourry, Marie-Noëlle. "Roman breton et mythes courtois: L'évolution du personnage féminin dans les romans de Chrétien de Troyes." *Cahiers de Civilisation Médiévale* 15 (1972): 193–204, 283–93.

Lefevre, Yves. "Du rêve idyllique au goût de la vraisemblance." *Le roman jusqu'à la fin du XIIIe siècle*, ed. Jean Frappier and Reinhold R. Grimm. Grundriss der romanischen Literaturen des Mittelalters 4: 1. Heidelburg: Carl Winter, 1978.

Lejeune, Rita. "Le rôle littéraire d'Aliénor d'Aquitaine et de sa famille." *Cultura Neolatina* 14 (1954): 5–57.

———. "Le rôle littéraire de la famille d'Aliénor d'Aquitaine." *Cahiers de Civilisation Médiévale* 1 (1958): 303–20.

———. "La femme dans les littératures française et occitaine du XIe au XIIIe siècle." *Cahiers de Civilisation Médiévale* 20 (1977): 201–17.

Levin, Carole and Jeanie Watson, eds. *Ambiguous Realities: Women in the Middle Ages and Renaissance*. Detroit: Wayne State University Press, 1987.

Lewis, Andrew W. *Royal Succession in Capetian France: Studies on Familial Order and the State*. Cambridge, Mass.: Harvard University Press, 1981.

Lewis, C. S. *The Allegory of Love*. Oxford: Oxford University Press, 1958.

Lochrie, Karma. "Women's 'Pryvetees' and Fabliau Politics in the Miller's Tale." *Exemplaria* 6, 2 (1994): 287–304.

Lomperis, Linda and Sarah Stanbury, eds. *Feminist Approaches to the Body in Medieval Literature*. Philadelphia: University of Pennsylvania Press, 1993.

Loomis, Roger Sherman. "The Strange History of Caradoc of Vannes." *Studies in Medieval Literature, a Memorial Collection of Essays*. New York: Burt Franklin, 1970.

Lot-Borodine, Myrrha. *La femme et l'amour au XIIe siècle d'après les poèmes de Chrétien de Troyes*. Paris: Picard, 1909.

Maddox, Donald. "Kinship Alliances in the *Cligés* of Chrétien de Troyes." *L'Esprit Créateur* 12 (1972): 3–12.

———. "Domesticating Diversity: Female Founders in Medieval Genealogical Literature and *La fille du comte de Pontieu*." *The Court and Cultural Diversity*, ed. Evelyn Mullaly and John Thompson. Bury St. Edmunds: D. S. Brewer, 1997. Pp. 97–107.

Marchello-Nizia, Christiane. "Amour courtois, société masculine et figures du pouvoir." *Annales: Economies, Sociétés, Civilisations* 36, 6 (1981): 969–82.

Martindale, Jane. "Eleanor of Aquitaine." *Richard Coeur de Lion in History and Myth*, ed. Janet L. Nelson. King's College London Medieval Studies 7. London: King's College London Centre for Late Antique and Medieval Studies, 1992. Pp. 17–50.

Mayer, Hans Eberhard. "Studies in the History of Queen Melisende of Jerusalem." *Dumbarton Oaks Papers* 26 (1972): 93–182.

McCann, W. J. "Tristan: The Celtic and Oriental Material Re-examined."

Tristan and Isolde: A Casebook, ed. Joan Tasker Grimbert. New York: Garland, 1995. Pp. 3–35.

McCartney, Elizabeth. "The King's Mother and Royal Prerogative in Early-Sixteenth-Century France." *Medieval Queenship*, ed. John Carmi Parsons. New York: St. Martin's Press, 1993. Pp. 117–41.

McCracken, Peggy. "The Body Politic and the Queen's Adulterous Body in French Romance." *Feminist Approaches to the Body in Medieval Literature*, ed. Linda Lomperis and Sarah Stanbury. Philadelphia: University of Pennsylvania Press, 1993. Pp. 38–64.

———. " 'The Boy Who Was a Girl': Reading Gender in the *Roman de Silence*." *Romanic Review* 85 (1994): 517–36.

———. "The Queen's Secret: Adultery in the Feudal Court." *Romanic Review* 86 (1995): 289–306.

Micha, Alexandre. "Le mari jaloux dans la littérature romanesque." *Studi Medievali* 17 (1951): 303–20.

Nederman, Cary J. and N. Elaine Lawson. "The Frivolities of Courtiers Follow the Footprints of Women: Public Women and the Crisis of Virility in John of Salisbury." *Ambiguous Realities: Women in the Middle Ages and Renaissance*, ed. Carole Levin and Jeanie Watson. Detroit: Wayne State University Press, 1987. Pp. 82–98.

Nelson, Janet L. "Queens as Jezebels: The Careers of Brunhild and Balthild in Merovingian History." *Medieval Women*, ed. Derek Baker. Oxford: Blackwell, 1978. Pp. 31–79.

———. "Women at the Court of Charlemagne: A Case of Monstrous Regiment?" In *Medieval Queenship*, ed. John Carmi Parsons. New York: St. Martin's Press, 1993. Pp. 43–61.

Newman, F. X., ed. *The Meaning of Courtly Love*. Albany, N.Y.: SUNY Press, 1968.

Newstead, Helaine. "The Equivocal Oath in the Tristan Legend." *Mélanges offerts à Rita Lejeune*. 2 vols. Gembloux: Duculot, 1969. 2: 1077–85.

Owen, D. D. R. *Eleanor of Aquitaine: Queen and Legend*. Oxford: Blackwell, 1993.

Paris, Gaston. "La légende de Saladin." *Journal des Savants* (1893): 284–99, 354–65, 428–38, 486–98.

———. "*Cligés*." *Journal des Savants*, ser. 3, 67 (1902): 57–69, 289–309, 345–57, 438–58, 641–55.

Parsons, John Carmi. "Ritual and Symbol in the English Medieval Queenship to 1500." *Women and Sovereignty*, ed. Louise Olga Fradenburg. Cosmos 7. Edinburgh: Edinburgh University Press, 1992. Pp. 60–77.

———. "Introduction: Family, Sex, and Power: The Rhythms of Medieval Queenship." *Medieval Queenship*, ed. Parsons. New York: St. Martin's Press, 1993. Pp. 1–11.

———. "Mothers, Daughters, Marriage, Power: Some Plantagenet Evidence, 1150–1500." *Medieval Queenship*, ed. Parsons. New York: St. Martin's Press, 1993. Pp. 63–78.

———. "The Queen's Intercession in Thirteenth-Century England." *The Power of the Weak: Studies on Medieval Women*, ed. Jennifer Carpenter and Sally-Beth MacLean. Urbana and Chicago: University of Illinois Press, 1995. Pp. 147–77.

———. "The Pregnant Queen as Counsellor and the Medieval Construction of Motherhood." *Medieval Mothering*, ed. John Carmi Parsons and Bonnie Wheeler. New York: Garland, 1996. Pp. 39–61.

———, ed. *Medieval Queenship*. New York: St. Martin's Press, 1993.

Payen, Jean-Charles. *Le motif du repentir dans la littérature médiévale française*. Geneva: Droz, 1967.

———. "Figures féminines dans le roman médiéval français." *Entretiens sur la renaissance du douzième siècle*, ed. Maurice de Gandillac and Edouard Jeauneau. Paris: Mouton, 1968. Pp. 407–28.

———. "La destruction des mythes courtois dans le roman arthurien: la femme dans le roman en vers après Chrétien de Troyes." *Revue des Langues Romanes* 78 (1969): 213–28.

———. "Lancelot contre Tristan: la conjuration d'un mythe subversif (réflexions sur l'idéologie romanesque au moyen âge)." *Mélanges de langue et de littérature médiévales offerts à Pierre Le Gentil*. Paris: SEDES and CDU, 1973. Pp. 617–32.

Poulet, André. "Capetian Women and the Regency: The Genesis of a Vocation." *Medieval Queenship*, ed. John Carmi Parsons. New York: St. Martin's Press, 1993. Pp. 93–116.

Pratt, Karen. *Meister Otte's Eraclius as an Adaptation of Eracle by Gautier d'Arras*. Göppingen Arbeiten zur Germanistik 392. Göppingen: Kümmerle Verlag, 1987.

Raynaud, Gaston. "La châtelaine de Vergi." *Romania* 82 (1992): 145–93.

Reed, Joselyn. "*La Chastelaine de Vergi*: Was the Heroine Married?" *Romance Notes* 16 (1974): 197–204.

Régnier-Bohler, Danielle. "Figures féminines et imaginaire généalogique: étude comparée de quelques récits brefs." *Le récit bref au moyen âge*, ed. Danielle Buschinger. Paris: Champion, 1980. Pp. 73–95.

Reilly, Bernard F. *The Kingdom of León-Castilla Under Queen Urraca, 1109–1126*. Princeton, N.J.: Princeton University Press, 1982.

Reinhard, J. R. "Burning at the Stake in Medieval Law and Literature." *Speculum* 16 (1941): 186–209.

Renzi, Lorenzo. *Tradizione cortese et realismo in Gautier d'Arras*. Padova: Casa Editrice Dott. Antonio Milani, 1964.

Rigolot, François. "Valeur figurative du vêtement dans le *Tristan* de Béroul." *Cahiers de Civilisation Médiévale* 10 (1967): 447–53.

Rokseth, Yvonne. *Polyphonies du XIIIe siècle: Le manuscrit H 196 de la Faculté de Médecine de Montpellier.* 4 vols. Paris: Editions de l'Oiseau-Lyre, 1935–39.

Rossi, Marguerite. "Sur l'épisode de Caradoc dans la *Continuation Gauvain*." *Marche Romane* 30 (1980): 247–54.

Rousset, Paul. "La croyance en la justice immanente à l'époque féodale." *Le Moyen Age* 54 (4th ser. 3) (1948): 225–48.

Said, Edward W. *Orientalism.* New York: Pantheon, 1978.

Schultz, James A. "Why Does Mark Marry Isolde? And Why Do We Care? An Essay on Narrative Motivation." *Deutsche vierteljahrs Schrift für Literaturwissenschaft und Geistesgeschichte* 61, 2 (1987): 206–22.

Scully, Terrence. "The Two Yseults." *Medievalia* 3 (1977): 25–36.

Sedgwick, Eve Kosofsky. *Between Men: English Literature and Male Homosocial Desire.* New York: Columbia University Press, 1985.

Sherman, Claire Richter. "The Queen in Charles V's 'Coronation Book': Jeanne de Bourbon and the 'Ordo ad reginam benedicendam.'" *Viator* 8 (1977): 255–98.

Shirt, David. "Cligés—a Twelfth-Century Matrimonial Case-Book?" *Forum for Modern Language Studies* 18 (1982): 75–89.

Sivéry, Gérard. *Blanche de Castille.* Paris: Fayard, 1990.

Skovgaard-Petersen, Inge, with Nanna Damsholt. "Queenship in Medieval Denmark." *Medieval Queenship*, ed. John Carmi Parsons. New York: St. Martin's Press, 1993. Pp. 25–42.

Southern, R. W. *Western Views of Islam in the Middle Ages.* Cambridge, Mass.: Harvard University Press, 1962.

Spiegel, Gabrielle M. "The *Reditus Regni ad Stirpem Karoli Magni*: A New Look." *French Historical Review* 7 (1971): 145–74.

Stablein, Patricia Harris. "Transformation and Stasis in *Cligés*." *An Arthurian Tapestry: Essays in Memory of Lewis Thorpe*, ed. Kenneth Varty. Glasgow: French Department of the University of Glasgow, 1981. Pp. 151–59.

Stafford, Pauline. *Queens, Concubines, and Dowagers: The King's Wife in the Early Middle Ages.* Athens: University of Georgia Press, 1983.

———. "The Portrayal of Royal Women in England, Mid-Tenth to Mid-Twelfth Centuries." *Medieval Queenship*, ed. John Carmi Parsons. New York: St. Martin's Press, 1993. Pp. 143–67.

Stary, J. M. "Adultery as a Symptom of Political Crisis in Two Arthurian Romances." *Parergon* n.s. 9, 1 (1991): 63–73.

Strayer, Joseph R. *The Reign of Philip the Fair.* Princeton, N.J.: Princeton University Press, 1980.

Strohm, Paul. *Hochon's Arrow: The Social Imagination of Fourteenth-Century Texts*. Princeton, N.J.: Princeton University Press, 1992.

Stuard, Susan Mosher. "Fashion's Captives: Medieval Women in French Historiography." *Women in Medieval History and Historiography*, ed. Stuard. Philadelphia: University of Pennsylvania Press, 1987.

Suleiman, Susan Rubin, ed. *The Female Body in Western Culture: Contemporary Perspectives*. Cambridge, Mass.: Harvard University Press, 1985.

Szkilnik, Michelle. "Les deux pères de Caradoc." *Bibliographical Bulletin of the International Arthurian Society* 40 (1988): 269–86.

Utley, Francis L. "Must We Abandon the Concept of Courtly Love?" *Medievalia et Humanistica* n.s. 3 (1972): 299–324.

Van Hamel, A. G. "*Cligés* and *Tristan*." *Romania* 33 (1904): 465–89.

Vinaver, Eugène. *A la recherche d'une poétique médiévale*. Paris: Nizet, 1970.

Vitz, Evelyn Birge. *Medieval Narrative and Modern Narratology: Subjects and Objects of Desire*. New York: New York University Press, 1989.

Walters, Lori J. "Introduction." *Lancelot and Guinevere: A Casebook*, ed. Walters. New York: Garland, 1996. Pp. xiii–lxix.

———, ed. *Lancelot and Guinevere: A Casebook*. Arthurian Characters and Themes 4. New York: Garland, 1996.

Wolfzettel, Friedrich. "La recherche de l'universel: Pour une nouvelle lecture des romans de Gautier d'Arras." *Cahiers de Civilisation Médiévale* 33 (1990): 111–31.

Wood, Charles T. *The French Apanages and the Capetian Monarchy, 1224–1328*. Cambridge, Mass.: Harvard University Press, 1966.

———. "Queens, Queans, and Kingship: An Inquiry into Theories of Royal Legitimacy in Late Medieval England and France." *Order and Innovation in the Middle Ages*, ed. William C. Jordan, Bruce McNab, and Teofilo F. Ruiz. Princeton, N.J.: Princeton University Press, 1976. Pp. 385–400.

York, Ernest C. "Isolt's Trial in Béroul and *La Folie Tristan d'Oxford*." *Medievalia et Humanistica* n.s. 6 (1975): 157–61.

Index

DATE D